Fun with the Family™ North Carolina

Praise for a previous edition of *Fun with the Family™ North Carolina*

"The author, a lifelong explorer of our state,
knows all of North Carolina's highways and byways firsthand,
and his energetic style keeps the guide entertaining throughout."

—*Our State* magazine

Help Us Keep This Guide Up to Date

Every effort has been made by the author and editors to make this guide as accurate and useful as possible. However, many changes can occur after a guide is published—establishments close, phone numbers change, hiking trails are rerouted, facilities come under new management, etc.

We would love to hear from you concerning your experiences with this guide and how you feel it could be improved and be kept up to date. While we may not be able to respond to all comments and suggestions, we'll take them to heart, and we'll make certain to share them with the author. Please send your comments and suggestions to the following address:

The Globe Pequot Press
Reader Response/Editorial Department
P.O. Box 480
Guilford, CT 06437

Or you may e-mail us at: editorial@GlobePequot.com

Thanks for your input, and happy travels!

INSIDERS' GUIDE®

FUN WITH THE FAMILY™ SERIES

fun WITH the Family™

NORTH CAROLINA

HUNDREDS OF IDEAS FOR DAY TRIPS WITH THE KIDS

JAMES L. HOFFMAN

SIXTH EDITION

INSIDERS' GUIDE®

GUILFORD, CONNECTICUT
AN IMPRINT OF THE GLOBE PEQUOT PRESS

To buy books in quantity for corporate use
or incentives, call **(800) 962–0973**
or e-mail **premiums@GlobePequot.com**.

INSIDERS' GUIDE®

Text design by Nancy Freeborn and Linda R. Loiewski
Maps by Rusty Nelson © Morris Book Publishing, LLC
Spot photography throughout © Photodisc and © RubberBall Productions

ISSN 1539-9044
ISBN 978-0-7627-4551-7

Manufactured in the United States of America
Sixth Edition/Second Printing

For Kaitlyn, Michaela, Jessie, Mike, Melissa, and Bonnie . . .
I love where we've been and look forward to many miles ahead.

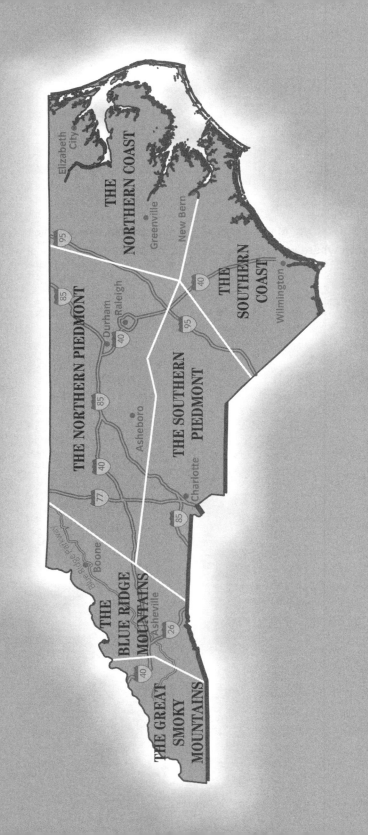

THE NORTHERN COAST

THE SOUTHERN COAST

THE NORTHERN PIEDMONT

THE SOUTHERN PIEDMONT

THE BLUE RIDGE MOUNTAINS

THE GREAT SMOKY MOUNTAINS

Elizabeth City

Greenville

New Bern

Wilmington

Durham

Raleigh

Asheboro

Charlotte

Boone

Asheville

Blue Ridge Parkway

95

85

40

77

26

Contents

Acknowledgments

With this edition we continue to strive to make a more user-friendly guide with updated hours, admission information, and other helpful details. I would like to thank all the people who have helped make this book possible. Originally, this work would not have been possible without many members of my family, including my parents, K. R. and Pat Hoffman, as well as Sara Pitzer, Dana Teague, and many other people throughout the years. The previous editions of this work would not have been possible without the assistance of my family and friends across the state, who recommended numerous hotels and restaurants. I am also grateful for the North Carolina Department of Tourism and all of the travel bureaus across the state too numerous to mention here, as well as a host of park rangers, museum guides, information center staffs, hotel clerks and concierges, waiters, and many, many others.

Introduction

I t seems to me that living in North Carolina is a privilege. My family and I are particularly lucky because we live in the Piedmont, where you can easily reach the mountains, the beaches, or the state's larger cities for travel and entertainment. I have many fond memories of my life here as a child, as a college student, and as an adult with my own family. We've been pretty much everywhere in the Tar Heel state, from Murphy to Manteo, as the expression goes. We've enjoyed the majesty of the mountains and the history and beauty of the coast. But one interesting thing occurred in the process of writing this book. I would ask the kids if they remembered going to the Native American village in the mountains or the loggerhead turtle that nested in front of the rental beach house, and almost every time the response would be a puzzled "no." That could be due to their young ages, or it could be a clever ploy to get me to take them back to these places. Oh well, I guess we'll have to do it all again.

Doing all that's in this book won't be much of a problem since the family has grown considerably since the first edition. Having grown children, along with one in Kindergarten and a couple in between makes for challenging vacation planning. We've fared well so far and hope we'll continue to explore together even as the older children get jobs and start their own families.

Traveling with children, especially with a large span of ages, creates unique challenges. The ubiquitous portable DVD player certainly does make life easier, but I've always been afraid that it would reduce our precious quality time together and dumb-down the vacation. The greatest joy we've found through the years is learning things about places we haven't been before. Utilize resources in planning. Take time to learn about the area in which you'll be traveling and share that along the way. Also, plan enough time to make short side trips. There's plenty in the pages that follow that make for good stops where you can stretch your legs and let the kids sip on a juice box.

Of course, there is always a need for quiet time. For that, you might try borrowing books on tape from your local library or even downloading files for your MP3 player from www.netlibrary.com. You'll find everything from Dr. Seuss to *Harry Potter,* so just take a look.

Our family also creates great memories by playing silly word games, like Count the Cows, Hangman, or I-Spy. Still, a healthy supply of crayons, activity books, and travel games can keep the mood in the car light and fun. You can keep those activities close at hand with a handy lap tray (made by Crayola and probably others as well) with a padded bottom and pockets for crayons, coloring books, and other items. Pocketed smocks that fit over the back of the front seat for easy access by back-seat passengers are also commercially available.

I've divided the state into six travel areas that roughly resemble the state's geographic regions. We begin our journey in the west in the Great Smoky Mountains and continue through the Blue Ridge Mountains, both part of the Appalachian Range. Next we go to the Northern Piedmont, traveling from west to east, and then back to the Southern Piedmont, where we again travel from west to east. Finally we move into the coastal plain, which I've divided into the Southern Coast and the Northern Coast. Traveling this route from south to north on the coast would take quite some time and require a number of ferry rides.

Each chapter is organized geographically, so you can use this guide to easily plan your itinerary or to find an adventure near you by flipping backward or forward a page or two. In addition, you'll find two indices—one general and one by type of activity—to help you select appropriate attractions and events for your family.

You'll also find listed throughout the book my recommendations for these attractions and events. In addition, I've included reference maps to help get you on the road. I wrote this book with the help of the map created by the North Carolina Department of Transportation, which is distributed free of charge. You can obtain a copy of it and more information by calling (919) 733–7600, or (800) 847–4848 if you are outside North Carolina.

For Quick **Reference**

Throughout this guide you will find recommendations for places to stay. We've mostly eliminated the larger chain accommodations, assuming one of these chains has already proven its efficiency to you. The accommodations listed are ones that have more local flare that you might not come across easily. We have tried to include a variety of price ranges, but in case you are set in your ways, here's how to get in touch with the larger chains that are found fairly prevalently throughout the state:

- **Best Western,** (800) 780–7234; www.bestwestern.com

- **Comfort Inn and Suites, Econolodge, Quality Inn, Clarion, Sleep Inn,** (877) 424–6423; www.choicehotels.com

- **Days Inn,** (800) 329–7466; www.daysinn.com

- **Hampton Inns and Suites,** (800) 426–7866; www.hamptoninn.com

- **Holiday Inn,** (800) 465–4329; www.ichotelsgroup.com

- **La Quinta Inns and Suites,** (866) 725–1661; www.lq.com

- **Marriott (including Residence Inn),** (888) 236–2427; http://marriott.com

I encourage you to use the Internet as a resource as much as you are able. Web sites from hotels and vacation realtors often provide peace of mind by giving you a look inside your accommodations. I've also included the Web addresses for as many attractions and visitor centers as possible, but don't let that hamper your sense of adventure. I encourage you to get out, take a chance, and see what might be off the beaten path.

One more thing: Have a great time exploring the great state of North Carolina!

Lodging, Restaurants, and Attractions Fees

In the "Where to Eat" and "Where to Stay" sections, dollar signs indicate general price ranges. For meals, the prices are for individual adult entrees. For lodging, the rates are for a double room, for a family of four, with no meals, unless otherwise indicated; rates for lodging may be higher during peak vacation seasons and holidays. Always inquire about family and group rates and package deals that may include amusement park tickets, discounts for area attractions, and tickets for concerts and other performing arts events.

Because admission fees change frequently, this book offers a general idea of the prices charged by each attraction.

Rates for Lodging

$	less than $50
$$	$50 to $75
$$$	$76 to $100
$$$$	more than $100

Rates for Attractions

$	less than $5
$$	$5 to $10
$$$	$11 to $20
$$$$	more than $20

Rates for Restaurants

$	most entrees under $10
$$	most $10 to $15
$$$	most $15 to $20
$$$$	most more than $20

The prices, rates, and hours listed in this guidebook were confirmed at press time. We recommend, however, that you call establishments to obtain current information before traveling.

Attractions Key

The following is a key to the icons found throughout the text.

SWIMMING		**FOOD**	
BOATING / BOAT TOUR		**LODGING**	
HISTORIC SITE		**CAMPING**	
HIKING / WALKING		**MUSEUM**	
FISHING		**PERFORMING ARTS**	
BIKING		**SPORTS/ATHLETICS**	
AMUSEMENT PARK		**PICNICKING**	
HORSEBACK RIDING		**PLAYGROUND**	
SKIING/WINTER SPORTS		**SHOPPING**	
PARK		**PLANTS /GARDENS /NATURE TRAILS**	
ANIMAL VIEWING		**FARM**	

The Great Smoky Mountains

The Great Smoky Mountains are just south of heaven. You'll find the beauty of the area unmatched as you climb to heights of more than 6,000 feet—some of the highest points in the eastern United States. The region includes the most popular national park in the country as well as one of the last virgin wildernesses. The trout fishing is great, too. Hiking trails, gorgeous flowing waterfalls, and crystal-like streams are waiting around just about every corner.

In this region you can take a wild rafting adventure down one of a number of rivers, mine precious stones, ride an old-fashioned railway, or visit a theme park. The heritage of the area is as important here as it is anywhere. You can visit a Cherokee

Jim's Top Picks in the Great Smoky Mountains

1. The Great Smoky Mountain Railway

2. Ghost Town in the Sky

3. White-water rafting on the Nantahala River

4. Oconaluftee Indian Village

5. Santa's Land Family Fun Park and Zoo

6. Tubing at Deep Creek in the Great Smoky Mountains National Park

7. Cruising the Blue Ridge Parkway

8. Folkmoot-USA

9. Mining in Franklin

10. Autumn in the mountains

THE GREAT SMOKY MOUNTAINS

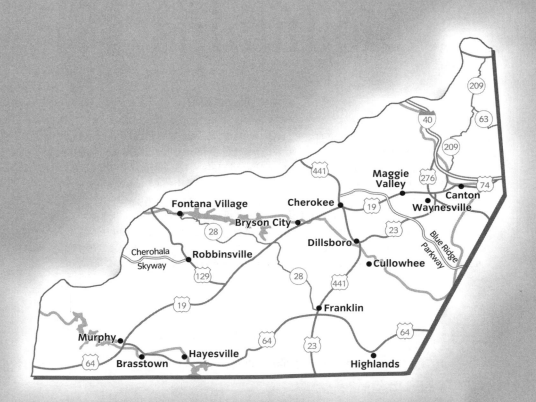

Maggie Valley
Canton
Waynesville
Fontana Village
Cherokee
Bryson City
Dillsboro
Cherohala
Skyway
Robbinsville
Cullowhee
Murphy
Franklin
Brasstown
Hayesville
Highlands
Blue Ridge Parkway

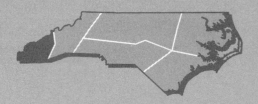

Indian reservation or learn about the Europeans who settled in this area. And don't miss all the country food and crafts the Great Smoky Mountains have to offer.

Travel is generally slow in this area, as it is over most of the mountains of North Carolina. Don't try to take in too much at one time, or you'll spend all your time driving and miss all the fun. U.S. Highway 64 runs through the southern portion of the state and is your best bet for long travel. U.S. Highway 74 runs from the northeast portion of the region to intersect with US 64. It combines with several other highways along the way, so don't let that confuse you. U.S. Highway 441 bisects the area and runs north to south.

For More Information

Smoky Mountain Host, (800) 432–4678; www.visitsmokies.org.

Murphy

Nestled in the westernmost corner of North Carolina is Cherokee County, and Murphy is where we begin our excursion. First settled by the Cherokee Indians, it offers an abundance of opportunities for outdoor activities.

Hanging Dog Recreation Area
Located on Hiwassee Lake, just 5 miles west of Murphy on US 64. Contact Nantahala National Forest at (828) 257–4200 for more information; www.cs.unca.edu/nfsnc. Free admission; camping $.

Hanging Dog offers a large campground, a picnic area, an opportunity for swimming, and hiking trails. Only small trailers are allowed at the campground.

Cherokee County Historical Museum (ages 5 and up)
87 Peachtree Street; (828) 837–6792; www.cherokeecounty-nc.gov. Open 9:00 a.m. to 5:00 p.m. Monday through Friday. Free.

Learn about the Cherokee Indians' presence in the western North Carolina mountains and about early American life at the Cherokee County Historical Museum. The museum features an extensive collection of more than 2,000 Native American artifacts and exhibits on early mountain life. You'll see tools, housewares, arrowheads, pipes, and games that have been used throughout the years, in addition to displays that explain the Trail of Tears—a forced westward march of more than 70,000 Native Americans following the U.S. Congress's 1830 passage of the Indian Removal Act.

Fields of the Wood (all ages)

Highway 294, southwest of Murphy; (828) 494–7855; www.fieldsofthewoodbiblepark .com. Open daily, generally from sunrise to sunset. **Free.**

This is probably the county's most unique attraction, a biblical theme park covering 200 acres of mountainside. You won't find any flashy rides or games at the Fields of the Wood. This very different park features the Ten Commandments displayed in concrete on one of those mountainsides, and the world's largest cross and altar. You can also see a depiction of Christ's tomb and displays on biblical teachings. You'll want to visit the park's Bible, book, and gift shop as well.

Where to Eat

Aldo's Restaurant, 399 Hill Street; (828) 837–8899. Aldo's serves classic Italian and seafood. $$

Captain Joe's, 1181 Andrews Road; (828) 837–4434. This is a nice cafe, serving seafood, chicken, sandwiches, and more. $–$$

New Happy Garden Chinese Restaurant, 2056 Highway 19; (828) 837–0711. This is a traditional Americanized Chinese restaurant with a buffet, so if the kids don't go for chow mein, they'll find something they like. $

Papa's Pizza To Go, 530 US 64 West; (828) 837–3335. Papa's offers eat-in and take-out pizza as well as a variety of other items from sub sandwiches to gyros. You'll find several Papa's Pizzas in the area. $

Showbooties Café, 25 Peachtree Street; (828) 837–4589. Clean your plate, because you'll want to check out the homemade desserts here. The cafe sometimes offers live jazz on weekend nights. $–$$

Wildflowers Treat Shop, 33 Peachtree Street; (828) 837–1415. Get baked goods sure to please any sweet tooth here. $

Where to Stay

Hamlet O Cabins, 451 Hilltop Lane; (800) 644–5957; www.hamletocabins .com. Small, rustic cabins are offered here. They accommodate up to six people and include full kitchens. $$

Hawkesdene House, 381 Phillips Creek Road, P.O. Box 670, Andrews; (800) 447–9549; www.hawkbb.com. This is a pretty bed-and-breakfast that is more family oriented and includes cabins. Lunch and dinner llama trips are offered in addition to the accommodations. $$$

For More Information

Cherokee County Chamber of Commerce, (828) 837–2242; www. cherokee countychamber.com.

Brasstown

Brasstown is located east of Murphy, just south on US 64.

John C. Campbell Folk School (all ages)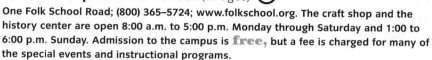

One Folk School Road; (800) 365–5724; www.folkschool.org. The craft shop and the history center are open 8:00 a.m. to 5:00 p.m. Monday through Saturday and 1:00 to 6:00 p.m. Sunday. Admission to the campus is free, but a fee is charged for many of the special events and instructional programs.

The 365-acre campus is home to what is recognized as the nation's only instructional folk program. The school, founded in 1925, has become a real asset to the small community and is in the National Register of Historic Places. A variety of special events, celebrations, and presentations are held throughout the year. The biggest, the Fall Festival, is held the first weekend in October and features crafts, music, and more. You can visit many of the campus buildings anytime and perhaps see one of the famous Brasstown carvers at work. The small museum of crafts in the log cabin, the sawmill, and the millhouse are also open to the public. In addition, the school offers minicourses lasting from two days to two weeks in blacksmithing, woodworking, pottery, wood carving, weaving, basketry, mountain music, folk dancing, gardening, jewelry making, and folklore. Most short courses are offered on weekends, and a catalog of listings is available. Children twelve years and older and parents can take week-long classes together during special summer programs that include everything from basket making to boat building. Campus visitors are welcome at the Olive Dame Campbell Dining Hall, too. The hand-forged bell signals the serving of each meal from the middle of campus. Staff serves a family-style meal, much of it from the college's organic garden, and visitors dine alongside students. Reservations are required by calling (800) 365–5724 or (828) 837–2775 by 10:00 a.m. ($).

Where to Stay

Trout Cove Cabins, 1629 Trout Cove Road; (888) 389–3584; www.troutcovecabins.com. This is a very quiet facility, offering two-bedroom cabins located on 184 acres. Each cabin is fully equipped. $$–$$$

Hayesville

Travel east on US 64 and exit to the north.

Hayesville offers plenty of opportunities to get out on the lake or simply out-of-doors. Lake Chatuge, which straddles the North Carolina–Georgia state line, offers facilities for camping, fishing, swimming, and picnicking. In addition you'll find hiking trails, boat rentals, and a visitor center. At **Jackrabbit Mountain** recreation area, off State Road 1155 (located off Highway 175), you'll find facilities for trailers up to 22 feet long with a few for trailers up to 32 feet. Jackrabbit has a sandy beach area as well as fishing access along the shoreline. If the sites are full at Jackrabbit, another nice campground is less than 30 miles east. **Standing Indian Mountain,** located just off US 64, offers remarkable trout fishing, hiking trails, and scenic drives around the area. The park has become popular for mountain biking enthusiasts, and both wilderness and developed camping sites are offered. Jackrabbit is open May through September; Standing Indian Mountain is open April through November. Call the Tusquittee Ranger Station at (828) 837–5152 for more information.

Nearby you'll find **Tusquittee Campground and Cabins** (9594 Tusquittee Road), which provides the perfect opportunity to head to the great outdoors, particularly for families with young children or those who simply refuse to camp in a tent. The park, located just east of Hayesville, provides full-service log cabins, creekside camper cabins for more rustic living, and traditional trailer and tent camping sites. The campground also has a heated bathhouse, hiking trails, a swimming hole, a swing set, and equipment for badminton, tetherball, volleyball, and horseshoes. The campground is open year-round. Call (828) 389–8520 for more information or to make reservations.

Peacock Playhouse (ages 5 and up) 🎵
301 Church Street; (828) 389–8632; www.licklogplayers.org. $$–$$$.

While you're in or near Hayesville, you might want to check out the Peacock Playhouse, where the Licklog Players present productions throughout the year. Licklog Players is a volunteer organization, but the group produces professional-quality performances ranging from drama to musicals to comedy. The theater seats about 250 people for the shows, and the annual playbill always includes some family-oriented productions.

Where to Eat

Country Cottage, 983 Highway 69; (828) 389–8621. This restaurant offers casual dining on home-cooked breakfast, lunch, and dinner complete with homemade desserts. $$

Mika's Pizza, US 64 Bypass; (828) 389–6366. Standard pizza fare is offered along with sandwiches and pasta dishes. $

Rib Country Restaurant, 495 US 64 Business; (828) 389–9597. A cafeteria-style buffet is offered here along with daily specials, steaks, snow crab legs, and baby back ribs. $$

Where to Stay

Chatuge Mountain Inn, US 64 East; (828) 389–9340. This is a very nice place near the lake. $$–$$$

Lakeview Cottages and Marina, Highway 175; (828) 389–6314. This facility offers nine cottages. One- and two-bedroom cottages are fully equipped with appliances, cooking utensils and dishes, and televisions. $$–$$$

For More Information

Clay County Chamber of Commerce, (828) 389–3704; www.claycounty-nc-chamber.com.

For more information on camping in the area, contact the **Nantahala National Forest** at (828) 257–4200; www.cs.unca.edu/nfsnc.

Franklin

Continuing east on US 64 and heading north on Highway 28 brings you to the town of Franklin, seat of Macon County.

In addition to the logging industry, tourism has become very important to the Franklin area economy. While accommodations—cottages, cabins, chalets, and vacation homes—fill the area, its natural beauty is still undisturbed. The biggest attractions for tourists are the mines, where you can hunt for and retrieve genuine rubies, sapphires, and other native stones. Precious stones are sometimes imported to make the hunt more interesting. There are nearly a dozen mining operations open to tourists in the area. A few require digging, while others confine your gem hunting to

Franklin Area **Mines**

- **Cherokee Ruby and Sapphire Mine,** 41 Cherokee Mine Road; (828) 349–2941

- **Cowee Mountain Ruby Mine,** 6771 Sylva Road; (828) 369–5271

- **Gem Mine at Gem World,** 1884 Georgia Road; (828) 349–5411

- **Gold City Gem Mine,** 9410 Sylva Road; (828) 369–3905

- **Jackson Hole Trading Post,** located on Highway 64 near Highway 28 between Franklin and Highlands; (828) 524–5850

- **Mason Mountain Mine (The Johnson's Place),** 5315 Bryson City Road; (828) 524–4570

- **Rose Creek Mine & Campground,** 115 Terrace Ridge; (828) 349–3774

- **Sheffield Mine,** 385 Sheffield Farms Road; (828) 369–8383

a flume and a single bucket. You'll want to call ahead to find out if equipment is included in the mining fee, which varies from mine to mine. Some charge per bucket, while others have an admission fee and then charge a nominal per-bucket fee. Most are open during daylight hours, and you can find one open any day of the week. Most mines operate April through October.

Franklin Gem and Mineral Museum (ages 5 and up)
25 Phillips Street; (828) 369–7831; www.fgmm.org. Open noon to 4:00 p.m. Monday through Friday and 11:00 a.m. to 3:00 p.m. Saturday, May 1 through October 31.
Free.

If you don't have much luck hunting for gems on your own, stop by one of the many shops in the area or at the Franklin Gem and Mineral Museum, located in the old jail. The museum, operated by the Franklin Gem and Mineral Society, features displays of all the native stones and a little bit about the history of the area's development.

Scottish Tartan Museum and Heritage Center (ages 5 and up)
86 East Main Street; (828) 524–7472; www.scottishtartans.org. Open 10:00 a.m. to 5:00 p.m. Monday through Saturday and 1:00 to 5:00 p.m. Sunday year-round except for major holidays. $.

This museum takes you to the Scotland of old. The Scottish Tartan Museum and Heritage Center, in downtown Franklin, is an extension of the Scottish Tartans Society. The museum includes displays on the tartan and Highland dress from as far back as 1700, as well as displays on the evolution of the kilt. A research library also provides information about the Scottish influence on the Appalachian and Cherokee cultures. If you have a Scottish background, you can try to find your roots.

Mountain Glides (ages 14 and up)
306 Depot Street; (828) 349–0506. $$$$.

This falls into the "why didn't I think of this" category. Sightseeing tours by Segway, a hi-tech, self-balancing scooter-like form of transportation, take visitors through and around town almost effortlessly. Mountain Glides offers tours alongside Little Tennessee River on the town Greenway, up Town Hill, and down Main Street. Each guest gets his own Segway and must be at least 14 years of age, giving the older kids in the family something fun to do. Tours start at around $50 and sell out well in advance.

Amazing North Carolina Facts

In 1973, the emerald was selected as North Carolina's precious stone. A 1,438-carat emerald is the largest ever found in the state.

Where to Eat

B&D Restaurant, 10 Palmer Street; (828) 524–3573. It looks like the B&D might have been an old hardware store at one time, but the burgers are great! $

The Boiler Room, 1024 Georgia Road; (828) 349–5555. The Boiler Room at The Factory game room features upscale dining in a family atmosphere where you can enjoy steaks, seafood, pasta, and gourmet desserts. $$

The City Restaurant, 1251 East Main Street; (828) 524–4948. You'll want to get breakfast here. The menu offers a variety of down-home selections. $$

Depot Bar and Grill, 577 Depot Street; (828) 369–9909. This is a pleasant casual restaurant decorated with antiques and a model train. Mom and Dad can enjoy a glass of wine and fine food, but there's also a children's menu and an old-time ice cream parlor. It's open Wednesday through Saturday only. $–$$

Sunset Drive-In Restaurant, 498 Harrison Avenue; (828) 524–4842. Drive-ins are just always fun when you can find them. $

Where to Stay

Carolina Mountaintop Homes, 150 Deer Crossing Road; (800) 820–1210. Located just outside Franklin on thirty-two acres, this company offers some pet-friendly options. $$$$

Colonial Inn, 3157 Georgia Road; (828) 524–6600. This inn, located on Highway 441, offers forty-two rooms, with basic amenities, on one level. $$

The Franklin Motel, 17 West Palmer Street; (800) 433–5507. Children under twelve stay **free** in this downtown motel. $$

Sapphire Inn, 761 East Main Street; (800) 401–0072. The Sapphire is a simple hotel in the middle of town. It does have a pool. $$$.

For More Information

Franklin Area Chamber of Commerce, (828) 524–3161 or (866) 372–5546; www.franklin-chamber.com.

Highlands

From Franklin take US 64 east to Highlands.

This region includes a particularly pleasing portion of a 61-mile scenic byway that begins to the north in Almond—a twenty-mile jaunt between Franklin and Highlands, the second-highest incorporated town in the eastern United States. The best idea is to bring along a picnic lunch—and don't forget the camera—for this ride. It takes about forty minutes and is truly lovely. In Highlands you'll find two of the most photographed waterfalls in the area. Heading east from Franklin, you first come to **Dry Falls** about 2 miles before you get to Highlands. From the parking lot an easy paved trail will take you behind, actually underneath, the 75-foot falls. Next, about 1 mile down the road, you come to **Bridal Veil Falls.** Here you can drive behind the 120-

foot falls, which you'll first see from the highway. You should be able to tell how this thin veil of running water got its name.

On the other side of the highway, about 2 miles to the west, are a campground and a picnic area. **Cliffside Lake** and **Van Hook Glade** offer picnic, camping, swimming, fishing, and hiking facilities. You can call the Highlands Ranger at (828) 526–3765 or the National Forest Office at (828) 257–4200 if you need more information or assistance while in this area.

To complete the 61-mile tour, you head north out of Franklin—that's west on US 64—to State Road 1310, also referred to as Wayah Road. Your drive takes you along Wayah Creek, which is mostly private, to **Wayah Bald**—the county's highest peak at 5,345 feet—named for the red wolves that once lived there. In this area you can hike part of the Appalachian Trail, have a picnic, see wildlife, and learn about how the natural beauty has been preserved despite more than a century of development.

Take Forest Road 69, a gravel road not on state maps, 1 mile to see the **Wilson Lick Ranger Station.** To find it, head west out of Franklin on State Road 1310. Built in 1913, it was the first ranger station in Nantahala National Forest. If you go 3 more miles up the road, you can park and take the paved trail to Wayah Bald Fire Tower. This tower, built by the Civilian Conservation Corps in the 1930s, provides a breathtaking view of the mountains of the Carolinas, as well as those of northern Georgia and southeastern Tennessee. A picnic area and two more hiking trails are located nearby. Some trails are more difficult than others, so you might want to check in with the Wayah Rangers District (828–524–6441) before you head out on any of them.

Your next destination should be **Nantahala Lake,** about 6 miles west of Wayah Bald on State Road 1310. With about 29 miles of shoreline, this lake offers fishing and boating (but no swimming). Picnic facilities are available on either side of the lake, accessible via State Road 1310. **Nantahala River** feeds the lake and provides excellent trout fishing, but you'll have to obtain the proper license.

State Road 1310 ends at Highway 19, near Andrews. Here you can finish your day trip and stop for a while to watch experienced water enthusiasts rafting, canoeing, and kayaking. A walkway gives you an excellent view of the brave ones traversing Nantahala Falls.

North Carolina **Fishing**

If you live outside North Carolina or you don't fish much, you can get a license to fish for up to three days. Most tackle stores can sell you the license best suited for your needs. Temporary licenses cost $5.00 per day for residents, $10.00 for nonresidents. You can buy them online at www.ncwildlife.org.

Where to Eat

Fireside Restaurant, located in Wright Square, West Main Street; (828) 526–3636. This nice family-style restaurant offers breakfast, lunch, and dinner. $$

Hilltop Grill, 326 South 4th Street; (828) 526–5916. Check out this old-fashioned grill that also offers soft-serve ice cream dips. $

The Log Cabin Steakhouse, Highway 106; (828) 526–3380. Located in a log cabin (duh), an interesting combination of steaks and Mexican fare are offered on both the adult and children's menus. $$$

Sports Page Sandwich Shoppe, 314 Main Street; (828) 526–3555. Drop in here for a quick lunch or a game-time meal. $–$$

Where to Stay

Highlands Suite Hotel, 205 East Main Street; (800) 221–5078. Few of the inns and B&Bs in Highlands are suitable for children, but this hotel is. It is a very nice AAA-approved suite hotel with all the amenities you would expect, including your own whirlpool and fireplace. $$$$

Whiteside Cove Cottages, Whiteside Mountain Road; (800) 805–3558. Five handsome log cabins are offered at the base of Whiteside Mountain between Cashiers and Highlands. The cabins are pet friendly. $$

For More Information

Highlands Chamber of Commerce Visitor's Center, (828) 526–2114; www.highlandschamber.org.

Robbinsville

Traveling northwest of Nantahala Lake to the intersection of US 129 and Highway 143 takes you into the town of Robbinsville.

Joyce Kilmer Memorial Forest 🅿️ 🚶

You can call the forest ranger's office at (828) 479–6431. Free.

Robbinsville lies at the eastern edge of one of the most impressive, undisturbed wilderness areas you will find in the country. Dedicated in 1936 to the poet who wrote *Trees*, the Joyce Kilmer Memorial Forest is truly a site to behold. Some of the trees in the forest are hundreds of years old, stand more than 100 feet high, and are 20 feet in diameter at the base. Here you will see a wide variety of trees, including yellow poplar, hemlock, sycamore, basswood, dogwood, beech, and oak, that burst into a blaze of red, yellow, and orange in early October. In spring, wildflowers, rhododendrons, mountain laurels, and azaleas take over the 3,800 acres, but you can't take the beauty with you when you go; removing any vegetation is prohibited by law. Let your camera capture your souvenirs. The forest is part of the 14,000-acre **Slickrock Wilderness Area,** where you'll find more than 60 miles of hiking trails that run along ridges and beside cool mountain streams. A 2-mile loop is easy enough for families to navigate and a picnic area is located on Route 416 at the entrance parking area.

Camping (A)

The U.S. Forest Service operates several campgrounds near Joyce Kilmer Memorial Forest. Contact the Nantahala National Forest office at (828) 479–6431; www.cs.unca .edu/nfsnc/.

To camp close to the forest, you'll probably want to head to **Horse Cove Campground,** located northwest of Robbinsville near the **Slickrock Wilderness Area.** In addition, **Cheoah Point Campground,** located on Santeetlah Lake off US 129, offers a host of recreational activities. Campsites cost $8.00 per night. Horse Cove is open year-round, but Cheoah Point closes between October and April. **Tsali Trail and Camping Area,** located off Route 28, has forty-one campsites and offers restrooms and showers. Here you can hike, bike, and enjoy all the fun the lake has to offer. **Cable Cove,** located just east on Highway 28, is a smaller recreation area. Tsali and Cable Cove campgrounds are open April through October.

For More Information

Graham County NC Travel and Tourism Authority, (800) 470–3790; www.grahamcountytravel.com.

Cherohala Skyway

Located off Highway 143 West and Santeetlah Road, the $100 million Cherohala Skyway, though less famous and shorter than the famed Blue Ridge Parkway, is majestic in its own right. One of twenty National Scenic Byways, it climbs to elevations of 5,300 feet and runs for 50 miles through the Cherokee and Nantahala National Forests. (Chero-hala, get it?) In North Carolina it begins in the town of Robbinsville overlooking Snowbird, Slickrock, and Joyce Kilmer Forests until drivers get to the state line and travel into Tellico Plains, Tennessee.

Scenic overlooks and strategically placed picnic tables give travelers ample time to while away the hours. Hiking trails, which vary greatly in degrees of difficulty, will take you into the forest. The Skyway also has rest facilities but no gas stations. For information call (800) 470–3790.

Fontana Village

Fontana Village is an expansive resort located north of Robbinsville along Highway 28. For information on Fontana Village attractions, call (800) 849–2258 or log on to www.fontanavillage.com.

This is the largest established resort in the area. Built by the Tennessee Valley Authority (TVA) in the early 1940s to house construction workers who were building Fontana Dam, the town was turned into a family resort following World War II. Today it has maintained its rustic, historic charm but offers everything you need for a wonderful, relaxing vacation. When you visit Fontana Village, you'll want to see **Fontana Dam,** an elaborate engineering feat for the time. Not only is the dam impressive, so is the fact that the TVA built a railroad and an entire community—including a hospital, bank, library, post office, and schools—essentially overnight. Fontana Dam is a massive concrete structure that stands 480 feet above its rock foundation, creating a 10,600-acre lake. From the visitor center at the top of the dam, you can take a tram or cable car into the powerhouse, where you'll see educational displays on the production of hydroelectricity. There is no admission charge. The visitor center is open from 9:00 a.m. to 8:00 p.m. daily, May through October.

Great Smoky Mountain Stables (all ages)
On Highway 28. $–$$$.

These stables offer pony rides for children under the age of ten ($$). For older children and adults, rides on trails through the dense forests of the area are offered ($$$).

Log Cabin Museum (all ages)
On Welch Road West. Open 9:00 a.m. to 7:00 p.m. daily year-round. Free.

You can take a self-guided tour of the Log Cabin Museum, built in 1875. Here you'll see many of the tools and relics that tell the history of the area's development. You'll learn about the Trail of Tears and the removal of the Cherokee people, and the arrival of the logging industry. The cabin is located in the heart of the village.

Amazing North Carolina Facts

Fontana Dam is 480 feet high, 2,365 feet wide, and includes 2.8 million cubic yards of concrete. It cost $74 million to build in the 1940s.

Fontana Marina ⚠

Located on Highway 28 about 1½ miles from the village on Fontana Lake; (800) 498–2211. Fees vary by activity.

This establishment offers canoe, kayak, and jet ski rentals, and fishing trips. Fishing licenses are available here as well. To get out on the water with someone else doing the work, try one of the two cruises the marina offers during the day. You can take a picnic cruise at noon ($$$) or a sightseeing cruise at 2:00 p.m. ($$). At 9:30 a.m. and 3:00 p.m., you can ride down the lake to the location where the 1994 motion picture *Nell*, starring Jodie Foster, was filmed ($$–$$$).

Where to Eat

Finding a place to eat won't be a problem at Fontana Village.

Mountview Bistro, located in The Lodge at Fontana Village, on Woods Road. The bistro serves breakfast, lunch and dinner that usually includes fresh-baked bread and pastries alongside home-style meals. $

The Wildwood Grill, located in Fontana Village on Welch Road West. The Grill offers a bit more atmosphere with dining on the patio and music inside. $$

Where to Stay

Fontana Campground, located on Highway 28 on the Little Tennessee River near the dam; (800) 849–2258. You'll find something for everyone in the family at this self-contained resort, which offers tent and trailer camping sites from May through October. There are three swimming pools, including one indoor pool, and a number of hot tubs that you can enjoy year-round. The kids will certainly love the village's nearby water slide. A crafts workshop (828–498–2211) (with gift shop) provides instruction in copper tooling, enameling, basketry, leather crafting, and stenciling. The kids might like the opportunity to learn the craft of shirt painting or birdhouse building. An activities center provides equipment for bike riding, archery, badminton, tennis, volleyball, shuffleboard, and horseshoes. The recreation department also plans structured activities such as softball and basketball games, pony rides, and guided hikes and bike rides. $

Fontana Village Resort, Highway 28; (800) 849–2258; www.fontanavillage.com. Fontana Inn offers ninety-four rooms, in addition to the resort's 150 cottages. The cottages, ranging from one to three bedrooms, come with all cooking and eating utensils. $$–$$$$

Bryson City

Drive east from Fontana Village to US 74/Highway 28 to find Bryson City.

Great Smoky Mountains National Park

Bryson City is an outdoor recreation center for the area and one of two North Carolina entrances to the Great Smoky Mountains National Park. Contact the Great Smoky Mountains National Park office at (615) 436–1200 or at www.greatsmokies.com for information on the park and its campgrounds.

Fontana Lake forms the southwestern border of the Great Smoky Mountains National Park, which covers a total of 520,000 acres and is bisected by the North Carolina–Tennessee state line. This is the most-visited national park in the United States, but don't worry if you're looking for space to stretch out. You'll find plenty of room to fish, hike, and camp.

The mountains of the park are among the oldest in the world and rise more than 6,000 feet. Plant and animal life is varied, with more than 140 species of trees and 200 species of wildflowers identified in the park. In the spring, the park comes alive with color as azaleas and wildflowers begin to bloom. Among the animal life that you might spot in the park are deer, wild turkey, ruffed grouse, and bear. You'll also find 900 miles of horseback riding and hiking trails and 735 miles of fishing streams. Many area campgrounds have organized activities, including presentations by park rangers and by people from the Cherokee Indian Reservation.

Make sure you take a drive up **The Road to Nowhere** from Bryson City to the national park. It was meant to be a route from Bryson City to Fontana Village when construction was begun following World War II. Bits and pieces of the road were built until the 1960s to the east side of Fontana Lake. Now it's one of the prettiest drives in the park.

Great Smoky Mountain Railway (all ages)

226 Everett Street; (800) 872–4681; www.gsmr.com. Trips run April through December. $$$–$$$$; free for children under two. Reservations are recommended.

One of the best ways to see the area is by taking a ride on the Great Smoky Mountain Railway. The railway offers regularly scheduled trips originating in Bryson City, Dillsboro to the south, and Andrews to the west on a train pulled by a steam locomotive or one of four conventional diesel locomotives. While the railway offers a number of different trips, the most popular is a four-hour excursion along Fontana Lake to the Nantahala Gorge and back. Beverages and snacks are available on the trains, and you can ride either in a comfortable enclosed coach or in an open car, which provides breathtaking views and excellent photo opportunities.

Outdoor Adventure

Two of the largest rafting outfitters, Wildwater, Ltd. (800–451–9972) and the Nantahala Outdoor Center (800–232–7238), offer special packages in conjunction with the railway. Other Bryson City outfitters include Adventurous Fast Rivers Rafting (800–438–7238), Endless River Adventures (800–224–7238), Paddle Inn Rafting Company (800–711–7238), Rolling Thunder River Company (800-408-7238), USA Raft (800–872–7238), Great Smokies Rafting Co. (800–581–4772), Nantahala Rafts (800–245–7700), and Carolina Outfitters Rafting (800–468–7238). Most offer other outdoor adventure equipment rentals and sales, too.

White-Water Rafting (ages 7 and up)
Prices vary; check with individual outfitters (see "Outdoor Adventure" sidebar).

Perhaps the most popular activity in the Bryson City area is rafting, and you can combine the railway trip with a white-water rafting trip. The area has several rivers that accommodate adventure seekers ready to get out on the water, but the Nantahala is by far the most popular. While some rivers may be too dangerous for a family excursion, the Nantahala is considered safe for children. Most outfitters will allow children as young as seven (a minimum of sixty pounds) on the trips. Check with several to find a trip that suits your needs.

Deep Creek Campground
1090 West Deep Creek Road, Bryson City; (828) 488–6055.

This great campground is located on the edge of the Great Smoky Mountains National Park. To get there follow the signs from the railway depot. The sites get crowded next to the creek, but you can find quieter sites on the hill in Section D. The most popular activity here is tubing.

You can rent a tire inner tube with a plastic or wood seat crafted in the middle ($). The plastic seats glide better over rock.

Going Tubular

Companies that provide tube rentals for tubing on Deep Creek include J. J. Tubes (828–488–3018), Deep Creek Store & Tubes (828–488–9665), Deep Creek Lodge/Creekside Tubing (828–488–2587), and Deep Creek Tube Center (828–488–6055). All are easy to find on your way to Deep Creek by vehicle and by tube as you finish your day.

Amazing
North Carolina Facts

The U.S. Fish and Wildlife Service and the National Park Service attempted the reintroduction of the red wolf into the Great Smoky Mountains in 1991. However, none of the thirty pups born in the wild since 1992 are known to have survived. Since then, the Western North Carolina Nature Center, the North Carolina Zoological Park, and the North Carolina Museum of Natural Sciences have joined forces to study, breed, and release red wolves on the Alligator River in eastern North Carolina.

Where to Eat

Anthony's Italian Restaurant, 103 Depot Street; (828) 488–8898. Conveniently located on Depot Street next to the train, hand-tossed pizzas, subs, and salads hit the spot after a long train ride. $

Everett Street Diner, 126 Everett Street; (828) 488–0123. Get a country breakfast as well as a variety of sandwiches, homemade soups, salads, and desserts. Local artwork is also displayed. $

Nantahala Village Restaurant, 9400 Highway 19 West; (828) 488–2826. The Village Restaurant offers a family-friendly atmosphere and a pretty good rib eye. The menu also includes trout and salmon along with children's selections. $$

Papa's Pizza To Go, 165 Everett Street; (828) 488–3700. If it's pizza time, this is the place to go. Papa's, one of a small chain, also serves sandwiches. $

Slow Joe's Cafe at Nantahala Outdoor Center, U.S. Highways 19/74 West; (828) 488–2176. If anyone stays behind on the rafting trip, they can grab a bite at Slow Joe's while enjoying the action on the river. $

Where to Stay

Almond Boat and RV Park, 1165 Almond Boat Park Road; (828) 488–6423. Almond offers RV sites as well as a dozen cottages with kitchenettes. $–$$$

Bryson View Cabin Rentals, 120 Sturken Drive; (828) 488–0220. These cabins, located in town, accommodate up to ten people and their pets. $$$–$$$$

The Cabins at Nantahala, 299 Dills Road; (888) 447–4436. These two-bedroom cabins are perfect for small families but you have to provide your own bathtowels and utilize the nearby bathhouse. $$

Carolina Mountain Vacations, 40 Greenlee Street; (828) 488–7500. This agency offers cabins, homes, and cottage rentals that are privately owned. $$$$

Creekside Cabins, 1044 West Deep Creek; (828) 488–2235. Located on the banks of the creek, you'll find eight rustic cabins and a country home that sleeps eight. $$–$$$

Euchella Sports Lodge, 9698 Highway 19 West; (800) 446–1603. The Euchella offers rooms at this site plus cabins and cottages from here to Almond. $$–$$$$

Freeman's Motel and Cottages, Highway 28 North, Almond; (828) 488–2737. Located just outside Bryson City, this relatively small operation offers a variety of accommodations. $–$$$$

Galbreath Creek Cabins, 24 Fry Street; (877) 943–8252. Twenty modern cabins with hot tubs and other amenities are tucked away just outside the national park. $$$

Heart of the Smokies Log Cabin Rentals, 504 Cline Road; (828) 488–6658. This company offers one- and two-bedroom cabins, front porch rocking chairs, and welcomes pets. $$$

Lands Creek Log Cabins, 3336 Balltown Road; (828) 488–9793. Some of these cabins already have established places for campfires. You'll find Jacuzzis in some. $$$–$$$$

Smoky Mountain Retreat, 51 Green Valley Acres; (828) 488–6347. Amazingly elegant custom-crafted log homes are offered for rent at the foot of a mountain, just outside Bryson City. $$$$

For More Information

Swain County Chamber of Commerce, (800) 867–9246; www.great smokies.com.

Parent's **Tip**

Bryson City, as well as many of the other mountain resort towns, offers a number of country inn and bed-and-breakfast dining rooms that make for a quiet, romantic evening. Some restaurants allow you to put a tie on junior and take him along, but I recommend leaving him with an older sibling.

Cherokee

Just a few miles east of Bryson City on US 19 is the town of Cherokee and the Cherokee Indian Reservation.

A visit to Cherokee is an interesting experience in that it combines the best of how things once were and good old-fashioned tourism marketing. Cherokee is the sole town located in the 56,000-acre Qualla Boundary Cherokee Indian Reservation, which is home to roughly 8,500 members of the Eastern Band of the Cherokee. It is nestled between the Great Smoky Mountains National Park and the western end of the Blue Ridge Parkway. The town has become a burgeoning tourist attraction. And amid all the glitz and glitter, you'll find much to do and learn.

Museum of the Cherokee Indian (all ages)

Located at U.S. Highway 441 and Drama Road; (828) 497–3481; www.cherokee museum.org. Open 9:00 a.m. to 6:00 p.m. Monday through Sunday, May to mid-June; 9:00 a.m. to 8:00 p.m. Monday through Saturday and 9:00 a.m. to 5:00 p.m. Sunday, mid-June through August. $$; free for children under six.

You'll want to take a lot of time to explore this area, and the best place to begin is at the Museum of the Cherokee Indian. The museum gives you an introduction to the Cherokee heritage, history, and culture. In front is a 20-foot California Redwood statue of Sequoyah, who invented the Cherokee alphabet. In addition to a big collection of clothes, crafts, weapons, and artifacts—some of which are more than 10,000 years old—the museum also has an art gallery and theaters where you can learn about this culture's history through audiovisual shows. Especially interesting are special phones allowing you to hear the Cherokee language spoken.

Oconaluftee Indian Village (ages 5 and up)

Located just off US 441; (828) 497–2315; www.oconalufteevillage.com. Open 9:00 a.m. to 5:30 p.m. daily, mid-May through late October. $$–$$$.

While you will see a number of people dressed in Native American attire, complete with headdress and ready to be photographed throughout Cherokee's tourist activity, these are not authentically dressed Cherokee. The real way the Native Americans lived can be seen at several attractions on the reservation. One of the most enlightening places to visit in the Cherokee area is the Oconaluftee Indian Village, where the past comes alive. The village is an authentic re-creation of an eighteenth-century Cherokee Indian community. Here costumed guides take you on a tour of the village, where you will see local people working at the ancient arts of basket making and pottery, and demonstrating blowguns, canoe hulling, and finger weaving, an art that involves using the fingers in place of a shuttle to produce colorful belts, headbands, and other articles. You can also visit the seven-sided council house—a wood and dirt structure—and learn how the Cherokee tribes functioned.

Unto These Hills (ages 5 and up)

Located on US 441, north of downtown; (828) 497–2111; www.untothesehills.com. Shows are presented at 8:30 p.m. Monday through Saturday, mid-June through late August. $$–$$$.

Near the village is the Cherokees' Mountainside Theater, where *Unto These Hills* is performed during the summer. The outdoor drama, written by Kermit Hunter, is an inspirational piece that captures the history of the Cherokee Indians from the mid-1500s to the tragedy of the Trail of Tears in the late 1830s. The Cherokee people originally settled much of this land, but many were forced off it by the U.S. government and made to march to Arkansas and Oklahoma. During these marches more than 4,000 of the 15,000 Native Americans involved died of disease or exposure. Others, whose descendants still live here, managed to escape into the mountains. The play, produced by more than 130 performers and technicians, runs about two hours.

Santa's Land Family Fun Park and Zoo (all ages)

US 19 or Soco Road, 3 miles west of downtown; (828) 497–9191; www.santaslandnc .com. Open 9:00 a.m. to 5:00 p.m. daily, May through October, and on weekends in November. $$$; children two and under free. The admission includes all rides, entertainment, and exhibits.

Celebrate Christmas during the summer at Santa's Land Family Fun Park and Zoo. An especially good attraction for younger children, it is a few minutes' drive east of Cherokee. The kids get an early order to Santa and his elves and visit the animals in the petting zoo, where they will see dozens of domestic and exotic animals. You'll also find paddleboats, train rides, and the Rudi-Coaster.

Cherokee Fun Park (all ages)

US 441; (828) 497–5877; www.cherokeefunpark.com. Hours vary according to season and weather. Prices vary by attraction.

More modern recreation is waiting at Cherokee Fun Park, located near the entrance to the Great Smoky Mountains National Park. The park features four acres of go-karts, bumper boats, miniature golf, and a big game room. The kids will let you know where it is. Yeah, it even looks fun.

Oconaluftee Islands Park

US 441, near downtown; (800) 438–1601. Free.

This is an attractive little grassy island park with a lovely river running through it, where you can get away from the tourist activity that abounds in Cherokee. Kids can wade in the creek, build a dam, or just chill!

The Great Outdoors

Don't forget about all the outdoor activities the Cherokee area has to offer. Trout fishing on the Cherokee Indian Reservation is excellent, and you'll find hundreds of miles of streams and several ponds in the area. Two North Carolina trout fishing records have been established on the reservation in recent years. A special reservation fishing license costs $7 per day, and children younger than twelve can fish on a parent's license.

Whether you want to stay in a luxury hotel, a cabin, or at a campground, you won't have any problem finding a place to suit your recreational needs. One of the best campgrounds nearby is **Smokemont Campground,** 6 miles north of Cherokee off US 441 in the Smokemont community. In addition to fishing streams and hiking trails, you'll also find great horseback riding trails and stables where you can make arrangements to rent horses. Smokemont Campground is open year-round, and sites cost $17 to $20. **KOA Kampgrounds,** located on Star Route north of Cherokee, is the largest commercial campground in the area. It offers a wide range of sites, from primitive tent sites to paved sites with full hookups to rustic cabins on the creek, that fit any budget. You will also find a wide variety of activities at the thirty-five-acre campground, including swimming, tennis, volleyball, a game room, and more. The campground's Fun Bus is ready to take you on a fun-filled day trip or shuttle you up the river for a 3-mile tubing trip. Call (828) 497–9711 or log on to www.cherokeekoa .com for more information.

Where to Eat

Grandma's Pancake and Steak, US 441 and 19; (828) 497–9801. Want pancakes in the middle of the day? Get 'em here. Grandma also serves country-style food. $

Tee Pee Restaurant, US 441; (828) 497–5141. The Tee Pee is located next to Mountainside Theater and has a buffet and menu. $

Where to Stay

Baymont Inn, Acquoni Road; (828) 497–2102. There are sixty-six rooms in this three-story hotel. You can walk to a fishing stream, and other attractions aren't much farther away. $$$

Craig's Motel, US 19 North; (828) 497–3821. This AAA-approved motel offers thirty-one rooms near a stream with picnic tables and grills. $$–$$$

Drama Inn, 62 Tsali Boulevard; (828) 497–3271. The Drama Inn, on the banks of the Oconaluftee River, is within walking distance to The Museum of the Cherokee Indians and other attractions. $$$

Pageant Hills Motel, 739 Tsali Boulevard; (828) 497–5371. Located on US 441, this motel offers forty-two rooms. $–$$

Pioneer Motel and Cottages, US 441 near US 19; (828) 497–2435. This motel offers rooms as well as riverside cabins. Lots of extras, such as horseshoes and basketball courts. $$–$$$

Riverside Motel and Campground, US 441 South; (828) 497–9311. This small motel features all riverfront rooms and a covered area with picnic tables and grill. The campground has thirty sites for camper, RV or tent. $

Smoky Mountain Cabins, US 19 North; (828) 497–0088. You can find quieter accommodations by calling Smoky Mountain Cabins. $$$$

For More Information

Cherokee Welcome Center, (800) 438–1601, (828) 497–9195, or (828) 497–5737; www.cherokee-nc.com.

Maggie Valley

Keep heading east on US 19, and you'll be in Maggie Valley.

You can plan to spend several hours in downtown Maggie Valley, its streets lined with specialty shops, restaurants, and various amusements. The community is a popular tourist resort and gets crowded during peak vacation times, but that doesn't spoil the old-time country feel of the town. Accommodations are as varied here as they are throughout the Smoky Mountains, but the best thing about this area's hotels and cottages is the spectacular view of the landscape that many of them offer.

Clingman's Dome

In the next chapter we'll learn about North Carolina's highest peak, but we'll break here to include Tennessee's highest peak because it shares the state line with North Carolina. Clingman's Dome earns its title at 6,643 feet and was named after U.S. Senator Thomas Lanier Clingman. It is the tallest mountain in the Smoky Mountains National Park.

Clingman's Dome is accessible via a paved road, that's closed from November through March, off US 441 (Newfound Gap Road) north of Cherokee. A paved road leads to within 300 feet of the summit, and from there visitors can walk a trail to the top. A wheelchair-accessible tower is located at the summit, and on clear days visitors can see four states (Tennessee, North Carolina, South Carolina, and Georgia). The area is developed with picnic tables and restrooms. For more information call the Great Smoky Mountain National Park office headquartered in Gatlinburg, Tennessee at (423) 436–1200.

The Cataloochee **Valley**

The Cataloochee Valley area of the Great Smoky Mountains National Park has taken on some new residents—elk. In 2002, the U.S. Department of Fish and Wildlife successfully reintroduced the species that once thrived in the area but were hunted out before the turn of the nineteenth century. They can often be seen grazing in the Cataloochee Valley, accessible from Maggie Valley, in the early morning and in the evenings.

Ghost Town in the Sky (all ages)
US 19; (828) 926–1140; www.ghosttowninthesky.com. Open 9:30 a.m. to 6:00 p.m. daily, the first Saturday in May through the last Sunday in October. $$–$$$$; free for children ages two and under.

A great western theme park should be first on any family's itinerary during a trip to this area. Here you can relive the adventures of frontier life against a beautiful mountain backdrop. You enter the park up a steep, 3,300-foot mountainside by an inclined railway or chairlift (a shuttle bus is available for the queasy). Stay alert as you browse through the Old West shops and displays because, just as in the frontier days, you never know when you'll be in the middle of a "gunfight" or "bank robbery." The park includes more than thirty rides and shows, including a roller coaster that almost casts you out over a mile-high mountainside. You can enjoy music and dancing at the old city hall or belly up to the bar at the Silver Dollar Saloon, where you will see the honky-tonk piano and can-can dancers. Country music abounds, and shows are presented continuously at the Mile High Fun Center. Plenty of grub—snacks, full meals, as well as picnic facilities—is available at Ghost Town.

The Stompin' Ground (ages 3 and up)
3116 Soco Road; (828) 926–1288. Shows begin at 8:00 p.m. nightly May through October. $$.

Get out your dancing shoes when you visit The Stompin' Ground. Here you get a glimpse of mountain heritage through clogging and mountain dancing adapted from the area's Irish and Scottish heritages. You'll be moved to stomp your feet yourself during the shows that are presented nightly.

Wheels Through Time Museum (ages 5 and up)
Soco Road, Maggie Valley; (828) 926–6266. Open 9:00 a.m. to 6:00 p.m. daily April through November, and 10:00 a.m. to 5:00 p.m. daily December through March. $; free for children four and under.

This museum features commercial, police, and military motorcycles that date back as far as 1909 when motorcycles began to emerge as a reliable form of transportation.

More than sixty working machines and other memorabilia create a sort of timeline through the twentieth century and into the twenty-first. From classic Harleys to one-off production models that just didn't catch on, the museum takes guests right up to the machines that thrill today's riders.

Cataloochee Ranch (all ages; horseback riding for ages 6 and up)

119 Ranch Drive; (800) 868–1401; www.cataloochee-ranch.com. $$$$.

To get out of the crowds, give Cataloochee Ranch a try. Located just a few miles north of Maggie Valley, the resort has been operating for more than sixty years. Here you not only find the aura of a rugged sheep and cattle farm, but you can also enjoy all the amenities of a modern vacation. The 1,000-acre ranch is one of only three private entrances to the Great Smoky Mountains National Park. The ranch offers individual cabins as well as rooms at the Silverbell Lodge and at the ranch house. The vegetable garden produces a great variety of food that makes its way to your dinner table in a hearty family-style setting. In addition to meals, the only structured activity at the ranch is horseback riding ($$$$). The rest of the time is your own, as the lodge offers tennis, hiking, trout fishing, horseshoes, table tennis, badminton, and croquet. You can relax by the swimming pool, take a hayride, or walk through the ranch's glorious meadows, where wildflowers abound in spring and summer. Bonfires, complete with storytelling and roasted marshmallows, round out the day.

Cataloochee Ski Area (all ages)

1080 Ski Lodge Road; (800) 768–0285; www. cataloochee.com. $$–$$$$.

Perhaps the best thing about the ranch is that it's right next door to the Cataloochee Ski Area. With the help of snowmakers, the North Carolina ski season usually starts in early December. Cataloochee has ten slopes and trails that range from gentle slopes for beginners to the monstrous 5,400-foot Moody Top plus a snowtube park. The Cataloochee Ski School offers skiing and boarding lessons; inquire about special lesson packages for children and family-special days. Hours of operation may vary according to weather.

Where to Eat

Arf's Restaurant, 1316 Soco Road; (828) 926–1566. Get the baby back ribs here. $$

Mountaineer Buffet, US 19; (828) 926–1730. This is a great place to relax following a long day at Ghost Town.

Where to Stay

You'll find dozens of places to stay in Maggie Valley, but here's a short list to get you started.

Jonathan Creek Inn, 4324 Soco Road; (800) 577–7812. This inn has forty-two rooms plus suites and a cottage and is very family oriented with a playground and children's programs. $$–$$$

Laurel Park Inn, 257 Soco Road; (800) 451–4424. This is a small, very afford-able inn. $–$$

Smoky Falls Lodge, 2550 Soco Road; (877) 926–7440. A game room and miniature golf make this thirty-two-room facility a great place from which to explore the area. $$–$$$

For More Information

The Maggie Valley Area Convention and Visitors Bureau, (800) 785–8259 or (828) 926–1686; www.maggie valley.org.

Waynesville

US 19 east to U.S. Highway 23 will take you to Waynesville.

This small, quaint mountain community still has brick sidewalks in the downtown district. Here you'll find more than one hundred charming shops, galleries, and restaurants. Among them are the **Mast General Store** (828–452–2101) and **Smith's Drugs** (828–456–8607), where you can get a drink from the old-fashioned soda foun-tain. Everything from antiques to clothes is available in the shopping district, but you might want to schedule your trip here for late July. Waynesville is home to North Car-olina's Official International Festival, **Folkmoot USA,** a two-week celebration of the world's cultural heritage through folk music and dance. Held in late July, Folkmoot features performances by more than three hundred artists representing more than a dozen countries. It also includes parades and workshops. Events demon-strate cultural heritage through colorful, authentic costumes; lively dance; music; and lots of food. For more information call (828) 452–2997 or log on to www.folkmoot.com.

Museum of North Carolina Handicrafts

(ages 5 and up)

307 Shelton Street; (828) 452–1551. Open 10:00 a.m. to 4:00 p.m. Tuesday through Friday, May through October; hours vary at other times. $

While you are in Waynesville, stop in at the Museum of North Carolina Handicrafts. Housed in the Shelton House, a farm home built in 1875, the museum features works by some of the state's best-known artisans. Here you'll see hand-carved dulcimers, unique carved bowls, and items children will love, like wooden, mule-drawn wagons and sleds. The Indian room features a collection of Navajo rugs, baskets, and jewelry as well as Cherokee crafts and artifacts.

Fishing Fun

If you lack experience with fishing, but want a successful experience with the kids, try a trout farm. The farms provide rod, line, and bait and it's not difficult to bring home a catch for dinner. They typically charge by the pound. Here is a list of area places to try your luck. Ferguson's Trout Pond, Clyde, (828) 627–6404; Holland's Trout Pond, Maggie Valley, (828) 926–0313; Maggie Valley Trout Pond, Maggie Valley, (828) 926–0766; Marvin's Soco Gap Trout Ponds, Maggie Valley, (828) 926–3635; Sorrell's Creek Trout Farm, Canton, (828) 648–9903; and Tusquitee Trout Ranch, Hayesville, (828) 389–6598.

Where to Eat

Carroll's Fine Food and Game World, 1840 South Main Street; (828) 456–9149. A large game room comes with your hot dogs and burgers here. $

O'Malley's On Main Pub & Grill, 172 North Main Street; (828) 452–4228. The name probably gives away the fun Irish theme in a grill that's typically crowded. $

Where to Stay

Hemphill Mountain Campground, 32 Woods Road; (828) 926–0331. This campground features pony rides for kids as well as a complete stable. $

Oak Park Inn, 314 South Main Street; (828) 456–5328. Rooms, condos, and efficiencies are offered at this AAA-approved motel. $$–$$$

Parkway Inn, 2093 Dellwood Road; (828) 926–1841. This is another AAA-approved motel that's very pleasant and affordable. $$

For More Information

Haywood County Tourism Development Authority, (800) 334–9036; www.smokymountains.net or www .waynesville.com.

Canton

Canton is a few miles east of Waynesville on US 74.

Canton Area Historical Museum (ages 5 and up)
36 Park Street; (828) 646–3412. Open 9:00 a.m. to 4:00 p.m. Monday through Friday. Open by appointment on Saturday and Sunday. Free.

The Canton Area Historical Museum, just a few miles east of Waynesville, is a small but interesting museum that also serves as the area visitor center. It offers a look at how this area, once a hunting and fishing ground for the Cherokee Indians, was developed. Following European settlement, it became a popular stopping point for western ranchers moving their cattle and swine to market in the East. In addition, the Pigeon River made it an important shipping point, leading to the establishment of the Champion Paper Mill, which remains the area's biggest employer. This history is presented in displays of the mill and with area artifacts, pictures, and records that provide a glimpse into life from the late 1800s to the present.

A Hoffman **Family Adventure**

Wahoo's Adventures sounded like the perfect outfit to take the kids (in middle school at the time) on their first white-water rafting trip. Our guide was eager to ensure we didn't have a dull moment, leading us in a game of "king of the boat" on the slowest part of the river and spinning yarns about his fifteen years leading trips. About four hours into the five-hour tour, blue skies clouded over and became grayer and grayer until finally, the heavens opened up. Raindrops pelted us like needles falling from the sky. Crackles of lightning from within the clouds reminded us that water and electricity definitely do not mix. We had been paddling feverishly to reach the end of the trip, but the guide gave the order to beach the rafts, saying he had never experienced anything like this on the river. We went ashore and propped the rubber rafts up on the oars to create shelter from the storm. We huddled together under our lean-to until the storm passed and the sun began to burn through the clouds. The kids and I were no worse for the wear, even though we were scared to death. The guide also handled the situation rationally and professionally. Our only disappointment: The photographer hired and waiting on the bank of the river to document the trip didn't wait out the storm.

Dillsboro

Dillsboro is located at the junction of US 23/441 and 74, southwest of Waynesville.

Maintaining the distinction of an old railway town, Dillsboro has been turned into a charming shopping and historic district. The Dillsboro Historic District is nestled at the edges of the Great Smoky Mountains on the Tuckasegee River. Log cabins and homes from the late 1800s provide showcases for handmade crafts and homemade treats. You can get a walking map of the district by calling the Jackson County Visitor's Center at (800) 962–1911. Then just park your car and stroll through the village, where you find very friendly shopkeepers and artisans. Visitors will find more than sixty shops, restaurants, and more in a 3-block area. So if the kids aren't exactly thrilled with the thought of going shopping, point out the blown glass, pottery, candles, and other items you'll see being made before your eyes. **Nancy Tut's Christmas Shop** (800–742–7155) might catch their attention for a while, and if you promise them a sample from the **Dillsboro Chocolate Factory** (828–631–0156), a good time is a lock. You might also check out **Bradley's General Store** (828–586–3891), a "Family Tradition Since 1888" (at least that's what they say). This old-time soda fountain sells local honey, jams and jellies, antiques, gifts, T-shirts, Yankee Candles, and Amish furniture. You might also stop in at **The Nature Connection** (828–586–0686) which carries cool metal sculptures, birdhouses, and mountain toys. **Peppermint Patti's Ice Cream & Candy Shoppe** comes right out of the 1950s with shakes, sundaes, banana splits, and floats.

Great Smoky Mountain Railway (all ages)

119 Front Street; (800) 872–4681; www.gsmr.com. Trips run April through December. $$$–$$$$; Free for children under two. Reservations are recommended.

Dillsboro is the "other end" of the Great Smoky Mountain Railway. You might find this location a little less crowded than the Bryson City end. The town has great charm and more than enough opportunity to soak up mountain life. This is also a good location to visit for special events conducted by the railroad such as the Santa Express, when the kids can have brunch with Santa, or "A Day Out with Thomas the Train."

Where to Eat

Dillsboro Smokehouse, 403 Haywood Street; (828) 586–9556. Locals like this barbecue restaurant as much as tourists. It has great ribs! $$

Beats and Eats, 164 Front Street; (828) 631–3647.You'll find burgers and other fast food selections on the menu here, but you should try the chili hot dogs. $

Where to Stay

Apple Realty, Macktown Road; (800) 766–2775. Fifty cabins are offered for rent. $$

Dillsboro Inn, 146 North River Road; (866) 586–3898. Riverfront suites here include balconies overlooking the waterfall. The inn also serves a continental breakfast. $$$$

Smoky Mountain Getaways, 12 Young Lane, Sylva; (866) 586–8058. This agency offers a wide variety of rental vacation homes in woods on the river and at the lake. $$$$

For More Information

The Dillsboro Merchants Association, www.visitdillsboro.org.

Cullowhee

To get here from Dillsboro, take Highway 107 South.

The Mountain Heritage Center (ages 5 and up)

Robins Administration Building, WCU; (828) 227–7129; www.wcu.edu/mhc/. Open 8:00 a.m. to 5:00 p.m. Monday through Friday and 2:00 to 5:00 p.m. Sunday, June through October, except during university holidays. **Free.**

The Mountain Heritage Center is part of Western Carolina University in Cullowhee. The center promotes the rich tradition of the southern Appalachian Mountains through exhibits, educational programs, and demonstrations. Exhibits at the center present life in the mountains through the years. You'll see photographs, artifacts, relics, and other displays that relate to the migration of the Scotch-Irish people who settled the area in the eighteenth century. The center also presents temporary exhibits on mountain crafts and works such as blacksmithing as well as programs on the natural beauty of the area. Thousands of people from across the Carolinas, Georgia, and Tennessee come to Cullowhee the last Saturday of each September for **Mountain Heritage Day,** which is sponsored in part by the Mountain Heritage Center. The usually quiet town of Cullowhee comes alive with crafts, mountain music, food, storytelling, and more during this event. Admission and events are **free.** For more information call the Mountain Heritage Center.

Other Things to See and Do
in the Great Smoky Mountains

- **Chunky Gal Stables,** Hayesville, (828) 389–4175
- **The Factory,** Franklin, (828) 349–8888
- **Franklin Family Entertainment Center,** Franklin, (828) 524–8567
- **Great Smoky Mountain Fish Camp and Safaris,** Franklin, (828) 369–5295
- **Cherokee Bear Zoo and Exotic Animals,** Cherokee, (828) 497–4525
- **The Mini-Apolis Grand Prix,** Maggie Valley, (828) 926–1685
- **Maggie Valley Carpet Golf,** Maggie Valley, (828) 926–3255
- **Fantasy Golf and Gameroom,** Maggie Valley, (828) 926–8180
- **Canton Recreation Park,** Canton, (828) 646–3411
- **Old Pressley Sapphire Mine,** Canton, (828) 648–6320
- **Queen's Farm Riding Stables,** Waynesville, (828) 926–0718
- **Waynesville Recreation Park,** Waynesville, (828) 456–8577

The Blue Ridge Mountains

Y ou'll never know how much fun a waterfall can be until you go to North Carolina's Blue Ridge Mountains. In this land of waterfalls, each one is a beautiful sight, but one waterfall stands out from all the rest and promises hours of fun in the water for your family. In addition, western North Carolina's biggest city, including the largest private residence in the United States, is here, ready to provide great family adventure. This region also offers an opportunity to learn about some of the state's most prominent residents or to take a trip with the help of a llama.

Interstate 40 is the main route in the Blue Ridge from points east. Interstate 26 or U.S. Highway 321 will get you here from the south. One of the main attractions here is the Blue Ridge Parkway, and you'll easily discover all the activities it has to offer in

Jim's TopPicks in the Blue Ridge Mountains

1. Tweetsie Railroad
2. Sliding Rock and surrounding area in Pisgah National Forest
3. Chimney Rock Park in Chimney Rock
4. Grandfather Mountain
5. Biltmore Estate in Asheville
6. Linville Falls and Linville Gorge Wilderness Area
7. Ski areas
8. Canoeing on the New River
9. Pack Place in Asheville
10. Mount Mitchell State Park

THE BLUE RIDGE MOUNTAINS

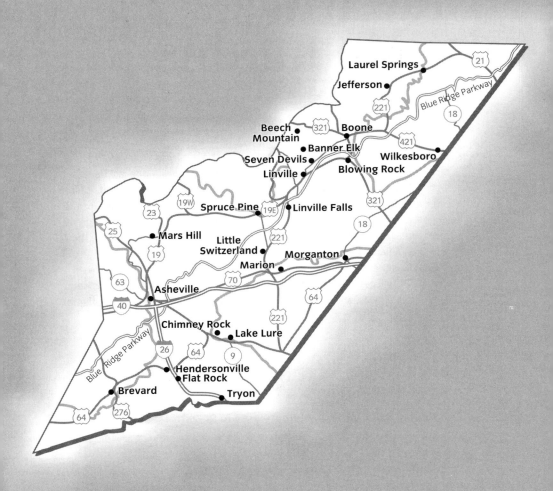

Laurel Springs

Jefferson

Blue Ridge Parkway

21

221

18

Beech
Mountain

321

Boone

421

Banner Elk

Wilkesboro

Seven Devils

Blowing Rock

Linville

19W

Spruce Pine

19E

Linville Falls

321

23

221

18

25

Mars Hill

Little
Switzerland

19

Marion

Morganton

63

70

Asheville

64

40

221

Chimney Rock

Lake Lure

Blue Ridge Parkway

26

64

9

Hendersonville

Flat Rock

Brevard

Tryon

64

276

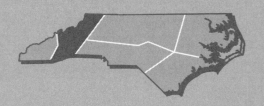

addition to its breathtaking views. If you're looking for quick travel, however, stick to the other highways because the parkway speed limit is 45 miles per hour.

Brevard

Brevard is located on U.S. Highway 276 south of the Blue Ridge Parkway.

Brevard and Transylvania County are known as the land of waterfalls. The Davidson and French Broad Rivers and their tributaries account for more than 250 waterfalls and 200 miles of cool mountain streams winding through the area. You can actually make a day out of visiting some of the lovely falls in this area. Start by heading west from Brevard on U.S. Highway 64, then south on Highway 281 to Whitewater Falls, where you can hike the short trail for a panoramic view of the falls. At 441 feet, the upper part of this two-level cascade is believed to be the highest in the eastern United States. Also on Highway 281 you'll find Rainbow Falls, which drops more than 200 feet. On US 64 is Toxaway Falls, which cascades 123 feet, with the highway running across the top. For more information on some of the beautiful sites in this area, contact The Brevard/Transylvania County Visitors Center at (800) 648–4523 or check out www.visitwaterfalls.com.

Sliding Rock (ages 7 and up)

A series of falls is located along Pisgah Highway and included is this fun attraction. A large paved parking area is located on Pisgah Highway. Call the Pisgah National Forest office at (828) 877–3350 or visit www.cs.unca.edu/nfsnc. Free.

North of Brevard you head into **Pisgah National Forest,** which provides a wide range of camping facilities and great fishing streams. You'll find waterfalls here, too, and more adventure than you might expect. Sliding Rock was named Sliding Rock for just that reason. The 150-foot natural water slide is a favorite of visitors to the area who aren't afraid to get wet. It's an exhilarating blast as you speed down the huge rock along with the 11,000 gallons of sixty-degree water that flow each minute. Your ride down the rock ends in a pool, so if the kids want to make the slide, be sure they are strong swimmers. You can walk smaller children down the rock and let them make a short slide. Use extreme caution: The rocks are very slippery. After your slide, stop by **Looking Glass Falls** and **Looking Glass Rock,** believed to be the largest single piece of granite in the southern Appalachians. You can park at the side of the road and walk down to the bottom of the 85-foot falls.

Cradle of Forestry (all ages)

2002 Pisgah Highway, Pisgah Forest; (828) 877–3130; www.cradleofforestry.com. Open 9:00 a.m. to 5:00 p.m. daily, April through October. $–$$; free for children under age five.

What would a national forest be if it didn't provide an opportunity to study nature? The Cradle of Forestry is a great hands-on museum that gets you on the road to discovering the wide variety of plant and animal life that inhabits this forest. Nearly one hundred years ago the Cradle of Forestry was opened as the country's first school of forestry. The museum is now operated by the U.S. Forest Service and is a National Historic Site. It's located about 14 miles north of Brevard on the main forest road (US 276). In addition to the displays of plant and animal life, the museum also displays tools and other relics that relate to the history of the area. Young children will love learning about forest conservation at the Forest Fun Exhibit, where they can play with puzzles, puppets, and costumes. A touch-screen monitor lets them find more information on selected topics. Then head out on one of two nature trails that interpret more of the history of forestry and logging. On one trail you see an old logging locomotive. On another, occasional demonstrations of spinning, weaving, blacksmithing, and quilting are held.

Pisgah Forest Fish Hatchery (all ages)

Located on a forest service road off US 276; (828) 877–4423; www.ncwildlife.org. The hatchery is open to the public from 8:00 a.m. to 4:00 p.m. daily. **Free.**

You can actually see why the trout fishing in this area is so good when you visit the Pisgah Forest Fish Hatchery. The hatchery breeds and raises 500,000 brown, brook, and rainbow trout annually for stocking in area streams during the month of March, when no trout fishing is permitted. At the hatchery you can walk along the troughs the fish are raised in to see their various stages of growth. Displays in the center provide information on the hatchery and how the fish are raised. In addition to an exhibit hall that includes aquariums with native species, the hatchery also features a short, paved trail that provides a look at other wildlife. From the trail, visitors can see dioramas, including preserved specimens such as bear and other woodland creatures.

Blue Ridge Corn Maze (all ages)

1605 Everett Road; (828) 884–4415. Operating mid-summer through Halloween. $–$$; **free** **for children age five and under.**

Escaping the Blue Ridge Corn Maze is a challenge for children and adults, who are asked to figure out a riddle as they wander through the rows of corn. Special events such as concerts throughout the period the maze is open adds to the fun.

Sapphire Valley Ski Resort

4000 US 64 West, Sapphire; (828) 743–1169; www.skisapphire.com. $$$

Winter is, of course, peak season of Sapphire Valley Ski Area and its Frozen Falls Tube Park; but it is a year-round resort just west of Brevard. With average elevation of 3,600 feet the resort consists of "The Sapphire Streamliner," and two other gracefully carved slopes. Since the ski area is smaller, it's less crowded than other slopes and offers a great low-pressure atmosphere for beginners. The rustic mountain-style lodge at the base of the mountain includes Jimmy-Mac's Restaurant and shopping.

A Hoffman **Family Adventure**

Michaela was eight when we took her for her first trip to Sliding Rock, cautioning her about how cold the water would be. She wasn't worried. She was going to slide! We watched from an observation deck overlooking the foot of the waterfall, ready to snap photos as she and her cousin stepped onto the rock and got into position. I snapped a photo as they began the 120-foot slide. I snapped another as they went airborne into the pool below. But we knew something was wrong as the girls' heads poked out of the water. Michaela was a little angry and more than a little frightened. "I didn't know I had to swim," she said. In our haste to warn her about the cold, we had neglected to tell her the pool at the bottom was over her head. It's good she is a strong swimmer. It's OK, Michaela. Dad didn't slide that day because he can't make it across the creek leading to the rock without slipping.

Where to Eat

Cardinal Old-Fashioned Drive-In, 728 South Broad Street; (828) 884–7085. Burger and fries are, of course, the specialty of the house. $

Casey Jones Restaurant, 4 McLean Road; (828) 884–3733. You'll find good, simple Italian dishes here. $

The Clock of Brevard, 1015 Asheville Highway; (828) 884–4010. Chicken is the specialty of the house. $

The Corner Bistro, corner of Broad and Main Streets; (828) 862–4746. Stop in here whether you have a vegetarian or a beer drinker in the family. The bistro serves standard bistro fare. $

Where to Stay

Davidson River Campground, US 276 in Pisgah National Forest; (828) 862–5960. This is a great campground with fairly private spaces, a swimming hole, and showers and it is conveniently located. $

Earthside Mountain Lodge, Route 1, Golden Road, Lake Toxaway; (828) 862–4207. This beautiful cedar log lodge has rock fireplaces and porches to help you kick back. It includes ten guest rooms, all with patchwork quilts, stained glass lamps, log beds, and private baths, some with lofts that seem to come right out of *Little House on the Prairie*. Activities on site include a challenging rope course, hiking trails, scavenger hunts, and many evening entertainment events. $$$$

Imperial Motor Lodge, US 64 and 276; (828) 884–2887. This is a larger hotel and very conveniently located. $$$

The Red Lion Inn, 4259 Pickens Highway, Rosman; (828) 884–6868. This inn includes rooms by the creek as well as cabins on the mountain way behind the inn. $$–$$$$

Sunset Motel, 415 South Broad Street; (828) 884–9106. This motel also offers a few efficiencies. $$$

For More Information

Brevard/Transylvania County Tourism, (800) 648–4523; www.visit waterfalls.com.

Hendersonville

From Brevard, head east on US 64 to the junction with Highway 25 to reach Hendersonville.

Holmes Educational State Forest (all ages)

1299 Crab Creek Road, 8 miles southwest of Hendersonville; (828) 692–0100; www.dfr .state.nc.us/esf/holmes_esf.htm. Open 9:00 a.m. to 5:00 p.m. Tuesday through Friday and 11:00 a.m. to 8:00 p.m. Saturday and Sunday from mid-March through mid-November. Free.

Have you ever seen a talking tree? You will if you go to Holmes Educational State Forest, where there's a lot of them. Everyone in the family will get something out of a visit to the trails in the 235-acre forest. The short Talking Tree Trail features various hardwood trees that relate their origin and history on push-button tape recordings. Another trail, which is slightly longer at 3 miles, allows you to touch various forest objects in special boxes that give you a chance to guess what it is without seeing it. Both picnic facilities and campsites are available in the forest, and park rangers present various interpretive programs throughout the year.

Historic Downtown Hendersonville

Henderson County Travel & Tourism Visitor Center, 201 South Main Street; (800) 828–4244; www.historichendersonville.org.

Start off a trip to historic downtown Hendersonville at the centrally located visitor center for information about the area. A visit here won't be a tremendously wild adventure, but you'll find a little something for everyone in the family. Main Street is beautifully adorned with seasonal plantings and benches scattered along the sidewalks, providing an opportunity for a short break or to sit back and people-watch. Be sure to drop in at **Days Gone By,** 303 North Main Street (828–693–9056), an old-fashioned drugstore that has been in town since 1882. After a drink or snack, head out to any one of the variety of stores downtown has to offer. You'll find everything from a specialty toy store to antiques to clothing stores and boutiques. Among the shops are one of five **Mast General Stores** (828–696–1883), **Dancing Bear Toys** (800–659–8697), and **Narnia Studios** (828–697–6393), a whimsical art gallery full of flowers, fairies, and other fanciful items. Although some stores are open seven days a week, most shops are closed on Sunday.

North Carolina features a number of apple festivals, but downtown Hendersonville is the site of the "official" **North Carolina Apple Festival.** The festival is a four-day event that is usually held in early September. Downtown and the surrounding area come alive during the festival, which features sporting events, arts and crafts, entertainment, and of course lots of apples—applesauce, apple jelly, apple cider, and more. The celebration is highlighted by the King Apple Parade. Call (800) 828–4244 for more information.

Hands On! (ages 1 to 10)
318 North Main Street, Suite 2; (828) 697–8333; www.handsonwnc.org. $.

This new child's gallery provides interactive educational exhibits and programs that stimulate the imagination of young children up to age ten. The attraction includes a costume theater, nature area, and areas dedicated to mountain music, food, and art.

North Mills River and Campground
The park is located in Pisgah National Forest off Highway 191 North, 13 miles from Hendersonville; (800) 283–2267. Open year-round.

If the hotels or inns in the area don't suit your needs, a good place to camp is North Mills River and Campground. In addition to fine fishing, the area offers picnic sites with grills and campsites for tents as well as trailers up to 22 feet. It's also a good place to take a trip down the river in an inner tube. Another plus this campground has to offer is the large, grassy playing area where the kids can run off some steam.

Where to Eat

Apple Annie's Cafe, US 64 West; (828) 685–8890. The cafe is open for breakfast and lunch seven days a week and serves just about everything under the sun. $

Haus Heidelberg, 630 Greenville Highway; (828) 693–8227. This restaurant features German beer for Mom and Dad and apple strudel for the kids. Oh, yeah, they serve dinner, too. There is a children's menu with German cuisine. $$

Mills River Restaurant, Highway 191; (828) 891–4039. This is another good restaurant for families with a variety of favorites. Items on the menu range from spaghetti to steak to seafood. $

The Poplar Lodge Restaurant, 2350 Laurel Park Highway; (828) 693–8400. This is a nice historic lodge, but casual dress and kids are acceptable. $$$

Where to Stay

Cedarwood Inn, 1510 Greenville Highway; (800) 832–2032. A few efficiencies are offered in addition to the rooms. $$

Cranmore Cottages, 220 Millard J. Drive; (888) 868–1779. Two- and three-bedroom cottages provide respite from a full day of sightseeing. $$

Echo Mountain Inn, 2849 Laurel Park Highway; (828) 693–9626. Rooms and apartments offer very nice views. $$–$$$$

For More Information

Henderson County Travel & Tourism, (800) 828–4244; www.historic hendersonville.org.

Flat Rock

Flat Rock is south of Hendersonville on Highway 25.

Connemara (ages 5 and up)

81 Carl Sandburg Lane; (828) 693–4178. Open 9:00 a.m. to 5:00 p.m. daily. Admission is free; guided tours ($; free for children sixteen and younger) are available (call ahead for a schedule).

Flat Rock, one of the oldest resort towns in the state, was for more than twenty years home to poet-historian Carl Sandburg. You can visit Connemara, Carl Sandburg Home National Historic Site, located west of Highway 25. Sandburg's works ranged widely from children's books to stark political and social commentary, and his homesite offers insight into how he lived and worked. The home was built around 1838; Sandburg moved into it in 1945 with his wife and daughters. While he wrote, his family managed to maintain the home as a working goat farm. The home has been largely preserved as it was when Sandburg died in 1967. More than 10,000 manuscripts, books, and notes are still scattered throughout the home.

Where to Stay

Lakemont Cottages, 100 Lakemont Drive; (828) 693–5174. Waterfront cottages are offered here. $$$

The Woodfield Inn, 2905 Greenville Highway; (800) 533–6016. Offers a wide range of amenities. $$$$

Tryon

From Flat Rock, head south on Highway 25 and east on Highway 176 to Tryon.

Foothills Equestrian Nature Center (FENCE) (all ages)

3381 Hunting Country Road; (828) 859–9021; www.fence.org.

Located at the western edge of the Blue Ridge Mountains, Tryon is home to numerous equestrian events year-round. The Foothills Equestrian Nature Center is host to most of these events and also includes nature trails and interpretive nature programs. Among the most popular events are the Tryon Horse Show, which has been held each June since 1929, and the Block House Steeplechase, which is held each April.

Pearson's Falls (all ages)

Located 4 miles west of Tryon off Highway 176. Open 10:00 a.m. to dusk daily. $.

For a slow-paced trip, head to Pearson's Falls. The falls, which cascade down a gentle 90-foot slope, are beautifully maintained by the Tryon Garden Club. The area includes several hundred acres of wildlife preserve and botanical gardens. Paths through 200 species of ferns and plants wind around the falls. Picnic facilities are available, but no fires are allowed.

The Green River (ages 5 and up)

The Green River, which runs from the center of Polk County, north of Tryon, to the county's eastern edge, provides a great opportunity to take an adventurous cruise in an inner tube or specially made kayak ($–$$). **Green River Cove Campground** (828–749–3781), located at 5200 Green River Cove Road, off Highway 9 (take Highway 108 north out of Tryon to the junction with Highway 9 and continue north); **Wilderness Cove,** 193 Green River Cove, Saluda (828–817–1095); and **Green River Adventures,** 1734 Holbert Cove Road, Saluda (800–335–1530) can set you up with all the equipment you need for a trip down the river. While the pace of the Green River is slower than the white water of the rivers at higher elevations, there are several series of rapids that make it fun for the younger as well as older members of the family. The outfitters offer tube, raft, and inflatable "funyak" rentals, as well as shuttle service so you can simply float back to your car. Trips range from 3 to 6 miles.

Where to Stay

Orchard Lake Campground, 460 Orchard Lake Road, Saluda; (828) 749–3901. Fully furnished A-frame cabins here will sleep up to six people, and their pets are welcome. It's on site with two lakes for swimming and fishing. $

Pine Crest Inn, 200 Pine Crest Lane; (828) 859–9135. This is a luxurious country inn. $$$$

Lake Lure

Located near US 74, north on Highway 9 from the Green River.

Bottomless Pools (all ages)

Located on Pool Road off US 74/Highway 64; (828) 625–8324. Open 10:00 a.m. to 4:00 p.m. Monday through Friday and 10:00 a.m. to 5:00 p.m. Saturday and Sunday, April through October. $; free for children under the age of seven.

Twenty-seven-mile-long Lake Lure provides an opportunity for fishing, swimming, and boating in this upscale resort town. The lake is surrounded by an unusual mountain range that has been the cause of some interesting geological formations. Faults in the mountains have caused landslides and exposed caves in the rock along the upper slopes. In addition, bottomless pools have been created as a result of stream erosion in the underlying rock. You can hike the trails and bring a picnic lunch along the way.

Lake Lure Tours (all ages)

2930 Memorial Highway; (877) 386–4255; www.lakelure.com. Tours depart on the hour typically from 10:00 a.m. until about one hour before dusk, March through November. $$–$$$; free for children under age four.

Get a lakeside view of this charming town by boat. Tours coast past local attractions and landmarks as the skipper tells tales of local legend and natural and cultural history. Both lunch and dinner tours are also offered.

The Beach at Lake Lure (all ages)

Memorial Highway; (877) 386–4255; www.lakelure.com. Open Memorial Day through Labor Day 10:00 a.m. to 6:00 p.m., weather permitting. $$; free for children under age four.

A sandy beach surrounded by the beauty of the Blue Ridge Mountains provides for an incredible relaxing day. The beach area admission also includes a small water park, including slides, water cannons and more.

Where to Stay

Many of the accommodations in the Lake Lure area are more suitable for adults, but you can find a place here and there that has kids in mind.

Geneva Motel, 3147 Memorial Highway; (828) 625–4121. Fish from the shore while Mom watches from a hammock just a few feet away. The motel has a playground, grill, and lawn games and offers cottages, cabins, and apartments in addition to rooms. $$–$$$$

Premier Properties Vacation Rentals, Highway 74, #7 Arcade Building; (800) 742–9556. You can probably find a place for Fido to stay in one of the facilities offered here.

Chimney Rock

Head north on Highway 74 from Lake Lure.

Chimney Rock Park (all ages)
US 64 and Highway 74A, Chimney Rock; (800) 277–9611; www.chimneyrockpark.com. Open year-round except Thanksgiving, Christmas, and New Year's Day, but trails may be closed due to inclement weather. The ticket office is open 8:30 a.m. to 4:30 p.m. daily, and until 5:30 p.m. during daylight savings time. $$–$$$.

On a clear day you can see almost 75 miles east as you stand on top of the 500-million-year-old rock at Chimney Rock Park, which is easy to find at its location on Highway 74A north of Lake Lure. Plan to spend at least several hours climbing on the rocks and exploring the caves at this great park. Safety rails guard most of the dangerous places, but you'll still want to keep a close eye on the little ones. An elevator installed in the rock will take you up the equivalent of twenty-six stories to the top of Chimney Rock, or you can explore the outside of it on a unique hiking trail. As you walk along the trail, you can take a subterranean shortcut and hike on the walkways that take you from rock to rock. You can also climb down the wooden stairs to see a moonshiners' cave. Two other trails will take you to views of **Hickory Nut Falls,** which cascades down 404 feet. While you're at the park you'll enjoy panoramic, breathtaking views all around. Snacks are available at the top of Chimney Rock, and picnic facilities and a nature center are also available.

Where to Stay

Carter Lodge, 273 Main Street; (828) 625–8844. All sixteen rooms at the Carter Lodge have balconies overlooking the river or a covered sitting area outside your room. It's located within walking distance of Chimney Rock Village. $$–$$$$

Chimney Rock Inn, 3207 Memorial Highway; (828) 625–1429. This motel isn't elegant, but it gets the job done nicely. $$

For More Information

Rutherford County Tourism Development Authority, (800) 849–5998; www.rutherfordtourism.com.

Asheville

Asheville is easy to find from almost any direction. It's located on I-40 and Highway 74.

If you plan a trip to Asheville, western North Carolina's biggest city, plan on being here a while. With a population of about 67,000, it's a great place for family adventure—to escape the heat of summer, to enjoy the color of fall and spring, or to spend a cozy weekend during the winter holidays. Although Asheville, nestled at the edge of the Smoky Mountains where I-26 and I-40 cross, has become a cultural and educational center for the western part of the state, its mountainous beauty remains.

Biltmore Estate (ages 5 and up)

1 Approach Road; (800) 624–1575; www.biltmore.com. Open daily 8:30 a.m. to 5:00 p.m. April through December; 9:00 a.m. to 4:00 p.m. January through March; closed Thanksgiving and Christmas. Some hours for attractions at the estate may vary. $$$–$$$$; free for children nine and younger.

A trip to North Carolina's mountains, or anywhere nearby, wouldn't be complete without seeing the Biltmore Estate, the 255-room French Renaissance mansion that, although no longer occupied by the Vanderbilt family, is the largest private residence in the country. You'll be dazzled as you approach this 8,000-acre estate, located on U.S. Highway 25 just off I-40, that was built by George Vanderbilt in 1895. Vanderbilt, the grandson of a railroad tycoon, originally bought more than 125,000 acres of land in this area, including what is now Pisgah National Forest. He is best known for having led an effort to manage forestry, instead of simply cutting down trees anytime the logging companies needed them. The home includes more than 50,000 works of art, furnishings, and antiques, which Vanderbilt spent years collecting in Europe and the Orient. Among the works you'll see at the home are pieces by Renoir and Whistler, in addition to a chess table once owned by Napoleon Bonaparte.

The home was constructed over a five-year period and took a total of one million hours of labor, much of it from European designers whom Vanderbilt brought here. In addition to the twenty-two rooms in which the Vanderbilt family lived, the home also includes an indoor swimming pool and bowling alley. The home is especially beautiful during the evening candlelight tours during the Christmas holidays. Your trip to the estate won't be complete without a visit to the winery, where sparkling, red, white, and rosé wines are produced. Finally, take a stroll around the lovely forty-acre gardens and pools. **The Inn on Biltmore Estate** provides a gracious environment and outstanding views. A carriage ride or meal in one of the Biltmore's four restaurants tops off a day trip nicely.

Historic Biltmore Village (all ages)

Located on US 25, adjacent to the Biltmore Estate; (828) 274–5570; www.biltmore village.com. Most shops are open 10:00 a.m. to 5:30 p.m. Monday through Saturday and 1:00 to 5:00 p.m. Sunday.

Adjacent to the Biltmore Estate is Historic Biltmore Village, a group of restored homes that now contain shops, restaurants, and galleries. At these shops you'll find handcrafted jewelry and pottery, blown glass, fine art, children's books and games, collectible dolls, and more. In all you'll find more than thirty shops and most likely something for everyone in the family. Of particular interest for children are **Biltmore Village Dolls & Gifts, Claying Around, Once Upon a Time,** and **William & Grace . . . A Children's Boutique.** Also, **Biltmore Village Historic Museum** presents photographs, maps, and artifacts on the history of the village.

Pack Place (all ages)

2 South Pack Square; (828) 257–4500; www.packplace.org. Admission varies by activity.

The next thing you'll want to do while in Asheville is pay a visit to Pack Place, the city's downtown center of arts, education, and science. It includes several museums as well as space for performing arts. (See the next three entries.)

Asheville Art Museum (ages 5 and up)

(828) 253–3227; www.ashevilleart.org. Open 10:00 a.m. to 5:00 p.m. Tuesday through Saturday (Friday until 8:00 p.m.) and 1:00 to 5:00 p.m. Sunday. $$; free for children under four. Additional fees may apply for selected exhibitions.

Modern American art makes up the biggest permanent collection at the Asheville Art Museum. The collection also features a wide range of work from Impressionists as well as contemporary abstract artists.

Colburn Earth Science Museum (ages 5 and up)

(828) 254–7162. Open 10:00 a.m. to 5:00 p.m. Tuesday through Saturday and 1:00 to 5:00 p.m. Sunday. $.

This museum is like many of the mineral museums in the mountains. It has local stones as well as displays of 4,500 precious stones and other specimens, including fossils, from around the world. Weather, Climate, and You is a fun and interactive exhibit that uncovers the science behind the weather report. It illustrates what happens when wind hits a mountain, teaches visitors about the history of weather in the region, and lets kids do their own TV weather report. The History of Mining in North Carolina takes visitors from the very earliest mining by Native American and early Spanish explorers through the present day. The exhibit also chronicles the major role that gold mining played in the state's history.

Health Adventure (all ages)

**(828) 254–6373; www.thehealthadventure.org. Open 10:00 a.m.
to 5:00 p.m. Tuesday through Saturday and 1:00 to 5:00 p.m.
Sunday. $–$$; free for children under age two.**

The best family feature Pack Place has to offer is the
Health Adventure, a spectacular interactive facility that
has dozens of exhibits and displays about the human
body. Here you can touch a 5-foot-high brain and challenge your own gray matter in a display that introduces
you to a number of creativity-testing games. Next, enter
the Bodyworks Gallery, where you can try to jump as
high as Michael Jordan or take a journey through a
giant replica of your bloodstream. At the Miracle of
Life Gallery you'll learn all about heredity and life
before birth. Children younger than eight will get a
kick out of dressing up as cowboys, pirates, and other characters at the Creative
PlaySpace. Here they can also put on a puppet show or take a slide down the
giant tongue.

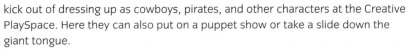

YMI Cultural Center (ages 5 and up)
39 Market Street; (828) 252–4614. Hours vary. $–$$.

The YMI Cultural Center is formerly the Young Men's Institute, founded by George Van-
derbilt in 1893. The center houses a few permanent and temporary art exhibits
related largely to the African American heritage of the area. The center also develops
programs for local residents and youth and stages various performances in its small
informal theater.

Thomas Wolfe Memorial (ages 5 and up)
**52 North Market Street; (828) 253–8304; www.wolfememorial.com. Open 9:00 a.m. to
5:00 p.m. Tuesday through Saturday and 1:00 to 5:00 p.m. Sunday, April through October; 10:00 a.m. to 4:00 p.m. Tuesday through Saturday and 1:00 to 5:00 p.m. Sunday,
November through March. $.**

The Thomas Wolfe Memorial, located at North Market and Woodfin Streets (the
entrance is next to the Radisson Hotel), was the childhood home of the world-famous
author. Although Wolfe left the home at age fifteen to attend school in Chapel Hill, he
wrote about it in his novel *Look Homeward, Angel,* published in 1929. The Wolfe
House was the victim of arson in 1998, but historians restored it and reopened the
house in 2004. Kids will also enjoy the visitor center next door, which includes a small
exhibit hall, a theater, and many items from the home.

Western North Carolina Nature Center (all ages)

75 Gashes Creek Road; (828) 298–5600; www.wildnc.org. Open 10:00 a.m. to 5:00 p.m. daily. It's closed Thanksgiving Day, December 24 through 27, December 31, January 1, and Martin Luther King Day. $–$$.

The Western North Carolina Nature Center offers an opportunity to study wildlife up close in its exhibit halls and along a nice wooded trail. The center is a living nature museum that shows visitors how animals, the environment, and people work together to shape the world. The center's World Underground exhibit demonstrates the importance of this unique environment; if you look really closely you'll find more life than you could imagine. Other exhibits include spiders, snakes, and even the least weasel. Along the trail you'll come face to face with gray and red wolves, otters, mountain lions, a huge bear, deer, and more. The petting zoo gives the kids an opportunity to pet a goat or even milk a cow.

Botanical Gardens at Asheville (ages 5 and up)

151 W. T. Weaver Boulevard; (828) 252–5190; www.ashevillebotanicalgardens.org. Open daily during daylight hours. Free.

More natural beauty awaits at the Botanical Gardens at Asheville, on the campus of the University of North Carolina at Asheville. Here you'll find hundreds of species of plants and flowers that are native to the southern Appalachian Mountains. Within these ten acres you'll find a large azalea garden and a charming rock garden. In addition, you can visit the renovated earthworks from the Battle of Asheville as well as a garden for the blind.

Grove Park Inn (all ages)

290 Macon Avenue; (800) 438–5800; www.groveparkinn.com. $$$$.

While you'll have your choice of a variety of accommodations in and around Asheville, clearly the best place to stay is the Grove Park Inn. This resort is one of the state's top hotels, first opened in 1913 and nestled in the hills of the Blue Ridge. Made of huge local granite stones, the hotel has 510 guest rooms, including twelve suites in the main building and the two wings. You can also play a round of golf on the eighteen-hole course, play tennis inside or out, swim inside or out, rent a mountain bike from the fitness center, or relax in the spa. Planned children's programs are also scheduled from week to week. The Inn's Cub's Adventure Camp for kids over age three includes activities such as nature hikes, swimming, lawn games, arts and crafts, and team competitions. Sign the kids up for a full or half day. Kid's Night Out gives a night out for parents, too. Activities include themed dinner parties, outdoor activities, games, swimming, face-painting, and movies *for the kids!* Even visitors who are not guests can play golf or visit the spa.

Zebulon B. Vance Birthplace (ages 5 and up)

Reems Creek Road, just off US 25, Weaverville; (828) 645–6706. Open 9:00 a.m. to 5:00 p.m. Tuesday to Saturday, April through October; and 10:00 a.m. to 4:00 p.m. Tuesday to Saturday, November through March. **Free.**

Just a few miles north of Asheville, but off the beaten path, you can visit the Zebulon B. Vance Birthplace. Vance, born in 1830, was a revered U.S. senator and served as governor of North Carolina during the Civil War. His home takes you back to the pioneer farm life of the eighteenth century. The two-story pine log structure has been reconstructed around the original chimney. Some of the furnishings in the home belonged to the Vance family, and all of it is representative of the late eighteenth and early nineteenth centuries. You can also visit the museum, which includes exhibits relating to Vance's life, and the six outbuildings that surround the house. Special living history re-creations are presented in the spring and summer, and free guided tours are conducted year-round on the hour.

Where to Eat

Asheville Pizza and Brewing Company, 675 Merrimon Avenue; (828) 254–1281. There used to be two screens here, but you can still catch a movie on the one active movie house after pizza. The joint includes a game room, too. $

Corner Kitchen, 3 Boston Way; (828) 274–2439. Located in historic Biltmore Village, this cozy restaurant provides options for outdoor dining with a varied menu. $

DJ's Family Diner, 1363 Tunnel Road; (828) 299–4888. This is a traditional diner from years gone by. $

El Chapala, 868 Merrimon Avenue; (828) 258–0899. A Mariachi band plays occasionally at this Mexican restaurant with six locations in the area. $

Hunter's Lodge, 330 Weaverville Highway; (828) 645–8383. Inside the walls of this log cabin, staff serves everything from trout to pan-fried chicken with thick creamy gravy. $$

Marble Slab Creamery, 14 Biltmore Avenue; (828) 225–5579. You pick your favorite ice cream, match it with just the right mixin's, and watch staff cut them together on a frozen marble slab. $

Mellow Mushroom, 50 Broadway; (828) 236–9800. Located in an old gas station, this Mellow Mushroom serves up stone-baked pizzas and calzones. $

Oliver & Annabelle's, One Page Avenue, Suite 139, Grove Arcade Market; (828) 350–8366. Located in the historic Grove Arcade Market downtown, this duo serves home-style meals. $

Three Brothers Restaurant, 183 Haywood Street; (828) 253–4971. This is a casual, family-style restaurant with a lot of variety. $

Where to Stay

Asheville is a large enough destination to support many hotels, including larger chains, so you shouldn't have much trouble finding a place to stay. Watch, however, for inns and B&Bs that are not equipped to handle children. Here are a few places in various parts of the city with local flair:

Forest Manor Inn, 866 Hendersonville Road; (828) 274–3531. Located near Biltmore Estate, this inn offers a heated outdoor pool, a playground, and shuffleboard. $$$$

Haywood Park Hotel, 1 Battery Park Avenue; (828) 252–2522. Located in the heart of Asheville's downtown, the Haywood Park Hotel is an extremely upscale inn offering rooms and suites. $$$$

The Mountaineer Inn, 155 Tunnel Road; (828) 254–5331. This historic landmark is located outside busy tourist areas but near Asheville Mall. $$$

The Pines Cottages, 346 Weaverville Highway, Asheville; (828) 645–9661. If you plan an extended stay in Asheville, you might want to try The Pines, which offers two-bedroom cottages. $$–$$$$

For More Information

Asheville Convention and Visitors Bureau, (800) 257–1300; www.explore asheville.com.

Blue Ridge Parkway

In Asheville you'll find the most-used entrance to the Blue Ridge Parkway, which runs from the Great Smoky Mountains National Park near Cherokee into Virginia at Interstate 77. You'll find a great deal to do along the parkway's nearly 500 miles, and the section near Asheville is no exception. Get recorded information on weather, road conditions, recreation, and more by calling (828) 298–0398 or check out www.blue ridgeparkway.org.

Southern Highlands Folk Art Center (ages 5 and up)

Blue Ridge Parkway, Milepost 382; (828) 298–7928; www.southernhighlandguild.org. Open 9:00 a.m. to 5:00 p.m. daily, January through March; 9:00 a.m. to 6:00 p.m. daily, April through December. The center is closed Thanksgiving, Christmas, and New Year's Day. Free.

In addition to some beautiful overlooks, the biggest parkway attraction in this area is the Folk Art Center. Opened in 1980, this is southern Appalachia's oldest and best-known crafts shop. The center is operated by the Southern Highland Craft Guild, the Appalachian Regional Commission, and the National Park Service. The 30,000-square-foot center is also one of the largest crafts shops you will find. A museum in the upstairs portion of the center is dedicated to displaying changing exhibits created by its members. You'll also have an opportunity to purchase quilts, toys, furniture, and stoneware made by guild member artisans. In addition, live demonstrations are held most of the time the center is open.

Amazing North Carolina Facts

Dr. Elisha Mitchell, the University of North Carolina mathematician for whom Mount Mitchell is named, died in 1857 while attempting to prove the mountain's height, some accounts say. He made a number of attempts to measure the mountain as early as the 1830s. Mitchell's grave is on the top of the mountain.

Craggy Gardens (ages 5 and up)

Blue Ridge Parkway between Mileposts 363 and 369; (828) 298–0398. Open daily, generally during daylight hours, May through October. Free.

The gardens are a beautifully sculptured sight when colorful rhododendron are at their peak bloom in early summer. Here you'll see a wide variety of other mountain wildflowers as well. You'll also find a visitor center, nature trails, and picnic facilities.

Mount Mitchell State Park

Exit off Blue Ridge Parkway at Milepost 355 onto Highway 128, Burnsville; (828) 675–4611 or www.ils.unc.edu/parkproject/. Open generally 8:00 a.m. to sunset. Free.

From Craggy Gardens you are only a few minutes away from Mount Mitchell State Park. At 6,684 feet, Mount Mitchell is the tallest peak east of the Mississippi River. This extraordinary peak pokes out of the Black Mountains, which are among the oldest mountains on Earth. From an observation tower at Mount Mitchell's peak, you can see the Smoky Mountains. You'll also find a small interactive museum as well as a restaurant that's open in the summer. In addition you can enjoy a number of outdoor activities at the 1,600-acre park, including hiking, picnicking, and some camping (although camping is not recommended for families). The park is open according to weather conditions, so call ahead. Because of the elevation it has been known to snow here as early as September and as late as May, not at all common in North Carolina.

Mars Hill

Drive north from Asheville on U.S. Highway 23.

Wolf Ridge Ski Resort (all ages)
**Located north of Asheville on US 23; (800) 817–4111; www.skiwolfridge.com.
$$$–$$$$.**

Before you leave Asheville you can get in a little skiing, tubing, or snowboarding only about forty minutes away. Wolf Ridge features twenty slopes for various skill levels and activities. In addition, the ski school there features a special program for children ages four through seven offering simple lessons and instructions, as well as races, games, and other planned activities. The lodge here is nice, too. The resort has food ranging from snacks to full meals, in a restaurant that provides beautiful views of the slopes. Accommodations are available at Wolf Ridge Lodge as well as at vacation homes that surround the area. Snowmaking machines allow this slope to open in late November.

Spruce Pine

If you're looking for a scenic drive, make your way back from Mars Hill to the Blue Ridge Parkway by taking U.S. Highway 19 north to Highway 80 South, or you can head straight over to Spruce Pine by staying on US 19.

As you twist through these mountain highways, you'll see that they are lined with handicraft shops and galleries, where you usually see local crafters and artists at work. If you want to see more, you can obtain a guidebook for a scenic drive that highlights this local work by contacting the Yancey County/Burnsville Chamber of Commerce (828–682–7413; www.yanceychamber.com).

Gem Mountain (ages 5 and up)
13780 Highway 226; (888) 817–5829; www.gemmountain.com. Open 9:00 a.m. to 5:00 p.m. Monday through Saturday (until 7:00 p.m. during the summer), March through December. Free admission to Gem Mountain, including the museum; mining buckets start at $$$.

In addition to the local crafts, this area's biggest attraction is its mines. Gem Mountain features flumes where you can hunt for gems for a per-bucket fee. In addition, you can visit Gem Mountain's Sands of Time museum, have a picnic by the stream, eat at the restaurant, or enjoy an ice cream cone.

Little Switzerland

From Spruce Pine, travel south on Highway 226.

Everything that makes the mountains of North Carolina so great—the crafts, the mines, the beautiful scenery, the lodging, the shopping, and the dining—can be found in Little Switzerland.

Emerald Village (ages 5 and up)
McKinney Mine Road off Highway 226A; (828) 765–6463; www.emeraldvillage.com. **Open 10:00 a.m. to 4:00 p.m. daily in April; 9:00 a.m. to 5:00 p.m. Monday through Friday and 9:00 a.m. to 6:00 p.m. Saturday and Sunday, May through October; 10:00 a.m. to 4:00 p.m. Saturday and Sunday in November. Fees vary by activity.**

This is probably one of the biggest and most popular public mining operations in the mountains. Dozens of different minerals, gems, and rocks have been found here, including aquamarine, emerald, garnet, and uranium. Attendants are on hand to help you identify your finds, as are artisans for cutting and mounting your stones. Additionally you can visit the **North Carolina Mining Museum,** located in an underground mine, where you'll see old mining equipment and displays on the area's mining heritage. Other **free** village attractions include the Company Store and Discovery Mill, where you'll see more displays related to mining as well as souvenirs and gifts.

Where to Eat

Switzerland Café & General Store, Highway 226 near the Blue Ridge Parkway; (828) 765–5289. Light items, soups, and salads are served in an old-time general-store atmosphere. $

Where to Stay

Big Lynn Lodge, Highway 226A; (800) 654–5232. This is a very nice country inn with rooms, cottages, and condos. $$$$

Skyline Motel, Highway 226; (828) 765–9394. The Skyline is located just off the parkway on a mountaintop. $$

Marion

Travel south from Little Switzerland to Highway 126 to find the town of Marion and a very popular lake.

Lake James State Park
Northeast of Marion on Highway 126; (828) 652–4496. **Open year-round, generally during daylight hours. Free.**

Lake James State Park is a great place to play golf, fish, camp, swim, and hike. The lake, which is fed by two mountain streams and the Catawba River, offers 150 miles

Brown Mountain **Lights**

I have never experienced the Brown Mountain Lights personally but many North Carolinians swear they are there. The mystery purports that on certain clear evenings, small, brilliant orbs can be seen wavering, bobbing up and down, disappearing, and reappearing from several points in this area. Sometimes they are red, sometimes blue. This mystery has attracted thousands of curiosity seekers, who have set up camp here since 1771. Extensive scientific research by the U.S. Geologic Survey has failed to explain the phenomenon. There are several vantage points along Highway 181, and from Wiseman's View on the Kistler Memorial Highway (State Road 138) near Linville Falls where you can try to catch a peek of the Brown Mountain Lights.

of shoreline along beautiful, crystal-clear water. A sandy beach is located near the park office. Ten golf courses are located in this area, and the park contains great campsites for low-impact camping. Each site has a grill, water, and a picnic table, and the sites are located away from traffic. Along the park's nature trails, you never know when you'll get a glimpse of a deer, flying squirrel, fox, or muskrat, and the lake offers great bass, crappie, and catfish fishing.

Where to Eat

Carolina Chocolatiers, 8 North Main Street; (828) 652–4496. That's right, kids—lunch in a chocolate factory! It serves deli sandwiches in addition to handmade chocolate and ice cream. $

Countryside Bar-B-Que, 2070 Rutherford Road; (828) 652–4885. Countryside serves a variety of homestyle dishes in addition to barbecue. $

Harvest Drive-In, 861 North Main Street; (828) 652–4155. This is a really peachy 1950s drive-in. $

Where to Stay

Barn House Inn, 11611 Montford Cove Road; (866) 690–9182; www.barnhouse inn.com. This rustic barn-style inn is located on a piece of property that's just as quaint. Enjoy creek walking, swimming, and hiking, and picnicking in the gazebo. A fully equipped kitchen stocked with breakfast items including homemade jellies and jams, local eggs, and honey is waiting for you to check in. Families with children and pets are welcome. $$$–$$$$

Budget Inn, 728 Highway 70 West; (828) 652–7276. This is a small, but cool, 1950s-style hotel. $$

For More Information

McDowell County Tourism Development Authority, (888) 233–6111; www.mcdowellnc.org.

Linville Falls

Located just off the Blue Ridge Parkway on U.S. Highway 221 is the town of Linville Falls and the Linville Gorge Wilderness Area.

These 7,600 acres of land have been preserved as a natural area, but you can hike a number of trails for various views of the falls and the Linville River, which descends more than 2,000 feet in only 12 miles. The upper part of the falls rolls over 50 feet and disappears into the mountain, then the lower falls drops another 60 feet. If it's hot you can hike down the rocks bordering the falls and wade in the cool waters, watching more adventurous hikers scale the vertical rocks. The gorge below the falls is part of **Pisgah National Forest** and is maintained for hunting and fishing. Two observation points, one on the east and one on the west side of the gorge, provide excellent panoramic views. You'll also come across plenty of picnic facilities around this area.

Linville Caverns (ages 5 and up)
US 221 North, Marion; (800) 419–0540; www.linvillecaverns.com. Open 9:00 a.m. to 5:00 p.m. daily (until 6:00 p.m. in the summer; 4:30 p.m. November through March and weekends only December through February). $–$$; free for children under five.

It's impossible to ignore the signs urging you to visit Linville Caverns, where the fifty-two-degree year-round temperature is more than welcome during a humid North Carolina summer. The caverns, the only ones in the state that are open to the public, are located on US 221 near its intersection with the Blue Ridge Parkway. At the caverns you'll get a lesson on stalagmites, stalactites, and other natural formations. In addition, you'll see unusual blind fish in the underground stream and experience total darkness. Guided tours on the marked trail are held about every half hour. One caution: The part of the tour that includes total darkness may frighten younger children.

The Orchard at Altapass (all ages)
1025 Orchard Road, at milepost 328.3 on the Blue Ridge Parkway, Altapass; (888) 765–9531.

More than just your average orchard, the one-hundred-year-old Orchard at Altapass, just south of Linville Falls, is a tribute to Appalachian culture and history. Built by the Clinchfield Railroad in some of the most beautiful country the state has to offer, the orchard has become a significant attraction for the area. In addition to mountain-grown apples and apple products, the orchard offers regular helpings of authentic mountain music each Saturday and Sunday from mid-May through October. Harvest time begins around July 4 when you can pick your own, or take home a pre-picked bag of apples. Visitors are also invited for hayrides while listening to the stories that have shaped our area for centuries. Hayrides are offered hourly every Saturday and Sunday from late May through October, from noon to 4:00 p.m.

Where to Eat

Famous Louise's Rockhouse Restaurant, Highway 221 near Highway 183; (828) 765–2702. A favorite of the locals, Louise's has homestyle cooking. $

Spears Restaurant, Linville Falls Lodge, Highway 221 North near Highway 183; (800) 634–4421. Brochures say this restaurant serves the best barbecue in the Carolinas. $

Where to Stay

Linville Falls Lodge and Cottages, Highway 221 North near Highway 183; (800) 634–4421. This is a small inn that also offers cottages. $$–$$$

Linville

Linville is located north of Linville Falls on US 221.

Grandfather Mountain (all ages)

Located on US 221, 1 mile from the Blue Ridge Parkway; (800) 468–7325; www
.grandfather.com. Open 9:00 a.m. to 5:00 p.m. daily during the winter; 9:00 a.m. to
6:00 p.m. in spring and fall; and 9:00 a.m. to 7:00 p.m. in summer. Closed Thanksgiving
and Christmas. $$–$$$.

Don't let the similar names confuse you—Linville and Linville Falls are two different towns. Linville is known for what is probably the top scenic attraction in the North Carolina mountains—Grandfather Mountain. This is a great place to spend the day hiking and learning about nature. The 5,964-foot peak was named for its profile as it appears from about 7 miles north. As the name suggests, from this vantage point the mountain looks like a bearded grandfather. Grandfather Mountain has been recognized by the United Nations as an international reserve where people and nature live together in harmony. You enter the park off US 221 and can drive through a lot of it, but you'll have to park at the visitor center and walk to get to the top. You'll also find picnic and limited camping facilities here.

No matter what time of year you visit Grandfather Mountain, there is always plenty to do. As you drive into the park, the first attraction you come to is the nature museum, a small museum with a gift shop that kids will adore. At the shop they will find toys and all sorts of knickknacks related to animals, nature, and the Blue Ridge Parkway. The museum offers an unusual look at the area's natural past with displays and films on nature and the mountains. You'll see gold nuggets, precious gemstones, a billion-year-old rock, and displays of rare plants and animals. The kids will surely want to have their picture taken with the big bear. They'll also love the Daniel Boone exhibit.

Celtic **Celebration**

A good time to visit Grandfather Mountain is the second weekend in July, when the Highland Games are held. While there are other Scottish celebrations in the state, this is one of the best. It includes traditional Scottish athletic competitions, spiced up with authentic Scottish music, dance, and other attractions from the Scottish tradition. For more information on the Highland Games, call (828) 733–1333 or log on to www.gmhg.org

Probably the most popular attraction is the Mile-High Swinging Bridge. It extends majestically over a natural gorge filled with hardwood trees and rhododendron. You'll find overlooks on both sides of the bridge if you can't make the walk across. A variety of animals—including black bears and cubs, cougars, deer, and eagles—are on display in what resembles natural habitats. Many of these animals have been injured and will never be able to return to the wild.

Seven Devils

Just north of Linville on Highway 105 is Seven Devils.

Hawksnest Golf and Ski Resort (all ages)
2058 Skyland Drive; (828) 963–6561; www.hawksnest-resort.com. $$$$.

This year-round resort not only has become known for one of the steepest slopes among the North Carolina ski areas but is also popular with snowboarders. Ten slopes are available as well as lessons and rentals. Hawksnest also includes a snow-tubing park. Bargain hunters will find the best deals early in the ski season, from late November through December. Free ski lessons are offered on Thursday. Visitors can enjoy the golf course during the more temperate months.

Banner Elk

From Seven Devils, take Highway 184 north to Banner Elk.

Sugar Mountain Ski Resort (all ages)
1009 Sugar Mountain Drive; (828) 898–4521; www.skisugar.com. $$–$$$$.

This ski resort is the area's largest, with twenty slopes and eight lifts. A 1,200-foot drop provides plenty of thrills for the advanced skier, while lessons are offered for

THE BLUE RIDGE MOUNTAINS 55

beginners. A ski school for kids ($$$$) offers lessons from 10:00 a.m. to 3:00 p.m. Tubing is also offered at the Sugar Mountain Golf Course.

For More Information

Avery/Banner Elk Chamber of Commerce, (800) 972–2183; www.avery county.com.

Beech Mountain

Continue north from Sugar Mountain to find Beech Mountain.

Ski Beech (all ages)

1007 Beech Mountain Parkway; (800) 438–2093; www.skibeech.com. $$$–$$$$; children under five get a free lift ticket when accompanied by a ticketed adult.

Ski Beech, located on Highway 184 in Beech Mountain, north of Banner Elk, is at the highest elevation of the area's ski resorts and as a result offers the most natural snow. Fourteen slopes and eleven lifts tend to keep you on the slope more here. Skaters in the family will appreciate the ice-skating rink, and special programs are offered for children. A tube run provides additional adventure and snowboarders will appreciate the freestyle terrain.

For More Information

Beech Mountain Chamber of Commerce, (800) 468–5506; www.beech mtn.com.

A Hoffman **Family Adventure**

When the kids were young and we'd take one of our mountain getaways, they always seemed to bring a little of the mountain home with them in the form of dirt. What a trip for a kid: Get as dirty as you want to, and Mom and Dad can't really do anything about it. On one trip, however, we made a stop at the laundromat. My wife and I were busy switching from washer to dryer and took our eyes off our son, Mike, for only a moment. When we turned around we discovered he was helping with the chore. He had his sister by the ankles and was struggling to angle her into the industrial dryer.

North Carolina **Skiing**

To the north of Linville is a skier's paradise. Between 5 and 8 feet of natural snow fall in this area each winter, depending on the elevation, but snowmaking machines provide good skiing conditions all winter long. You can call the High Country Ski Report at (800) 962–2322 or visit www.skinorthcarolina.com to get conditions at the area's ski resorts.

Boone

From Beech Mountain, head east on US 321. From Banner Elk, take Highway 194 East. From Linville, take the Blue Ridge Parkway to US 321.

Boone is a great central location for seeing this part of the Blue Ridge. Not only is there a lot to see and do in and around the city, but Boone also provides easy access to the Blue Ridge Parkway, the ski resorts, and other towns and attractions. Boone is named for the famous frontiersman Daniel Boone, who had a cabin here from 1760 to 1769. Today there are thousands of lodging rooms, ranging from bed-and-breakfast inns to chain hotels.

Horn in the West (ages 5 and up) 🎵
591 Horn in the West Drive; (828) 264–2120. Performances, which last about two hours, are held at 8:30 p.m. Tuesday through Sunday from late June to mid-August. $$–$$$.

Daniel Boone's legacy and contribution to the settlement of the area is portrayed in *Horn in the West,* a fabulous musical outdoor drama held at the Powderhorn Amphitheater just off U.S. Highway 421. The play, America's third longest-running outdoor drama running since 1952, is set during the time Boone lived here, when colonial unrest against British dominance was at its peak. The play reveals how Boone and his men struggled to settle this area and build the mountain culture that is still evident today. A favorite from the piece, for young and old alike, is a spectacular Cherokee Indian fire dance.

Hickory Ridge Homestead (all ages) 🏛
Located on the grounds at *Horn in the West;* (828) 264–2120. Hours vary according to showtimes.

Hickory Ridge is an eighteenth-century living history museum highlighting the daily lives of mountain ancestors. Visitors get a glimpse into the past as interpreters in period clothing explain pioneer life and culture. Regular demonstrations in weaving and hearthside cooking as well as crafts are presented. Guests can explore the historic buildings on the grounds such as the Tatum cabin, built in 1785, and learn how settlers survived.

Daniel Boone Native Gardens (ages 5 and up)

591 Horn in the West Drive; (828) 264–6390. The gardens are open from 1:00 to 8:30 p.m. while the *Horn in the West* is in production and 9:00 a.m. to 4:00 p.m. Saturday and 1:00 to 4:00 p.m. Sunday in autumn. $.

You can head to the outdoor theater early to see the Daniel Boone Native Gardens, which features plantings unique to the area, native gardens, and unique architecture. In addition to handsome hardscapes—a gatehouse, a complex of arbors and walks, and a reflecting pool—the garden features a bog garden, ferns, rhododendrons, and a whimsical meditation maze.

The Appalachian Cultural Heritage Museum (ages 5 and up)

Located on University Hall Drive just off US 321; (828) 262–3117. Open 10:00 a.m. to 5:00 p.m. Tuesday through Saturday and 1:00 to 5:00 p.m. Sunday. $; free for children under eight. Free admission on Tuesday.

This is a great little museum that features exhibits and audiovisual displays of not only the past but the present as well. Here you see antique quilts, arrowheads, handmade furniture, Junior Johnson's race car, and a bit of the yellow brick road from the Land of Oz, a now-defunct theme park based on the movie.

Wahoo's Adventures (ages 7 and up)

US 321; (800) 444–7238; www.wahoosadventures.com.

To schedule an active family adventure without doing all the planning yourself, call Wahoo's Adventures. No matter what kind of adventure you are looking for, Wahoo's can help you put it all together. White-water rafting trips are offered on four rivers in the area for all different ages and skill levels. Full- and half-day trips are conducted, and picnics are prepared for you by the crew. If an overnight trip is more to your liking, that can be arranged. The outfitter also plans four-wheel-drive trips, self-guided canoe trips, inner-tubing, and ski trips. Prices are as varied as the activities, so call ahead for information or to make reservations.

Appalachian Ski Mountain (all ages)

940 Ski Mountain Road; (800) 322–2373; www.appskimtn.com. $$$.

Just off the parkway near US 321 is another of North Carolina's ski resorts. Appalachian Ski Mountain has nine slopes and four lifts. The resort is home of the French-Swiss Ski College. The resort traditionally offers the best rate during its opening-anniversary period, when you ski for 1962 rates of $5.00 for an adult lift ticket, $2.50 for a junior lift ticket, and rentals for $6.50. Look for this special deal early in December.

Where to Eat

Bandana's Bar B Que and Grill, 1475 Highway 105; (828) 265–2828. Bandana's features barbecue of all kinds—pork, chicken, turkey, and babyback and St. Louis ribs in a relaxed family atmosphere. $$

Casa Rustica, 1348 Highway 105; (828) 262–5128. This Italian restaurant has a neat casual atmosphere and good pizza. $

Dan'l Boone Inn. 130 Hardin Street; (828) 264–8657; www.danlbooneinn .com. $–$$$; children under four eat **free.** If it's time for dinner, make sure you're hungry before you head to the Dan'l Boone Inn restaurant. One price gets you all you want to eat at this charming, rustic inn. You won't have to worry about menus or deciding what you're going to eat because meals are served family-style just like at Grandma's house. If they run out of mashed potatoes, don't worry—if you want seconds you can have rice. There is plenty of variety on the dessert cart, too; save room if you can.

Knights on Main, 870 Main Street; (828) 295–3869. Knights serves breakfast, lunch, and dinner, offering great variety and a super atmosphere. $–$$$

Mountain House Restaurant, 1601 Blowing Rock Road; (828) 264-4680. Get breakfast any time of day here. Steaks, seafood, salads, and sandwiches are also offered. $

Troy's 105, 1286 Highway 105; (828) 265–1344. This 1950s-style restaurant serves standard diner selections. $

Where to Stay

ADN Log Cabin Rentals, Blowing Rock, Boone, and Valle Crucis; (800) 237-7975. This agency describes their rentals as elegantly rustic cabins. Enjoy the hot tub on the porch or go inside and curl up by the gas log fireplace on the elegant furnishings. Video games, Foosball, or other entertainment is available in each cabin. $$$$

Boone Trail Motel and Apartments, 275 East King Street; (828) 264–8839. This facility offers twenty-two units, including large apartments, near the center of town. $–$$$$

Broyhill Inn & Conference Center, 775 Bodenheimer Drive; (800) 951–6048. First-class service and accommodations are trademarks here. Rooms and suites are offered. It includes a play area. $$–$$$$.

High Country Inn, 1785 Highway 105; (800) 334–5605. This inn manages to maintain a great family atmosphere, even in the sports bar on the premises. The inn also manages Hummingbird Hill Cabin Village Rentals. $–$$$

For More Information

Boone Convention and Visitor's Bureau, (800) 852–9506; www.visit boonenc.com.

Blowing Rock

Blowing Rock is south of Boone on US 321.

This is a small resort town, and you'll find plenty to do near here. Plan to spend several hours in the village shopping center downtown. There are a dozen antiques shops, a great sports novelty shop, and local craftworkers making candles and other items.

Blowing Rock (all ages)

US 321 and Rock Road; (828) 295–7111; www.theblowingrock.com. Open 8:30 a.m. to 7:00 p.m. daily, Memorial Day weekend through Labor Day; 9:00 a.m. to 6:00 p.m. Sunday through Thursday and 9:00 a.m. to 7:00 p.m. Friday and Saturday, September and October; 9:00 a.m. to 5:00 p.m. daily, November and December; and 9:00 a.m. to 5:00 p.m. Saturday and Sunday, January through March. $–$$; free for children three and under.

Just south of the shopping district on US 321 you can learn how the town got its name at the Blowing Rock, where it snows upside down. The attraction is a large rock formation hanging over John's River Gorge. Plan to spend about an hour or so enjoying the views and walking the ridges and rock, as you discover the story of this mysterious formation. Legend says that a Cherokee brave who had thrown himself off the Blowing Rock was blown up out of the gorge to the Chickasaw maiden who had prayed for his return for three days. Today light objects thrown from the rock will be blown back up.

The Legend of **the Blowing Rock**

The legend of the Blowing Rock seems to vary a little from one account to another. Here's a summary of one I found in *North Carolina Legends* by Richard Walser (North Carolina Division of Archives and History):

A maiden named Starlight, at the age of sixteen, convinced her father to allow courting by suitors on a particular day. Among the braves who came was Kwasind, who some said had deserted his wife in a far-off land. Believing this to be true, Starlight rejected the brave, who, in a profession of his love, threw himself off the peak now known as Blowing Rock. At that moment Starlight shrieked, "O Strong West Wind, bring my lover back to me! O sweet South Wind, bear him up in your gentle arms." It worked, and the two were wed.

Tweetsie Railroad (all ages)

300 Tweetsie Railroad Lane, off US 321; (800) 526–5740; www.tweetsie.com. Open 9:00 a.m. to 6:00 p.m. daily, generally mid-May to September, and weekends only in September and October. $$$–$$$$.

You might think they need to beef up security when you take a ride on the Tweetsie Railroad, because it seems robberies occur on every single trip. Tweetsie, located just north of Blowing Rock, is a great park where you take a trip back to the Old West. You'll enjoy dozens of great rides as you walk through the theme park, where you are more than likely to meet up with a gunslinger or a Native American chief. You can also visit a century-old general store, a blacksmith shop, and a jail. Another option is a mining town, where the children can pan for gold or meet the animals in the petting zoo. But the biggest attraction here is old Number 12, a steam locomotive that takes you on a 3-mile journey around a mountain. You never know when robbers or Native Americans will hop on board, so stay alert. Plenty of traditional theme park rides provide hours of entertainment as well. In October you can enjoy a haunted house, visit a mad scientist's lab, and go trick-or-treating at the Tweetsie Railroad Halloween Festival, which features rides on the ghost train. While the escapades at Tweetsie might be amusing to adults and older children, they will seem very real to young children. Use your discretion when determining whether your children will enjoy a ride on the train.

Mystery Hill (ages 5 and up)

129 Mystery Hill Lane, off US 321/221; (828) 264–2792; www.mysteryhill-nc.com. Open 9:00 a.m. to 8:00 p.m. daily, June through August; 9:00 a.m. to 5:00 p.m. daily the rest of the year. Closed Thanksgiving and Christmas. $$; free for children under five.

As you drove to Tweetsie from Blowing Rock on US 321, you probably noticed Mystery Hill, a hands-on science museum that lets visitors decide if these strange exhibits are natural phenomena or illusions. It doesn't appear there's much to the old wood-sided building, but it's worth stopping here to see rocks that glow in the dark and exhibits that defy gravity, such as a ball that rolls uphill, or leave your shadow on the wall. Is it science or is it magic?

Where to Eat

Bistro Roca, 143 Wonderland Trail; (828) 295–4008. A wood-fired oven produces gourmet pizzas and roasted fish and meats. $

Blowing Rock Grill, 349 Sunset Drive; (828) 295–9474. Looking for trout? Look here. The grill also serves a great breakfast. $

Canyons, US 321 Bypass; (828) 295–7661. Asian, American, Mexican, and Southwestern dishes make for an interesting blend and a large selection on the menu. Sunday brunch features live jazz. $–$$

Pssghetti's Italian Restaurant, 7179 Valley Boulevard; (828) 295–9855. Authentic Italian cuisine served in a restaurant with an inauthentic spelling. $$

Woodlands Barbecue and Pickin' Parlor, US 321 Bypass; (828) 295–3651. We'll talk more about barbecue later, but you can get a pretty good plate here. $

Where to Stay

Because the ski slopes are located near here, there is no shortage of places to stay in Blowing Rock. Here's a short list of places you might look into first:

Alpen Acres Motel, 318 Old US 321; (828) 295–7981. This family-oriented motel with nineteen rooms has a playground, and children stay free. $$–$$$

Alpine Village Inn, 297 Sunset Drive; (828) 295–7206. Alpine is a very nicely decorated inn in a great location. $$

Blowing Rock Inn and Mountain Village, 788 North Main Street; (828) 295–7921. Very cozy rooms are offered at this inn that also has several villas for rent. $$–$$$$

Blowing Rock Resort Rentals, P.O. Box 2486, Blowing Rock 28605; (828) 295–9899. This company offers a large variety of cottages, condos, and cabins.

Chetola Resort at Blowing Rock, North Main Street; (800) 243–8652. With lodge rooms, condominiums, and a bed and breakfast, Chetola offers an indoor fitness center, massage therapy, kid's camp, and much more in some of the most luxurious accommodations in the Blue Ridge. $$$$

The Gathering Place, Blue Ridge Parkway, Glendale Springs; (800) 819–7643. This retreat is located on the Blue Ridge Parkway outside of Boone and caters to larger families and groups. $$$

Hillwinds Inn, 315 Sunset Drive; (828) 295–7660. Selections include standard rooms, suites and cottages, some with fireplaces and full kitchens. Complimentary continental breakfast is offered, and pet-friendly rooms are available. $–$$$

The Village Inn, 7876 Valley Boulevard; (828) 295–3380. Beautifully landscaped with a lake and the New River. Accommodations include guest rooms, suites, and cottages. Pet friendly rooms are available. $$–$$$$

For More Information

Blowing Rock Chamber of Commerce, (800) 295–7851; www.blowing rock.com.

Back on the Parkway

The Blowing Rock area is one of the best places to explore the Blue Ridge Parkway. Nearby is a small lake where you can rent canoes and paddleboats, plus two great parks where you can have a picnic and let the kids run. **Moses Cone Memorial Park,** located at Milepost 297, has grills at the sites, stepping-stones in the stream that runs through the park, and a big field that's great for tossing a football or baseball. **Julian Price Park,** also located at Milepost 297, features great hiking trails around the lake as well as boat rentals. Just south of the park is the **Linn Cove**

Viaduct, the most complicated concrete bridge in the world. It took fifteen million pounds of concrete and steel to wind the road around the cove without damaging the environment.

The Jeffersons

Heading north on the Blue Ridge Parkway, you escape a lot of the common tourist activity that you find in the larger towns. Two towns, Jefferson and West Jefferson, seem to blend into one.

Mount Jefferson State Natural Area (all ages)

State Road 1152 off Highway 163; (336) 246–9653. Generally open during daylight hours. Free.

The slopes and summit of this mountain area are home to an immensely diverse population of trees, shrubs, and wildflowers—a canopy of oak, shade rhododendron, mountain laurel, azaleas, and dogwoods. Wildflowers include trillium, pink lady slipper, and false lily of the valley. Until the early twentieth century, American chestnut trees were abundant in the area but the chestnut blight, introduced from Europe in 1910, destroyed the species here and elsewhere. Rangers give occasional programs, and you can hike one of several trails. A picnic site with grills is available.

Ashe County Cheese Factory (ages 3 and up)

106 East Main Street, West Jefferson; (336) 246–2501. The factory is open to the public 8:30 a.m. to 5:00 p.m. Monday through Saturday, but you should get there by 2:00 p.m. to see cheese being made. Call ahead since they often stop production at least one day a week. Free.

Founded in 1930, this is North Carolina's only cheese factory. Forty-five-minute tours of the plant are conducted by the staff, who will show you how they make cheese. They demonstrate how they turn milk into cheddar, Colby, and several other types of cheese, totaling 50,000 pounds per week.

Amazing North Carolina Facts

The New River, located in this area, is said to be the second oldest river in the world. Along its banks you'll find park areas that offer fishing, picnicking, and primitive camping. Also, you can "canoe the New" by calling one of the area outfitters: New River Outfitters, (800) 982–9190; Wahoo's Adventures (see the Boone entry), (800) 444–7238; and Zaloo's Canoes, (800) 535–4027.

Ben Long Frescoes

The most popular attraction here is the collection of contemporary paintings by Ben Long at two local churches. The Blue Ridge Mountain Frescoes, at **St. Mary's Episcopal Church,** 400 Beaver Creek School Road, in West Jefferson (336–982–3076), and **Holy Trinity Episcopal Church,** 120 Glendale School Road, in nearby Glendale Springs (336–982–3076), include *The Last Supper,* one of the largest frescoes in the country, and *Mary Great with Child.* Long, a Statesville native, has become known internationally, and his work is featured both in the United States and in Italy. Admission is free, and the churches are open to the public during limited hours.

For More Information

Ashe County Visitors Center, (336) 246–9550; www.main.nc.us/ashe.

Laurel Springs

Continue north on the Blue Ridge Parkway.

Doughton Park (all ages)

Blue Ridge Parkway at Milepost 241; (336) 372–4499. Open May through October. Free.

The largest recreation area on the parkway is Doughton Park. The park includes all the standard park facilities, and you can also stay at **Bluffs Lodge** ($$$–$$$$), a rustic lodge that offers twenty-four rooms with scenic views of the mountains and surrounding meadows. A coffee shop and crafts shop are located nearby. Here you can explore great scenic trails and several historic buildings. **Brinegar Cabin** and the **Caudill Family Homestead** give a glimpse of the secluded mountain life.

A Hoffman Family Adventure

My son and I went on his first canoe trip on the New River with his scout troop. The only ones to ride home wet were the leaders. Mitch, don't stand up in the canoe! What kind of a leader are you? You're setting a bad example for the rest of us.

Wilkesboro

Worth a detour south off the Blue Ridge Parkway from Laurel Springs is the Wilkesboro area. Backtrack to Highway 18 and travel south.

The W. Kerr Scott Dam and Reservoir (all ages)
Highway 268, 499 Reservoir Road; (336) 921–3390. The reservoir is generally open during daylight hours. Free.

The reservoir, located on the Yadkin River, is accessible by taking Highway 18 through Wilkesboro to Highway 268 West. This 1,470-acre lake at the edge of the Blue Ridge Mountains offers a dozen sites for outdoor recreation. There are more than 55 miles of shoreline for everything from swimming to boating. Picnic facilities are located throughout the area, and you can also camp at Bandits Roost and Warrior Creek Park. **Berry Mountain Park,** located 5 miles west of Wilkesboro on Highway 268, is a good place to spend the day swimming and sunning on the beach. **Bloodcreek Overlook,** located about 2 more miles west, has a fishing pier as well as picnic facilities that include grills. A state fishing license is required to fish here.

Old Wilkes (all ages)
"Old Wilkes" is how local folk refer to their charming downtown area that is incredibly rich with history. Call (336) 667–3712 for more information. Tours are free; donations accepted.

Make an appointment or take a walking tour of Old Wilkes, which includes thirteen buildings that are on the National Register of Historic Places. Some of the highlights of the tour are the Old Wilkes Jail, completed in 1860, which once held Tom Dooley, convicted of murdering his girlfriend and made famous in a ballad; Wilkes County Courthouse, a 1902 classical revival building that is known for the Tory Oak on the front lawn from which British sympathizers were hanged; and the Robert Cleveland House, a log home built in the 1770s and moved behind the jail.

Morganton

You can end your tour by swinging back west and south from Wilkesboro along Highway 18 to the junction with I-40 at Morganton.

This is the home of the late U.S. Senator Sam Ervin Jr., who became famous for presiding over the Watergate hearings in the early 1970s. This area offers a number of opportunities for recreational outdoor activities.

Other Things to See and Do
in the Blue Ridge Mountains

- **Brevard Music Center,** Brevard, (828) 884–2100
- **Backcountry Outdoors,** Brevard, (828) 884–4262
- **Pisgah Forest Stables,** Brevard, (828) 883–8258
- **Whitewater Equestrian Center,** Brevard, (828) 966–9646
- **Jump Off Rock,** Hendersonville
- **Western NC Air Museum,** Hendersonville, (828) 696–2482
- **High Mountain Expeditions,** Blowing Rock, (800) 262–9036
- **Blowing Rock Stables,** Blowing Rock, (828) 295–7847
- **Magic Mountain Mini Golf,** Boone, (828) 264–6959
- **Fun N Wheels,** Boone, (828) 262–3780
- **Mast General Store,** Valle Crucis, (828) 963–6511; Boone, (828) 262–0000; Waynesville, (828) 452–2101; Hendersonville, (828) 696–1883; Asheville, (828) 232–1883
- **Grassy Creek Speedway at Gem Mountain,** Spruce Pine, (828) 766–6007
- **Grandfather Trout Farm,** Banner Elk, (828) 963–5098
- **Judaculla Rock,** Cashiers
- *From This Day Forward Outdoor Drama,* Valdese, (828) 874–0176

Tuttle Educational State Forest (all ages)
US 64; (828) 757–5608. The forest is generally open during daylight hours. Free.
Located north of Morganton off US 64 near Lenoir, the forest is a 170-acre park that offers a range of educational nature programs. In addition, there is a family campground as well as primitive campsites.

South Mountains State Park (all ages)
Highway 18; (828) 433–4772. The park is generally open during daylight hours. Free.
South of Morganton off Highway 18 is South Mountains State Park, a great place for trout fishing or simply wading in the streams or stepping on stones. The 7,330 acres

of this park are largely undeveloped, but a series of bridges and walkways along the trails make the park more accessible, especially for younger children.

Where to Stay

Daniel Boone Campground, 7360 Highway 181 North; (828) 433–1200. Trailer and tent sites are here along with a nature trail, playground, and a store so you can pick up any items you forgot. $

Rose Creek Campground, 3471 Rose Creek Road; (828) 438–4338. This will get the kids' vote. It has a water slide, playground, and more. $

For More Information

Burke County Travel and Tourism Commission, (828) 433–6793; www.burkecountytourism.org.

NC High Country Host, (800) 438–7500; www.highcountryhost.com.

The Northern Piedmont

S ome of North Carolina's biggest metropolitan areas are located in the Northern Piedmont, and as a result there is no shortage of great things to see and do. Educational opportunities abound at the state capital and on the campuses of the state's leading universities. Here you'll also find one of the country's leading zoos, where you can come within an arm's length of a rare bird or any number of African and North American animals. In addition, some of the best parks are located here, as is a living-history eighteenth-century Moravian village.

The highway system here is tops, which means you won't have much of a problem navigating this area. Interstate 40 takes you here from the west and combines

Jim's
TopPicks in the Northern Piedmont

1. North Carolina Zoological Park, Asheboro

2. Chapel Hill (all of it)

3. Old Salem

4. Wet 'n Wild Emerald Pointe, Greensboro

5. North Carolina Museum of Natural Sciences, Raleigh

6. SciWorks, Winston-Salem

7. Carolina BalloonFest

8. North Carolina Museum of History, Raleigh

9. Durham Bulls

10. North Carolina State Fair, Raleigh

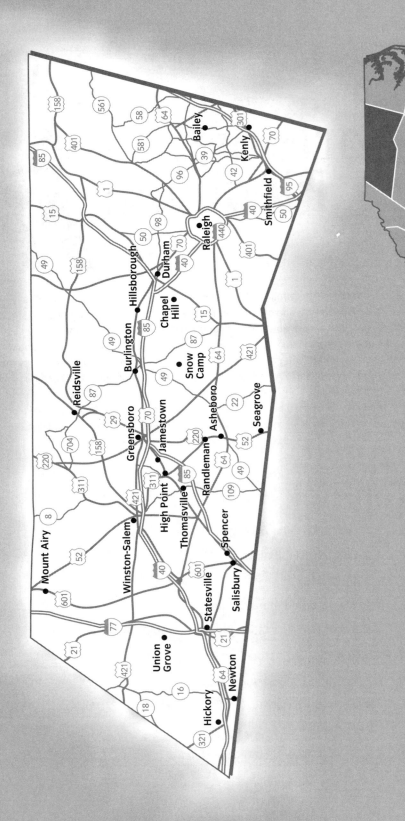

THE NORTHERN PIEDMONT

with Interstate 85 at Greensboro. I-40 then runs south through Raleigh, and I-85 runs north into Virginia.

Hickory

Hickory is conveniently located on Highway 321 and I-40.

Leaving the Blue Ridge Mountains, you descend quickly into the Catawba River Valley, originally inhabited by the Catawba Indians, the "people of the river." The Hickory area, the westernmost point of the Northern Piedmont, is the first city you come to and has become known as a national furniture capital. So if you are looking for new or antique furniture, this is the place to come.

Hickory Furniture Mart (all ages, but younger children will be more difficult to entertain)

2220 Highway 70 East; (800) 462–6278; www.hickoryfurniture.com. Open 9:00 a.m. to 6:00 p.m. Monday through Saturday and 1:00 to 5:00 p.m. on Sunday. Free.

In addition to the many stores you'll find throughout the area, the Hickory Furniture Mart features one hundred factory stores, outlets, and galleries. In the twelve acres of showrooms you can find everything you need to decorate your home, including bedding, linens, art, floor coverings, and furniture. Adjacent to the mart is an antiques center that includes North Carolina furniture as well as Oriental and European pieces. If shopping for furniture doesn't hold the kids' attention for very long, they might like learning more about the furniture industry that has been so important for this area for so long. The **Catawba Valley Furniture Museum** is located at the Furniture Mart on Level I. The museum traces the roots of the industry and features a reproduction of an early woodworking shop as well as a collection of vintage tools and furniture. You will also find the area visitor center here, making it well worth the stop.

Catawba Science Center (all ages)

243 Third Avenue Northeast; (828) 322–8169 or www.catawbascience.org. Open 10:00 a.m. to 5:00 p.m. Tuesday through Friday, 10:00 a.m. to 4:00 p.m. Saturday, and 1:00 to 4:00 p.m. Sunday. $; free for children under three.

The Catawba Science Center will provide hours of entertainment and education with a wide variety of hands-on exhibits. Don't miss the exhibit on the life cycle of a live mountain stream or the exhibits on health and fitness. The Physical Science Arcade offers opportunities to learn about physics, light, and sound. Climb a mountain wall and check out the exhibits in the Piedmont Treehouse. Kids can also take a walk down Energy Avenue where they will create and launch rockets, give themselves a lift with a pulley system, and take a spin in Spin Circle.

Hickory Museum of Art (all ages)
243 Third Avenue Northeast; (828) 327–8576; www.hickorymuseumofart.org. Open 10:00 a.m. to 5:00 p.m. Tuesday through Friday, 10:00 a.m. to 4:00 p.m. Saturday, and 1:00 to 4:00 p.m. Sunday. $; free for children under age three.

The city of Hickory has instituted a concerted effort over several decades to establish an art museum focused on American art to rival similar museums of bigger cities. And they have done that. The museum contains a significant collection of contemporary folk art and classic American work from significant artists such as Romare Bearden and Herb Jackson. The museum also contains an incredible collection of blown glass, including some amazing pieces by Dale Chihuly. Local clay works and pottery are also represented in the museum.

Where to Eat

Circus Hall of Cream, 211 Twenty-second Street; (828) 328–4214. This is a fun-themed ice cream place. $

Four Peas In a Pod, 1640 Tenth Avenue; (828) 267–0202. Friendly service in a family atmosphere is a trademark of this restaurant. $

Fuddruckers, 1510 Eighth Street Drive; (828) 323–1044. This small chain is kid-friendly and serves great burgers you complete yourself. $

Hickory Smokehouse, 2450 North Center Street; (828) 328–2300. Barbecue is the specialty here. $

J & S Cafeteria, 1949 Thirteenth Avenue Drive Southeast; (828) 326–8983. This is a great place for families with a wide variety of tastes. $

Where to Stay

Park Inn Gateway Center Hotel, 909 Highway 70 Southwest; (800) 789–0686. You get a buffet breakfast in this very nice hotel. $$

Chain hotels here also include Courtyard by Marriott, Comfort Suites, Hampton Inn, Holiday Inn Express, and Quality Inn and Suites.

For More Information

Hickory Metro Convention & Visitors Bureau, (800) 849–5093; www.hickory metro.com.

Newton

East and a bit south of Hickory is the town of Newton, the Catawba County seat, located off I-40.

Historic Newton Walking Tour (ages 5 and up)
Buildings on the tour are open 9:00 a.m. to 4:00 p.m. Tuesday through Friday, 10:00 a.m. to 4:00 p.m. Saturday, and 2:00 to 5:00 p.m. Sunday. Call (828) 465–0383 for more information. For a walking tour brochure, call (828) 465–7400. Free.

You'll find a number of historically significant sites on the Historic Newton Walking Tour, which includes 105 buildings. Among the sites on the tour are Murray's Mill, a fully restored corn and gristmill; and St. Paul's Lutheran Church, a two-story log, weather-boarded church that includes the balcony where slaves sat during services and a cemetery with tombstones in German dating back to 1771. Also on the tour is the **Catawba County Museum of History.**

Catawba County Museum of History (all ages)

30 North College Avenue; (828) 465–0383; www.catawbahistory.org. Open 9:00 a.m. to 4:00 p.m. Wednesday through Saturday and 1:30 to 4:30 p.m. Sunday. Free.

The historical settler reenactments are a key program at this small history museum, located in the former Catawba County Courthouse in Newton's Downtown Square. The Catawba County Museum of History pays tribute to the brave settlers of the Catawba River Valley and their descendants who are responsible for establishing a world-renowned furniture industry. The significant collections include agricultural tools and implements forged from hand-dug iron ore, produced by the area's Scotch-Irish, German, and English settlers. Handcrafted household cupboards, wagon benches, and other furniture items are on display. You will also find military uniforms, including a British Red Coat from the Revolutionary War era, Civil War weapons, and other objects. The museum has also re-created antebellum parlors and an early-twentieth-century medical office here. A gallery of looms, spinning wheels, and other items commemorates the area's textile heritage.

Where to Eat

Geppetos of Newton, 114 North College Avenue; (828) 464–7833. Pizza is the specialty of the house. $

Statesville

Continue east on I-40 or U.S. Highway 70 to where they intersect Interstate 77, and you'll be in Statesville. U.S. Highways 64 and 21 also converge here.

Carolina BalloonFest (all ages)

Statesville Regional Airport, I-40 West at Exit 146 or Exit 148. Call the Greater Statesville Chamber of Commerce at (704) 873–2892 or visit www.carolinaballoonfest .com for more information about the balloon fest or other special events. $$.

Balloons fill the sky over Statesville each October as one of the oldest and biggest balloon rallies on the East Coast gets under way. The Carolina BalloonFest, held in late October, is the city's best attraction. Thousands of spectators show up annually to watch the more than fifty beautiful, silent, colorful balloons ascend to the heavens. Standard festival amenities are also offered at the event, including a kids fun zone, a trick-or-treat event, crafts, and even an adult feature—a wine festival. Balloon rides are also offered, of course.

Museum of Arts and Heritage (all ages)

134 Court Street; (704) 873–4734; www.iredellmuseums.org. Hours are 10:00 a.m. to 5:00 p.m. Monday through Friday. Free.

The Museum of Arts and Heritage is located in the former 1920s courthouse in downtown Statesville. It exhibits the work of local and regional artists and displays a permanent collection of art and historical items, including paintings, drawings, Audubon prints, sculpture, pottery and even an Egyptian mummy. This, along with the courthouse architecture, really makes it worth the stop.

The Children's Museum and Play Space (all ages)

1613 East Broad Street; (704) 872–7508; www.iredellmuseums.org. Hours are 10:00 a.m. to 5:00 p.m. Monday through Friday, and 10:00 a.m. to 3:00 p.m. Sunday. $; free for children under age twelve.

Part of the Iredell Museums organization, the Children's Play Space operates in Signal Hill Mall. Its art exhibit includes an abundance of art supplies to allow children to experiment with a variety of media. A music exhibit helps children explore instruments from around the world, including African drums, bells, xylophone, tambourine, and rain stick. A costume and puppet stage invites children into a "barn" equipped with a variety of diverse puppets to help children to create their own puppet show. Nearby is a costume area and mirror where children dress up and put on their own performance. A child-sized kitchen and cafe exhibit puts children to work setting a table, preparing and serving "meals" to friends and family, and cleaning up and vacuuming. A blocks exhibit exposes children to architecture and the nature exhibit includes live fish, snakes, and painted turtles.

Fort Dobbs (ages 5 and up)

438 Fort Dobbs Road; (704) 873–5866. Open 9:00 a.m. to 5:00 p.m. Monday through Saturday and 1:00 to 5:00 p.m. Sunday, April through October; 10:00 a.m. to 4:00 p.m. Tuesday through Saturday and 1:00 to 4:00 p.m. Sunday, November through March. Free.

Just north of Statesville on US 21 is Fort Dobbs, built in 1756 and named after Royal Colonial Governor Arthur Dobbs. The fort was constructed at a time when tension between the colonists and the British was rising and settlers came into increasing conflict with Native Americans. On many occasions colonists in the area, including Daniel Boone and his family, were forced out of their homes and sought refuge at the fort, which was attacked only once in more than fifteen years. Today the fort, which includes little more than ruins and ground impressions, is the site of continual archaeological investigation. Archaeological finds and other artifacts are displayed along the trails and at the visitor center.

Love Valley Arena (all ages)
Highway 115, north of I-40; (704) 592–2299. Prices vary by activity.

During the summer months Statesville's Love Valley Arena features old-fashioned rodeos and other events. Love Valley is known throughout the state as a cowboy's paradise, complete with a saloon, hitching posts, and a general store, and it attracts horse enthusiasts year-round. During the Tar Heel Classic Horse Show, held in May, you can get a look at Tennessee Walkers, Arabians, and quarter horses as they go through various events and judging. Among the fun-filled rodeo events are junior competitions and events with a frontier theme.

Union Grove

Old Time Fiddler's and Bluegrass Convention (all ages)
Fiddler's Grove Campground, Highway 901 west of I-77. For more information call (828) 478–3735 or log on to www.fiddlersgrove.com.

One of the state's more unusual annual events is the Old Time Fiddler's and Bluegrass Convention, held each May near the town of Union Grove, located north of Statesville. It is the oldest event of its kind in the nation, running since 1924, and attracts musicians from around the country. The weekend-long event features continuous performances and competitions in all areas of bluegrass music, from clogging to fiddling. There are more than fifty bands that compete for various titles including the coveted Fiddler of the Festival award. Whether you're an experienced fiddler wishing to sharpen your skills or a beginner who has never held a fiddle before, the convention has a class—and often an instrument—available for you. Booths are situated throughout the campground, offering a variety of musical and craft items for sale.

For More Information

Statesville Convention and Visitors Bureau, (704) 878–3480; www.visit statesville.org.

Salisbury

Salisbury is located southeast of Statesville at the junction of US 70 and I-85.

Salisbury, the largest city in western North Carolina until the early 1900s, was once a center for trade and politics. Today the city celebrates its rich heritage with eight separate historic districts where you can take a walk back in time.

Salisbury Heritage Tour (all ages)

When you get to Salisbury, head to the Visitors Information Center, located in the Gateway Building, 204 East Innes Street (800–332–2343; www.salisburync.gov). Here you can pick up a brochure or **free** audiotapes for the Salisbury Heritage Tour and the Salisbury National Cemetery Tour. The sites that you won't want to miss are **Josephus Hall House** and the 1820 Federal-style home of the chief surgeon of the Salisbury Confederate Prison. A Civil War cannon rests on the lawn in front of the home, which has been renovated with Greek and Victorian touches. Free tours by costumed guides are given on weekends. Another interesting home is the **Old Stone House,** an impressive two-story stone structure built in 1766. On the second story you'll find two openings believed to be gunports used to fight off hostile Native Americans. In all there are 142 points of interest on the tour, which can be taken by trolley on Saturday April through October.

Lazy 5 Ranch (all ages)

Located on Highway 150 west of Salisbury; (704) 663–5100; www.lazyfiveranch.com. Open 9:00 a.m. to 7:00 p.m. Monday through Saturday and 1:00 p.m. to 7:00 p.m. Sunday. $$. Reservations for wagon rides ($$) are recommended.

You can take a drive through this ranch in your car or a horse-drawn wagon, but expect to see more than horses and cows. A road winds around 185 acres that include hundreds of exotic animals in somewhat natural habitats. There's also a petting zoo and a playground.

Dan Nicholas Park & Campground (all ages)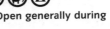

6800 Bringle Ferry Road; (704) 216–7800; www.dannicholas.net. Open generally during daylight hours. Free; fee for some activities.

This 400-acre park just southeast of Salisbury offers a big lake for paddle boating and fishing. Live animals in a petting barn and nature center are eager to greet the kids. The park also offers miniature golf, a carousel, gem mining, and a miniature train ride. You'll also find standard park amenities such as tennis courts, picnic shelters, a playground, volleyball, horseshoes, and ballfields. There are also eighty sites for tents and campers.

Barbecue Battle

Since we're coming up on the halfway point in the book, we'll pause for a moment and mention Lexington, which has gained considerable notoriety for its barbecue. The town, located on US 64, holds an annual barbecue festival in October, and restaurant guides proclaim Lexington to be the "Barbecue Capital of the World," listing twenty-one barbecue restaurants. The reason I put this in the middle of this guide is that there is some debate in the state over what is and is not "barbecue." In Lexington, you see, they serve western North Carolina barbecue, made of pork shoulder, cooked over hickory coals, and topped with a tomato-based sauce. In the east the whole pig is used and topped with a vinegar-based sauce. For more information about Lexington's festival call (336) 236–4218.

Where to Eat

Christo's Family Restaurant, 431 Innes Street; (704) 637–9050. Christo's offers subs, salads, pasta, and pizza. $

D.J.'s, 1502 West Innes Street; (704) 638–9647. A local favorite, D.J.'s serves an eclectic blend of Italian, Greek, and American including steak and seafood.

Escape the Daily Grind, 118 North Main Street; (704) 636–0160. You'll find great deli sandwiches and salads here. $

Las Palmas, 122 East Fisher Street; (704) 636–9475. This is a cool Mexican restaurant. $$

Where to Stay

You'll probably want to stick with the larger chain hotels if your trip calls for a stay in the Salisbury area. You'll find all of them here.

For More Information

Rowan County Convention and Visitors Bureau, (800) 332–2343; www.visit salisburync.com.

Great Train **Day Trip**

Amtrak operates two Piedmont train routes from Charlotte to Raleigh with seven stops in between. So if you find yourself in any one of these cities, you can combine a train trip with an attraction you want to see in one of the other cities. Rates range from $8.00 to $32.00 per person, and each summer a promotion has permitted children to ride **free.** Call (800) 878–7245 for details or visit www.amtrak.com.

Spencer

Just north of Salisbury on US 70 is the town of Spencer.

Historic Spencer Shops (all ages)

Located on South Salisbury Avenue; (704) 636–2889; www.nctrans.org. Open 9:00 a.m. to 5:00 p.m. Monday through Saturday and 1:00 to 5:00 p.m. Sunday, April through October; 10:00 a.m. to 4:00 p.m. Tuesday through Saturday and 1:00 to 4:00 p.m. Sunday, November through March. Museum admission is **free;** train rides ($–$$) are **free** for children under three.

Everything you want to know about transportation you can learn at the **North Carolina Transportation Museum** at Historic Spencer Shops. The Spencer Shops was once the largest steam locomotive servicing station operated by the Southern Railway. Built in 1896 and now a State Historic Site, it features exhibits on the development of vehicles, from the dugout canoe to the airplane. You can also see vintage automobiles and take a train ride through the fifty-seven-acre facility that includes thirteen buildings.

Thomasville

Thomasville is northeast of Spencer, just off I-85.

You might not plan an entire vacation around the town of Thomasville, but it is a beautiful, charming town to pass through. Thomasville's symbol is the World's Largest Duncan Phyfe Chair. You will know you are in furniture country when you stop at the town square to see the faux wood-framed chair that rests majestically on a granite pedestal for a total height of 30 feet with a seat 10½ feet wide.

In addition, the town is home of the oldest remaining railroad depot in the state, also located in the town square. Next, head north on I-85, and you'll find a rest stop

Fine **Furniture**

The 18-foot chair in Thomasville was once promoted as the **World's Largest Chair.** But officials discovered it was technically the World's Tallest Duncan Phyfe Chair—apparently another chair had it beat. By the way, the World's Largest Chest of Drawers is located not far away, in High Point. It's the four-story home of the High Point Jaycees.

that makes a great place for a picnic and a chance to see the **North Carolina Vietnam Veterans Memorial.** Located down a short trail, the memorial features crepe myrtles and brick walls in honor of the 216,000 North Carolinians who served in Vietnam and the 1,600 who died or are missing.

For More Information

Thomasville Convention and Visitors Bureau, (800) 611–9907; www.thomas villetourism.com.

High Point

High Point, north of Thomasville off I-85 or US 70, is North Carolina's main furniture manufacturing center, with 125 furniture manufacturing plants.

Furniture Discovery Center (ages 5 and up)
101 West Green Drive; (336) 887–3876; www.furniturediscovery.org. Open 10:00 a.m. to 5:00 p.m. Tuesday through Friday, 9:00 a.m. to 5:00 p.m. Saturday, and 1:00 to 5:00 p.m. Sunday. $–$$.

Furniture Discovery Center is a colorful museum that takes you through the furniture-making process in an innovative fashion, from lumber milling to detailed carving. The museum is laid out in color-coded stations that let you get hands-on experience with tools used in making furniture, including an air-powered nail gun and a paint-spray gun (Plexiglas keeps little fingers safe). You can also see several miniature collections. The gift shop at the museum has a wide selection of books on furniture making as well as crafts.

Angela Peterson Doll and Miniature Museum (all ages)
101 West Green Drive; (336) 885–3655. Open 10:00 a.m. to 4:00 p.m. Monday through Friday, 9:00 a.m. to 4:00 p.m. Saturday, and 1:00 to 4:00 p.m. Sunday. $.

Anyone who has ever played with dolls will love the Angela Peterson Doll and Miniature Museum, adjacent to the furniture center. Here you will find one of the greatest collections of dolls anywhere. It features more than 2,500 dolls, miniatures, and artifacts from around the world. This exquisite collection took more than fifty years of travel to put together, and Angela Peterson made many of the costumes, shadow boxes, and dollhouses herself. As you enter the main gallery you'll see dozens of glass cases filled with china dolls, along with dolls made of papier-mâché, wax, and tin, some dating back to the 1800s. A 3-foot-high Shirley Temple doll may prompt some stories from Grandma. Among the most interesting in the collection are an unusual doll made of seaweed and the dressed fleas you have to look at under a magnifier. And don't forget the more modern collection of Barbie dolls and the Pillsbury Doughboy.

All-a-Flutter Butterfly Farm (all ages)
7850 Clinard Farms Road; (336) 989–4507; www.all-a-flutter.com. Family days are Saturdays 10:00 to 11:00 a.m., late April to late September. $.

If you've ever been to a wedding during which the couple releases butterflies, they may have gotten them here. But the operators have developed a significant and fun educational program in conjunction with the wedding business. They present demonstrations of all stages of butterfly development from caterpillar to chrysalis to emergence of an adult butterfly. Plus you get a chance to hand feed the colorful creatures. The program, which covers the Monarch, its lifecycle, and the nectar plants on which it feeds, is presented in a small flight house. Laughter also emerges as audience members dress up as part of the show. Tip: Wear bright clothes, especially warm colors, and you just might make a new friend.

High Point Museum and Historical Park (ages 5 and up)
1859 Lexington Avenue; (336) 885–1859; www.highpointmuseum.org. The museum, house, and grounds are open 10:00 a.m. to 4:30 p.m. Tuesday through Saturday and 1:00 to 4:30 p.m. Sunday. Admission is free.

Make sure you see the High Point Museum and Historical Park and pick up a guide to High Point's other historical attractions. The museum contains woodworking tools dating back to the nineteenth century as well as local artifacts and Civil War items. Also on the grounds is **John Haley House,** an early brick Quaker house, the oldest structure still standing in Guilford County. Built in 1786, the house has been fully restored, and the grounds also include a weaving house, the Hoggett House built in 1801, and blacksmith shop.

Carolina Dynamo (all ages)
McPherson Stadium, 6105 Townsend Road; (336) 316–1266. $–$$; free for children under two.

One of the newer attractions on the family fun scene in High Point is the Carolina Dynamo, a soccer team that springs into action each April. Each home game brings an array of promotional events, including a fans' kick for $15,000 toward the purchase of a new car and a kids' competition for soccer gear. D. D., the 8-foot soccer dog, comes out of his house in the 10,000-seat stadium to give away premium items.

Piedmont Environmental Center (all ages)
1220 Penny Road; (336) 883–8531; www.piedmontenvironmental.com. Open 9:00 a.m. to 5:00 p.m., Monday through Saturday and 1:00 to 5:00 p.m., Sunday. Free.

Located at High Point City Lake, this nature preserve, with a staff of naturalists, includes a nature store and a center with small animal exhibits. There is also access to Greenway Trail, an 8-mile walk. In addition the center conducts hands-on family workshops on topics such as stargazing, birding, cultivating wildflowers, and mushrooms.

High Point City Lake Park (all ages)
602 West Main Street, Jamestown; (336) 883–3498; www.highpoint.net/pr/citylake.cfm. Open generally during daylight hours and activities vary by season. Free, fees for some activities.

Access to High Point's (and one of the state's) best parks is located in nearby Jamestown. The 340-acre lake is open for boating, fishing, and other fun. You can rent a fishing boat, a paddle boat, or a canoe or take a tour on the thirty-passenger excursion boat. For the younger set, there are amusement rides, including a carousel and train. A waterslide and the largest outdoor swimming pool in the state create more water fun, and you'll want to make time for miniature golf and the playgrounds.

Where to Eat

You won't have any trouble finding a variety of food in High Point. Among the dozens of restaurants are a slew of barbecue places, chain restaurants, and places with local flavor that include the following:

Carolina Diner, 201 Eastchester Drive; (336) 869–0660. This is a good family-style diner. $

K&W Cafeteria, 1661 Westchester Drive; (336) 886–4422. K&W is a small, popular chain cafeteria with standard fare. $

Where to Stay

Atrium Inn, 425 South Main Street; (888) 928–7486. Children under eighteen stay free in this smaller, standard hotel that was renovated in 2006. $$$–$$$$

Biltmore Suites Hotel, 4400 Regency Drive; (888) 412–8188. This is an upscale facility that caters largely to business travelers. Suites are available. $$$$

For More Information

High Point Convention and Visitors Bureau, (336) 884–5255; www .highpoint.org.

Winston-Salem

Northwest of High Point, via Highway 109 near I-40, is Winston-Salem.

Tanglewood Park

4061 Clemmons Road; (336) 778–6300. Open 7:00 a.m. to dusk. $–$$$.

While there are a number of hotels and other accommodations in the area, the most popular place to stay is Tanglewood Park, a great outdoor recreational facility operated by Forsythe County, about ten minutes from downtown Winston-Salem. It offers a bed-and-breakfast inn in an old manor house as well as cottages and a neat campground. Both welcome children. The park has 1,100 acres for golf, tennis, swimming, horseback riding, hiking, studying nature, and fishing. Included are two top-rate golf courses and a par-three course for families who just want to get out on the course for a couple hours. You'll also find miniature golf and horse stables.

Old Salem (ages 5 and up)

527 South Main Street; (888) 348–5420; www.oldsalem.org. Hours are 9:00 a.m. to 5:30 p.m. Tuesday through Saturday and 12:30 to 5:30 p.m. Sunday, January through March; and 9:00 a.m. to 5:30 p.m. Monday through Saturday and 12:30 to 5:30 p.m. Sunday, April through December. Hours of some facilities and exhibits may vary. $$–$$$$.

Winston-Salem's most popular attraction is Old Salem, a living-history eighteenth-century Moravian village. You'll want to spend most of the day here as costumed guides take you through the community from which the city evolved. More than eighty structures, dating back to 1766, have been fully restored. The most popular among kids is Winkler Bakery, where fresh sugar cakes, gingerbread cookies, and other tasty goodies are made using early methods and recipes. You can also see the Boys School; John Vogler House, which includes a collection of nineteenth-century toys; a structure that served as a meat market and firehouse; Shultz shop, the shoemaker's shop; and more. A film on Moravian life is presented in a theater inside Vierling Barn. In addition, you can take a half-hour carriage ride ($$$) on the cobblestone streets of the district.

The **Old Salem Children's Museum** is a play space that encourages children (and adults) to learn about colonial life. The hands-on exhibits include a marble run that teaches the concept of gravity and encourages children to imagine how the water traveled through clay pipes to the town of Salem. Children weave ropes on a weaving frame. They draw a profile to learn how memories of loved ones were captured before the camera was invented. Plus, they will play for hours if you let them, as they pretend to live and cook in a child's size Miksch house. A maze, puppet theater, and climbing structure finish off a fun visit.

Yes kids, there were toys before video games and **The Old Salem Toy Museum** shows us. More than 1,200 toys from Europe and America, dating back as far as A.D. 225, are on display here. Most of the exhibit focuses on toys that Moravian children played with in the nineteenth and twentieth centuries. German toys, ships, marbles, games, puzzles, cars, and trains all captured imaginations of the boys and girls who made this land their home more than 200 years ago. Dolls from the seventeenth century, teddy bears, puppets, doll houses, and toy zoos all add up to create a fascinating exhibit.

You can also see the nation's largest collection of furniture and decorative arts of the south here at the **Museum of Early Southern Decorative Arts.**

Southeastern Center for Contemporary Arts (ages 10 and up)

750 Marguerite Drive; (336) 725–1904; www.secca.org. Open 10:00 a.m. to 5:00 p.m. Wednesday through Saturday and 2:00 to 5:00 p.m. Sunday. $–$$; free for children age sixteen or younger.

More low-key adventure awaits you at the Southeastern Center for Contemporary Arts, located in the English-style manor house of the late industrialist James G. Hanes. Although this is a center for southeast arts, you can enjoy fascinating works from around the world in changing exhibits from well-known artists. In addition, the museum presents occasional interpretive programs on exhibits as well as performing arts programs. A wide array of contemporary crafts are also on display and for sale at the Centershop.

Historic Bethabara Park (all ages)

2147 Bethabara Road; (336) 924–8191; www.bethabarapark.org. Building tours ($) are 10:30 a.m. to 4:30 p.m. Tuesday through Friday and 1:30 to 4:30 p.m. Saturday and Sunday. Admission to the grounds is free.

More history awaits you at Historic Bethabara Park, located north of town off University Parkway. It's a great place for outdoor activities, to have a picnic, or to stroll along the walking trails, but history is alive here, too. Its 175 acres are a wildlife preserve, but the park is also part museum, telling the story of a group of Moravians who bravely settled the village beginning in 1753. You can visit Palisade Fort, originally built in 1756 during the French and Indian War and reconstructed on its original site. You'll also find the 1788 Gemeinhaus, a church; a 1782 Potter's House; and an 1803 Brewer's House.

Museum of Anthropology (ages 5 and up)

Located behind Kentner Stadium off University Parkway, Wake Forest University; (336) 758–5282. Open 10:00 a.m. to 4:30 p.m. Tuesday through Saturday. Free.

For those who like to meet people from around the world, check out the Museum of Anthropology, located on the campus of Wake Forest University. This is the only museum of its kind in the Southeast. The museum is dedicated to the study of world cultures and includes exhibits related to these studies. Featured are costumes, clothing, tools, and more, all depicting human development around the world. The museum also relates some of the greater achievements of the people from the Americas, Africa, Asia, and the Pacific. Even young kids will love the Discovery Room, which helps them explore anthropology through hands-on activities.

Reynolda House Museum of American Art (ages 5 and up)

2250 Reynolda Road; (336) 758–5150; www.reynoldahouse.org. Open 9:30 a.m. to 4:30 p.m. Tuesday through Saturday and 1:30 to 4:30 p.m. Sunday. Closed Thanksgiving, Christmas, and New Year's Day. $$; admission to the gardens is free.

Three centuries of American art are on display at Reynolda House Museum of American Art, located off Reynolda Road near Wake Forest University. The museum is located on the country estate and model farm built by tobacco magnate R. J. Reynolds and his wife, Katherine Smith Reynolds. The house, built in 1917, is filled with beautiful paintings, prints, sculptures, and furnishings, some of which date back to the seventeenth century. Also included is a ladies' costume collection that dates back to nearly 1900. Japanese cherry trees on the grounds bloom with magnificent color in late March, but a visit to the garden and greenhouses is fun anytime.

SciWorks (all ages)

400 West Hanes Mill Road; (336) 767–6730; www.sciworks.org. Open 10:00 a.m. to 4:00 p.m. Monday through Friday and 11:00 a.m. to 5:00 p.m. Saturday. $$; free for children under two.

Science lovers will get their fill in Winston-Salem at SciWorks, a 45,000-square-foot science center and environmental park that lets kids and adults alike uncover some of the mysteries of science. Here you can actually do experiments yourself, while staff members put on displays designed to astonish you. You can learn more about the sea at the aquariums, at the touch tank, and through CD-ROM computer programs of undersea adventure. The center also includes a 120-seat planetarium that presents various shows year-round. In addition, you can take a walk or have a picnic in the thirty-four-acre park. Here you're likely to come face-to-face with a deer or river otter, and the kids get a chance to meet farmyard animals.

Where to Eat

La Carreta, Inc., 725 Coliseum Drive, (336) 722–3709; 137 Jonestown Road, (336) 774–3010; 1989 North Peace Haven Road, (336) 768–7881. This Mexican restaurant chain has a very friendly staff. $

Lucky 32, 109 South Stratford Road; (336) 777–0032. This restaurant is upscale but casual, with a varied menu. $$

Old Salem Tavern Dining Room, 736 South Main Street in Old Salem; (336) 748–8585. Servers wear Moravian costumes. You'll want to make reservations here. $$

Winston's Eatery, 300 South Liberty Street; (336) 248–2828. Located in an old railroad building near Old Salem, this restaurant offers a little more elegant dining, but it's casual enough for kids. $$$

Village Tavern, 2000 Griffith Road, (336) 760–8686; 221 Reynolda Village Road, (336) 748–0221. Pasta, fish, and chicken are the mainstays of the menu here. $–$$

The Vineyards Restaurant, 120 Reynolda Village; (336) 748–0269. This restaurant fits in very well with its location. $$

West End Cafe, 926 West Fourth Street; (336) 723–4774. This is very casual, but it still offers great atmosphere near Old Salem. $$

Where to Stay

Brookstown Inn, 200 Brookstown Avenue; (336) 725–1120. Fresh-baked cookies every night. Wow! And children under twelve stay **free.** This historic inn is located in a restored factory and is very nice with exposed brick and beams on high ceilings. $$$$

The Hawthorne Inn and Conference Center, 420 High Street; (800) 972–3774. While this hotel caters largely to business travelers, it's a great place for the family. Suites and efficiencies are available. $$$$

For More Information

Winston-Salem Convention and Visitors Bureau, (800) 331–7018; www.visitwinstonsalem.com.

Amazing North Carolina Facts

The Eastern gray squirrel was selected as the state mammal in 1969. You'll find them everywhere from hardwood forests to backyards throughout the state.

Mount Airy

If you're staying in the triad area—Winston-Salem, High Point, or Greensboro—a great day trip is less than an hour northwest on U.S. Highway 52, where you'll find Mount Airy.

The town was made famous as the model for Mayberry in the popular television series *The Andy Griffith Show*. Griffith, the show's star (who later became the title character in television's *Matlock*), was born and raised here until he left to attend college in Chapel Hill. His house, at 711 East Haymore Street, and the **Andy Griffith Playhouse,** at 218 Rockford Street, have been preserved as landmarks and are on the town's tour of historical places. Memorabilia from the show and Griffith's career can be found throughout the town but his house is now a rental property. In addition, the playhouse is the venue for productions throughout the year. At the **Andy Griffith Museum** on Main Street you'll find a variety of memorabilia from his career.

Hanging Rock and Pilot Mountain State Parks

Hanging Rock is on Hanging Rock Road, and Pilot Mountain is at 1792 Pilot Knob Park Road. Both parks are open sunrise to sunset daily, year-round. Free.

To the south and west of Mount Airy you will find two state parks that are great for recreational activities. **Hanging Rock State Park** (336–593–8480), located off Highway 89, provides a great opportunity for picnicking, hiking, camping, and swimming. Six rustic cabins are available for rent in advance.

An interesting granite formation pokes 1,400 feet out of the earth at **Pilot Mountain State Park** (336–325–2355), located off Highway 52. Here a number of recreational activities are available in addition to a family campground ($), which operates on a first-come, first-served basis.

Where to Eat

Snappy Lunch, 125 North Main Street; (336) 786–4931. The Snappy Lunch was mentioned on *The Andy Griffith Show,* and Andy ate there as a young boy growing up in Mount Airy. It's famous for its pork chop sandwich. $

Where to Stay

The Mayberry Motor Inn, U.S. 52 Bypass North; (336) 786–4109. Great rates are offered at the AAA-approved hotel that takes advantage of "Mayberry's" fame. $$

For More Information

Call the town visitor center at (800) 576–0231 for more information on Mount Airy, or visit www.visitmayberry .com.

Greensboro

North Carolina's third largest city is easily accessible from I-85 and I-40.

With a population of more than 200,000, Greensboro regularly rates as one of the nation's most desirable places in the country to live. The Piedmont Triad International Airport has made it one of the Southeast's more economically successful business centers, with businesses ranging from textiles to tobacco to service-related industries such as insurance. For the visitor it hosts a wide variety of activities that includes outdoor sports, among them golf and tennis, as well as spectator sports that include Atlantic Coast Conference basketball action, Class A baseball, and arena football. Greensboro is a center for arts, history, and culture as well.

Guilford County Courthouse National Military Park (all ages)
2332 New Garden Road; (336) 288–1776; www.nps.gov/guco. The park is open 8:30 a.m. to 5:00 p.m. daily. Free.

Much of Greensboro's roots are tied up at one of the city's most popular attractions, the Guilford County Courthouse National Military Park. It is the country's first Revolutionary War park and features more than 200 acres of wooded trails, monuments, and memorials. It memorializes a bloody battle at Guilford Courthouse, then the county seat, that occurred in March 1781. In that battle American major general Nathaniel Greene, for whom the city is named, lost control of the area to the British—but in the process took out more than a quarter of their troops. The British soon lost North Carolina as a result. The entire battle is re-created at the visitor center through an audiovisual display and exhibits of period artifacts. A film, exhibits, and audio tour will take you through it all.

Tannenbaum Park (all ages)
2200 New Garden Road; (336) 545–5315. The heritage center is open 9:00 a.m. to 5:00 p.m. Tuesday through Saturday. The park closes at 4:30 p.m. in winter. Call for information on the center or a schedule of living-history events at Hoskins House. Free.

You can learn more about the state's history from the Revolutionary War period to the early 1800s at Tannenbaum Park, near the National Military Park. At the heart of the park is **Hoskins House** (circa 1778). It is nearly 45 percent original but has been restored to what historians believe to be its original condition. Occasional living-history programs bring the house—including the kitchen, barn, and blacksmith shop—alive with demonstrations from interpreters. The **Colonial Backcountry Farm** is host to field crop and gardening exhibits and presentations. The **North Carolina Colonial Heritage Center** at the park provides an opportunity for hands-on participation in learning about backcountry life. Here visitors can try on colonial clothes, feel the weight of a real musket, and see up close how colonial people made their clothes and furnishings.

Amazing
North Carolina Facts

On February 1, 1960, four African American North Carolina A&T State University students sat down at a segregated lunch counter at the F. W. Woolworth in Greensboro and asked for service. This fueled the campaign for racial desegregation in the South. A museum and international rights center have been planned to commemorate this event. Currently the event is memorialized at the Greensboro Historical Museum and at North Carolina A & T.

Greensboro Historical Museum (ages 5 and up)
130 Summit Avenue; (336) 373–2043. Open 10:00 a.m. to 5:00 p.m. Tuesday through Saturday and 2:00 to 5:00 p.m. Sunday. Free.

Much more history about the Greensboro area is waiting for you at the Greensboro Historical Museum, where you get a glimpse into the lives of some of the area's more prominent residents. Among them is Greensboro native William Sydney Porter, who gave his account of the city's occupation by Union troops in the stories he wrote under the name O. Henry. Other displays highlight the lives of First Lady Dolly Madison and famed television journalist Edward R. Murrow. The museum, housed in a Romanesque church built in 1892, also features changing exhibits and displays on early transportation, military history, and Native American settlements. You can also learn about the famous sit-in at the Woolworth lunch counter in 1960 that helped launch the national civil rights movement.

Blandwood Mansion and Carriage House (ages 5 and up) 🏛
447 West Washington Street; (336) 272–5003. Open 11:00 a.m. to 2:00 p.m. Tuesday through Saturday and 2:00 to 5:00 p.m. Sunday, February through December. $–$$.

Historical elegance is only a short drive away at Blandwood Mansion and Carriage House, a nineteenth-century Italian villa. The house, originally built as a farmhouse in the late eighteenth century, was redesigned and totally renovated in 1844. Blandwood served as home for former North Carolina governor and Whig party politician John Motley Morehead and today still contains many of its original furnishings. The adjacent carriage house serves as the site for many formal receptions and meetings.

Charlotte Hawkins Brown State Historic Site (ages 5 and up) 🏛
Located off I-85, northeast of Greensboro, 6136 Burlington Road, Sedalia; (336) 449–4846. Open 9:00 a.m. to 5:00 p.m. Monday through Saturday April through October, and 10:00 a.m. to 4:00 p.m. November through March. Free.

Greensboro's history continues into the twenty-first century at the Charlotte Hawkins Brown State Historic Site. North Carolina's first official site to honor an African American and a woman, it is the former location of the Palmer Institute, a prep school that Brown founded in 1902 when she was only nineteen years old. Eventually the school grew to 350 acres, included a farm, and received full accreditation by the Southern Association of Colleges and Secondary Schools. Today you can see displays about the school, Brown's life, and the civil rights movement. Also included are her home and gravesite.

Greensboro Cultural Center at Festival Park (ages 5 and up) 🖼

200 North Davie Street. Admission to all the museums and galleries is free, but hours vary. Call each museum for hours of operation or other details.

You'll find Greensboro's arts downtown at the Greensboro Cultural Center. The center features five galleries that include different types and themes in the visual arts. The **African American Atelier** (336–333–6885) exhibits original artwork by local African American artists and provides educational programs to the community's youth. The **Green Hill Center for North Carolina Art** (336–333–7460) features changing exhibits and programs that include works in glass, ceramics, jewelry, and painting. The **Greensboro Artists' League Gallery and Gift Shop** (336–333–7485) includes a sales gallery as well as changing exhibits of the works of artists in the Triad area. The **Guilford Native American Art Gallery** (336–273–6605) has contemporary Native American arts and crafts on display and for sale. The **Mattye Reed African American Heritage Center** (336–334–7108) is a satellite center located on the campus of North Carolina A&T State University. This museum has a seemingly unending collection of cultural exhibits from more than thirty African nations, New Guinea, and Haiti.

ArtQuest (all ages)

200 North Davie Street; (336) 333–2610; www.greenhillcenter.org. Public hours are 12:30 to 7:00 p.m. Tuesday through Saturday. $.

ArtQuest, located in Green Hill Center, is a hands-on children's gallery that offers creative learning and fun with interactive exhibits. Morning hours are often reserved for group tours, but it's open to the public the rest of the time. Families have the opportunity to discover the excitement of making art together through activities like building a castle or working on the loom. Wednesday from 5:00 to 7:00 p.m. is free family night.

Bur-Mil Park (all ages) 🖼 🖼

5834 Bur-Mil Club Road; (336) 373–3800. Generally open during daylight hours. Free.

This city/county park includes standard park facilities, but features a significant wildlife education facility and program. Visitors can take lessons on everything from fly fishing to landscape design. At the center of the park, in a renovated barn, is the Frank

Sharpe, Jr. Wildlife Education Center. You can borrow a fishing rod here or browse through the permanent and rotating exhibits on local wildlife and the environment.

Greensboro Children's Museum (ages 1 to 10)

220 North Church Street; (336) 574–2898; www.gcmuseum.com. Open 9:00 a.m. to 5:00 p.m. Tuesday through Saturday, 9:00 a.m. to 8:00 p.m. Friday, and 1:00 to 5:00 p.m. Sunday. $$.

This bright, colorful museum is a great place for families to spend hours. It is a wonderland of exciting exhibits that are the perfect size for kids and their imaginations. It includes themed learning stations for children ages one to ten. Visitors can swing by the kid-sized ATM at the bank, drive a fire truck, sound the siren on a police car, and bring a DC-9 jet in for a landing. Kids can help with a house under construction or deliver the mail in a U.S Postal Jeep. Whatever's in your town is likely to be in theirs. The "Tot Spot" offers activities to stimulate even the youngest children.

Spectator **Sports**

Greensboro has much to offer sports lovers. Forest Oaks Country Club (800–999–5446), located at 4600 Forest Oaks Drive, is the site of the **Wyndham Championship,** one of the richest and most prestigious golf tournaments on the PGA tour. Well-known golf stars come out for this event each October to compete for the purse.

In addition to pro golf, the **Greensboro Coliseum Complex** (336–373–7474), located at 1921 West Lee Street, is the site of a number of college events as well as the occasional host to the Atlantic Coast Conference basketball tournament. The coliseum additionally hosts such nonsporting events as the Ringling Bros. and Barnum & Bailey Circus, trade shows, flea markets, and more.

First Horizon Park at 408 Bellemeade Street (336–268–2255) is the new home of the Greensboro Grasshoppers, a Class A affiliate of the Florida Marlins. This state-of-the-art facility features a huge, open-air concourse that includes a kids' play park. The Grasshoppers have special promotions practically every game night. These include giving away hats, pennants, and other novelties. They also have special picnic packages that combine your dinner with a seat at the game. Check the local media for the dates of special dollar nights to attend a game in the 7,500-seat stadium at a bargain price.

Carolina Theatre (all ages)

310 South Greene Street; (336) 333–2605; www.carolina
theatre.com.

This historic landmark puts an old twist on a popular
pastime. Built in 1927, the historic Carolina Theatre
once hosted some of the era's most famous vaude-
ville performers, as well as being a first-run movie
house for silent films. Despite the decline of vaude-
ville, the dwindling of downtown's popularity, and
even a fire, the theater has returned to its old glory
and continues to welcome audiences in a rich
atmosphere of days gone by. It now hosts film and
live presentations.

Garden Variety (all ages)

Open 8:00 a.m. to sunset daily. Call (336) 373–2199 for more information. Free.

Three of the state's most beautiful and intriguing botanical gardens are located in
Greensboro. **The Bog Garden,** located at the corner of Hobbs and Starmount Farms
Roads, provides an interesting twist to this swampy land. The marsh has been trans-
formed into a beautiful area that includes more than 8,000 trees, shrubs, ferns, bam-
boo, and wildflowers. A wooden walkway takes you through the bog, where plants
are labeled for visitors' education. **Bicentennial Gardens,** completed in 1976 to
commemorate the nation's bicentennial and located at 1105 Hobbs Road off Highway
29 North, features spectacular rose gardens as well as a fragrance and herb garden.
It's hard to find a time of year when this garden isn't bursting with color. A favorite
among kids is the **Greensboro Arboretum,** located on Wendover Avenue, which
features seventeen acres of gardens, including a butterfly garden and eleven other
labeled plant collections.

Wet 'n Wild Emerald Pointe (all ages)

**Off I-85 at 3910 South Holden Road; (800) 555–5900; www.emeraldpointe.com. Hours
vary according to season and weather. $$$–$$$$.**

Those who want to get in on some action themselves and cool off during the warm
summer months can head to Wet 'n Wild Emerald Pointe. Splash and play here at the
Carolinas' largest water park, which offers twenty-two water slides, rides, and attrac-
tions, in addition to an exciting Sky Coaster ride that lets you fly suspended under a
giant arch. The Sky Coaster requires an additional charge.

Celebration Station (all ages)

Just off I-40 at 4315 Big Tree Way; (910) 316–0606. Open 10:00 a.m. to 10:00 p.m. Monday through Thursday and 10:00 a.m. to 11:00 p.m. Friday and Saturday. Fees vary by activity.

You'll find more than water fun at Celebration Station, a great family entertainment center. The park includes miniature golf, bumper boats, go-karts, batting cages, arcade games, a pizza restaurant, and a snack bar where you can grab a foot-long hot dog or a salad. The center is set up so each age group has its own area, making the activities safe for young children as well as their older siblings. It's also a lot of fun, especially if you have toddlers, to order a pizza and listen to the entertainment from the Dixie Diggers, an animated musical band of animals.

Natural Science Center (all ages)

4301 Lawndale Drive; (336) 288–3769; www.natsci.org. Open 9:00 a.m. to 5:00 p.m. Monday through Saturday and 12:30 to 5:00 p.m. Sunday. $$.

You can probably make a day out of a visit to the Natural Science Center of Greensboro. It's a real treat to visit this hands-on museum, zoo, and planetarium. If your kids like dinosaurs, and they probably do, they'll love visiting the fine dinosaur gallery as much as they'll like the snakes and amphibians at the herpetarium and the crabs and sea urchins in the touch tank. Here and at the touch labs they'll learn a lot about minerals and gems. The kids can meet animals up close at the petting zoo, where they will find donkeys, rabbits, goats, and more. They can also see a black bear and a jaguar at the zoo. The Edward R. Zane Planetarium is always ready to show an entertaining and educational show under its own stars.

Afterward you can spend the afternoon at **Country Park** (336–545–5343) adjacent to the science center. The park offers fishing at two stocked lakes, paddleboats, playgrounds, fields for running and playing, and trails for hiking and jogging. It's also a great place for a picnic. Admission to the park is free and it is open 8:00 a.m. to sunset daily.

Where to Eat

Greensboro is so large that there is no shortage of places to eat. The Greensboro Area Convention and Visitors Bureau can provide you with a thirty-page booklet of places to eat ranging from fast food to first class. Here are a few of the spots area families are likely to be:

Anton's Restaurant, 1628 Battleground Avenue; (336) 273–1386. This Italian restaurant is popular among local folks. You'll find a good variety of American dishes—steak, seafood, and chicken—in addition to the classic Italian food. $$

Arigato, 1200 South Holden Road; (336) 299–1003. Japanese food prepared at your table—who could ask for more? You'll also find a sushi bar, of course. $$

Chuck E. Cheese, 702-A Pembroke Drive; (336) 855–0234. You've probably been to Chuck's before, but we thought we would let you know it's here. $

Gate City Chop House, 106 South Holden Road; (336) 294–9977. While this is fairly upscale and a little on the pricey side, it does have a children's menu. $$$

Lucky 32, 1421 Westover Terrace; (336) 370–0707. If you like the Lucky 32 in Winston-Salem, you'll like the one here. $$

Where to Stay

Battleground Inn, 1517 Westover Terrace; (800) 932–4737. This is a good, affordable place to stay. $$

O. Henry Hotel, 624 Green Valley Road; (336) 854–2000. This hotel is conveniently located and has a pool, game room, and suites. $$

Park Lane Hotel at Four Seasons, 3005 High Point Road; (800) 942–6556. This is one of the nicer hotels in Greensboro. Look for a little pampering here. $$$$

For More Information

Greensboro Area Convention and Visitors Bureau, (800) 344–2282; www.greensboronc.org.

Reidsville

Head north from Greensboro on U.S. Highway 29, and you'll find the town of Reidsville, home of one of the prettiest plantations in the state.

Chinqua-Penn Plantation (ages 5 and up) 🏛

2138 Wentworth Street; (336) 349–4576; www.chinquapenn.com. Open 10:00 a.m. to 4:00 p.m. Saturday and 1:00 to 4:00 p.m. Sunday. $$–$$$; **free** for children under six.

This is the beautifully preserved home of businessman and farmer Thomas Jefferson Penn. The twenty-seven room mansion, built in 1925, is filled with an extensive collection of artwork and furnishings from Russia, Egypt, China, and France. Some pieces date as far back as 1100 B.C. Outside, the gardens reflect the same eclectic taste, from the fountains to the pagoda gardens.

Jamestown

Jamestown is just south of Greensboro on US 29.

Mendenhall Plantation (ages 5 and up)

603 West Main Street; (336) 454–3819; www.mendenhallplantation.org. Open for tours from April through the third week in December 11:00 a.m. to 3:00 p.m. Tuesday through Friday, 1:00 to 4:00 p.m. Saturday, and 2:00 to 4:00 p.m. Sunday. $.

Mendenhall is an early nineteenth-century Quaker plantation. It consists of a number of interesting structures, a museum, and one of only two false-bottom wagons still in existence. The wagon was used to transport escaped slaves during the operation of the Underground Railroad.

Castle McCulloch (ages 10 and up)

3925 Kivett Drive; (336) 887–5413; www.castlemcculloch.com. Open for gem mining Sunday 11:00 a.m. to 5:00 p.m., April through October. House and grounds are open year-round, except when they host private events. Grounds tours are available 11:00 a.m. to 4:00 p.m. Wednesday through Sunday. House tour hours are 10:00 a.m. to 4:00 p.m. Saturday and 1:00 to 4:00 p.m. Sunday. $–$$$.

Part panning operation, part wedding venue, you can't deny that Castle McCulloch is pretty cool to visit simply because it really does look and feel like a castle. Both a National and State Historic Site, the landmark was built by an enterprising Cornish engineer named Charles McCulloch as a gold refinery in 1832. Now tourists can mine for gold, emeralds, rubies, garnets, amethyst, and crystals. Special events such as the Christmas Castle are conducted throughout the year.

Randleman

Richard Petty Museum (ages 5 and up)

142 Academy Street; (336) 495–1143; www.pettyracing.com. Open 9:00 a.m. to 5:00 p.m. Monday through Saturday. $; free for children age six and younger.

This museum is a tribute to the king of NASCAR. Petty won seven Winston Cup Championships during his career, and today the museum, located in his hometown, houses a fine collection of memorabilia commemorating his career. Included are a number of cars he raced, his trophies, and tons of other awards and recognitions he received. You can also see on video some of the most exciting moments of his career, in addition to photos that include his crash at Daytona Speedway.

Amazing
North Carolina Facts

Richard Petty won his first stock car race in 1960 at the age of twenty-two on a half-mile dirt track at the Mecklenburg County fairgrounds.

Asheboro

Continue south on U.S. Highway 220 to reach Asheboro.

North Carolina Zoological Park (all ages)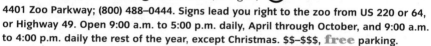
4401 Zoo Parkway; (800) 488–0444. Signs lead you right to the zoo from US 220 or 64, or Highway 49. Open 9:00 a.m. to 5:00 p.m. daily, April through October, and 9:00 a.m. to 4:00 p.m. daily the rest of the year, except Christmas. $$–$$$, free parking.

You'll want to head to one of the best family attractions in the state, the North Carolina Zoo, one of the largest walk-through zoos in the world. Great care has been taken to create this natural-habitat zoo to give you the best possible view of the animals on display. While you can walk through the zoo, a tram allows you to go back and see your favorite parts over and over. The North American Region, with more than 200 acres, features ten different exhibits that cover everything from deserts to swamps to prairies. In this region you'll see bison in an eleven-acre exhibit, roadrunners, rattlesnakes, and polar bears diving into a huge tank of water, as well as puffins, sea lions, and more at play. Also part of the North American Region is the Red Wolf Species Survival Plan, one element of the zoo's commitment to save the endangered animal and reintroduce it into the wild.

Next journey to Africa at the zoo's 500-acre region that includes nine exhibits. Among those is a 37-acre African Plains exhibit that includes some of the largest animals that naturally roam the plains of the African continent. Here antelope graze an open plain, giraffes tower at treetop level, and elephants get up close and personal. In this region you also get a chance to look massive gorillas in the eye and muse at the antics of monkeys and baboons. One of the best parts of the African exhibit is the R. J. Reynolds Forest Aviary, including more than 1,700 tropical plants and one hundred birds. A carousel and 4-D adventure ride round out this great experience. There is a picnic area located at the main entrance, and snack bars and refreshment stands are scattered throughout the park. Lockers are also provided.

Where to Eat

America's Roadhouse, 818 East Dixie Drive; (336) 633–1234. This restaurant offers a wide selection from seafood to ribs. $–$$

Taste of Asia, 127 East Taft Avenue; (336) 626–7578. You can get great Thai food in a friendly, unassuming atmosphere. $–$$

Where to Stay

Zooland Family Campground, 3671 Pisgah Covered Bridge Road; (336) 381–3422. This campground offers 200 sites, two pools, miniature golf, a game room, playgrounds, and modern bathhouses. $

Chains located here include Best Western, Comfort Inn, Fairfield Inn and Suites, Hampton Inn, and Holiday Inn.

For More Information

Randolph County Tourism Development Authority, (800) 626–2672; www.visitrandolph.org.

Seagrove

Seagrove, south of Asheboro on US 220, and the surrounding area could well be the pottery capital of the world.

Seagrove Area Potteries (ages 5 and up)

For more information call the Pottery Museum at (336) 626–0364; www.discover seagrove.com.

The Seagrove Area Potteries bring to life a tradition that has been passed down through the ages. In this area, you'll find something in the neighborhood of one hundred potteries where potters work and put their wares on sale. Pottery was first made here by Native Americans in the 1500s. Today's works have been refined, thanks to modern technology, but some of the potters here now come from families that have practiced the craft since the late eighteenth century. Here you can purchase a whole set of dishes or even a pottery bird feeder. The annual Pottery Festival, sponsored by the Friends of the Pottery Museum, is held in Seagrove each November on the Sunday before Thanksgiving. In addition to pottery, the crafts of doll making, candle making, wood carving, and more are demonstrated. The museum began making plans to move to a new, permanent, expanded location after operating in temporary locations for twenty-five years.

Burlington

If you choose to head east instead of south from Greensboro, I-40 or US 70 will take you to Burlington.

The city of Burlington has grown to become a shopping mecca for North Carolina residents, but it offers plenty of history and other attractions for your family to enjoy.

Alamance Battleground State Historic Site (ages 5 and up)
Located on Highway 62 South off I-85/40 on Alamance Battleground Road; (336) 227–4785. Open 9:00 a.m. to 5:00 p.m. Monday through Saturday. Free.

You can start a historical tour of the Burlington area at the Alamance Battleground State Historic Site. This is the site where Royal Governor William Tryon in 1771 led the North Carolina Militia into a battle against 2,000 Regulators, an army of colonial reformers who protested taxes, corrupt officials, and the lack of representation. You can learn more about the battle and the Regulator movement at the site. The visitor center presents an audiovisual display as well as other historical information. In addition, the **John Allen House,** a log home typical of this area in the late 1700s, has been restored and contains its original furnishings.

Cedarock Historical Farm (all ages)
Highway 49 South, 4252 Cedarock Park Road; (336) 570–6769. Open 9:00 a.m. to 4:00 p.m. Wednesday through Friday and 1:00 to 4:00 p.m. Saturday and Sunday. Free.

A great way to spend part of an afternoon is at Cedarock Historical Farm. This is a unique, 414-acre park that features a rolling terrain full of cedar trees and rock outcroppings, hence its name. Now restored to its original condition, this farm and its buildings were originally constructed in 1830 by John and Polly Garrett. Today a variety of livestock is kept on the farm, including goats, sheep, and cattle, as well as Jed and Jethro, the team of working mules. A museum includes antique farm equipment and demonstrations of long-lost farming techniques.

City Park (all ages)
Located at South Church Street and Overbrook Road; (336) 222–5030. The park generally is open during daylight hours. Free.

When you are in Burlington, make sure you visit City Park, especially if you have young children. This seventy-six-acre park offers miniature golf and amusement rides ($) in addition to traditional park facilities, such as picnic tables and a pool. But the centerpiece of the park is a Dentzel Menagerie Carousel made in 1910. This is a beautiful piece of work. The carousel has forty-six hand-carved animals, no two alike. Included are twenty-six horses with real horsehair tails and a variety of other bright animals ranging from pigs to reindeer. Other rides, including a train and boats, are small and great for younger children and even toddlers.

Where to Eat

The Cutting Board, 2619 Alamance Road; (336) 226–0291. Standard American dishes, especially steak, are offered in a sea-themed setting. $

Where to Stay

You'll find a number of large chain accommodations near I-40 and I-85.

For More Information

Burlington Convention and Visitors Bureau, (800) 637–3804; www.burlington-area-nc.org.

Snow Camp

From Burlington take Highway 87 South to Snow Camp.

Snow Camp Amphitheatre (all ages)

Located on State Road 1005 south of Burlington; (800) 726–5115; www.snowcamp drama.com. Evening shows are presented at 8:30 p.m. from mid-June through late August. $–$$$. Write to P.O. Box 535, Snow Camp, NC 27349 for tickets.

Although Snow Camp is a small town, it boasts one of the best drama societies in the state. The most popular annual production is *Sword of Peace,* which is presented alternately with *Pathway to Freedom.* Much of Alamance County's history is presented in William Hardy's *Sword of Peace,* a tribute to the Quakers and their role in the American Revolution. In this action-packed production, Simon Miller, a Quaker miller, must decide whether his faith allows him to take part in the Revolution. In *Pathway to Freedom,* playwright Mark R. Sumner tells the fictional story of the son of a slave-owning family and how he became involved with the Underground Railroad. In addition to these wonderful annual productions, Snow Camp also presents other plays that are especially appropriate for children. In the past such greats as *The Sound of Music* have been presented, and Saturday mornings are reserved for young children with productions such as *Cinderella.*

Where to Eat

Ye Old Country Kitchen, located on Drama Road at the amphitheater; (336) 376–6991. You can eat at the buffet here before going to the play. $

Ye Old Ice Cream Shop, on Drama Road at the amphitheater; (919) 376–6948. Not only will you find ice cream here, but also roasted peanuts and other confections. Outside, crafts and other displays are set up during performances. $

Chapel Hill

Three cities to the east of Burlington—Raleigh, Durham, and Chapel Hill—lie in a geometric shape known as the Triangle Area. If you visit this area in the winter months, you should be aware that you are in college basketball country. The state's three main universities are located in the Triangle Area, making for a long-standing rivalry among the teams vying for the Atlantic Coast Conference basketball championship. For years it has been one of the favorite athletic competitions for North Carolina residents.

University of North Carolina

Caution: Extreme bias exists in the following entry. It was composed by a Carolina fan.

Chapel Hill is home of the University of North Carolina, the nation's first (and always the best) state-supported university, chartered in 1789. This great town is, for all intents and purposes, the university—the town's population of 40,000 includes a largely diverse collection of 24,000 students and professors from across the country, making Chapel Hill a uniquely cosmopolitan town. Franklin Street, which forms the northern edge of the university campus, is full of opportunities for a wide variety of shopping and dining, while the campus provides a multitude of cultural and popular attractions. Parking is not available on campus, but you can use one of the municipal lots on Rosemary or Franklin Streets.

There are a few formal exhibits on the 700-acre campus, and the campus itself is well manicured and awe-inspiring. A free tape-recorded walking tour is available at the visitor center (919–962–1630) at the planetarium. Some of the sights you will see include the Morehead Patterson Bell tower on South Road, south of the art museum; and the Dean E. Smith Center, located on Skipper Bowles Drive on the southern part of campus, the home of the Tar Heels and named for the longtime men's basketball coach. You'll have to plan ahead, have connections, or very good luck to get tickets to a game on campus, but the center is host to other special events and concerts. Football tickets are easier to come by if you get them as soon as the schedule is finalized in early summer. In addition, you can get a glimpse of the university's rich athletic history in the center's Carolina Athletic Memorabilia Room. It features 3,000 square feet of exhibit space for artifacts, highlight tapes, and other souvenirs. The center is open 8:00 a.m. to 5:00 p.m. Monday through Friday. Admission is free if you want to come in and look around when there's no basketball game. Call (919) 922-2296 or visit www.unc.edu for more information.

Morehead Planetarium (all ages)

250 East Franklin Street; (919) 962–1236; www.moreheadplanetarium.org. Open 2:30 to 5:00 p.m. Sunday, 12:30 to 5:00 p.m. Monday and Tuesday, 10:00 a.m. to 4:00 p.m. Wednesday through Friday, and 10:00 a.m. to 5:00 p.m. Saturday. Shows are presented Thursday through Saturday evenings. Touring the planetarium and exhibits is free, but an admission fee ($) is charged for films and other programs.

The most easily accessible attraction is Morehead Planetarium, once used by NASA as a training center for astronauts. Part of the university, the planetarium houses a rare projector that casts nearly 9,000 stars onto the inside of the planetarium's 68-foot dome. In addition to the 350-seat theater, there are a host of related exhibits, art galleries, a digital theater, observatory, a science shop, rose gardens, and a huge sundial. Special programs for children are held most weekends. Call for a schedule of shows.

Ackland Art Museum (ages 5 and up)

South Columbia Street near Franklin Street; (919) 966–5736; www.acklandart.org. Hours are 10:00 a.m. to 5:00 p.m. Wednesday through Saturday and 1:00 to 5:00 p.m. Sunday. Free.

Next take a stroll through the oak trees that line brick walks of the campus to the Ackland Art Museum. Here you'll find a wide range of art—paintings, sculptures, drawings, photographs, and furnishings. Works in the museum's permanent collections come from Europe and Asia as well as the United States. Art from the Renaissance to the present is represented as well as North Carolina pottery and folk art.

North Carolina Botanical Garden (all ages)

Old Mason Farm Road; (919) 962–0522; www.ncbg.unc.edu. Open 8:00 a.m. to 6:00 p.m. Monday through Friday, 9:00 a.m. to 5:00 p.m. Saturday, and 1:00 to 5:00 p.m. Sunday. Free.

This is the largest natural botanical garden in the Southeast and consists of 600 acres of naturally preserved land. There are miles of walking trails and collections of North Carolina and southeastern plants arranged in habitats in natural settings. Here you will also see carnivorous plants, aquatic plants, herb gardens, and more in ten acres of display gardens.

Kidzu Children's Museum (ages 1 to 8)

105 East Franklin Street; (919) 933–1455; www.kidzuchildrensmuseum.org. Hours are 10:00 a.m. to 5:00 p.m. Tuesday through Saturday and 1:00 to 5:00 p.m. Sunday. $; free for children under age 2.

Kidzu offers an interactive, fun learning environment for children up to age eight through storytelling, art, crafts, music, and permanent and traveling exhibits, such as Mister Roger's Neighborhood. You'll also want to take time to visit Laughing Turtle Gift Shop.

A Hoffman **Family Adventure**

We didn't even have to leave North Carolina to take the longest car trip of my life. I was a young teen one March when we traveled from Gastonia to the Triangle to visit my older brothers who lived there. Temperatures were in the fifties when we left on Friday. When we woke up on Sunday the snow was falling. And it kept falling. My father insisted that we make the trip home. You see, in North Carolina we're not really equipped to handle a lot of snow. Towns pretty much shut down after a couple of inches. So you can imagine how a three-hour drive turned into nine looooong hours in what turned out to be 9 inches on the ground. We did make it home, safe and sound. My father did a superlative job handling the very adverse conditions—at least until he pulled into our driveway and slid onto the front yard. He left the car there until morning.

Where to Eat

Breadmen's, 324 West Rosemary Street; (919) 967–7110. Breadmen's serves great burgers and such, as well as breakfast all the time. $

Dip's Traditional Country, 405 West Rosemary Street; (919) 942–5837. Get your fried chicken here. Try the ribs or even the chitterlings. $

Il Palio Ristorante, 1505 East Franklin Street; (919) 929–4000. This is probably the best Italian restaurant in the town and the state. It can be great for a romantic dinner, but it also has a children's menu. Make reservations. $$$

The Ramshead Rathskeller, 157–A East Franklin Street; (919) 942–5158. You'll find a lot of local flavor here along with jukeboxes at each booth. The Rathskeller serves a variety of sandwiches and plates. $

Spanky's Restaurant & Bar, 101 East Franklin Street; (919) 929–5098. A tradition at Chapel Hill, the menu at Spanky's features burgers, its famed brown-sugar baby back ribs, and it has a kid's menu. $$

Top of the Hill Restaurant, 100 East Franklin Street; (919) 929–8676. Overlooking Franklin Street from the third floor patio, this microbrewery offers casual, upscale dining. $$

Where to Stay

Chapel Hill offers a selection of upscale hotels, all with a taste of the town. For more moderately priced accommodations, you'll have to look for hotel chains.

Carolina Inn, 211 Pittsboro Street; (800) 962–8519. This is a classic historic hotel located on the campus and "the" place to stay. Make sure you eat at Carolina Crossroads, the restaurant in the hotel. $$$$

The Siena Hotel, 1505 East Franklin Street; (919) 929–4000. This is another of Chapel Hill's AAA four-diamond hotels. Expect great service and accommodations here. $$$$

For More Information

Chapel Hill/Orange County Visitors Bureau, (888) 968–2060; www.chocvb.org.

Hillsborough

North of Chapel Hill on Highway 86 is the historic town of Hillsborough.

Hillsborough is listed on the National Register of Historic Places and has more than one hundred structures from the late eighteenth and nineteenth centuries, some of which provided a backdrop for a number of events during the Revolutionary War. Most notable is the site of the Constitutional Convention of 1788, where delegates demanded a Bill of Rights before they would ratify the Constitution. In addition, the town was significant in the Civil War and served as headquarters for Confederate general Joseph E. Johnston, who later negotiated terms of the South's surrender with Union General William T. Sherman.

Orange County Historical Museum (ages 5 and up)
201 North Churton Street; (919) 732–2201; www.orangecounty museum.org. Open 11:00 a.m. to 4:00 p.m. Tuesday through Saturday and 1:00 to 4:00 p.m. Sunday. Free.

The museum illustrates much of Hillsborough's past, depicting history and lifestyles from the time Native Americans inhabited the Eno River area through the Civil War. It was the site of the 1788 North Carolina Constitutional Convention. A gallery features works by a different artist every month.

Occaneechi Village Restoration (ages 5 and up)
Cameron Street on the Eno River; (919) 304–3723; www.occaneechi-saponi.org/. Free.

This project of the Occaneechi Band of the Saponi Nation is still in development, but you can visit now. Its village was reconstructed with a palisade (stockade fence), huts, a cooking site, and a sweat lodge, just as it was in this general area during the late seventeenth century. During that period tribes in south central Virginia and western North Carolina used it along their trading path. Future years will bring more attractions to the site.

Where to Eat

Tupelo's Restaurant & Tavern, 101
North Churton Street; (919) 643–7722.
Fusion cuisine fluctuates from Southern,
Creole, Southwestern, and other
regional flavors. It has an upscale feel-
ing, but also features a children's menu.
$$–$$$

Where to Stay

Southern Country Inn, 122 Daniel
Boone Street; (919) 732–8101. You'll find
great hospitality at this hotel that also
has a campground out back. $–$$

For More Information

Alliance for Historic Hillsborough,
(919) 732–7741; www.historic
hillsborough.org.

Durham

Although Durham is noted for its athletic heritage at Duke University and a history of
the tobacco industry, it is just as notable as a "city of medicine." The university
opened its medical school in 1930, there are five major hospitals and a number of
pharmaceutical research companies located here, and the city is largely connected
to Research Triangle Park, said to be the world's largest university-related research
park. To reach Durham from Hillsborough, take I-85 South.

Duke University

Duke University is located on another beautiful campus. Its stately architecture indicates its rich history and legacy as one of the leading private universities in the country. For more information the university Web site is www.duke.edu.

Duke University Chapel (all ages)

**Located on Chapel Drive; (919) 681–1704; www.chapel.duke.edu. Tour the church
8:00 a.m. to 10:00 p.m. daily, 8:00 a.m. to 8:00 p.m. in summer, or attend a nonde-
nominational worship service at 11:00 a.m. Sunday. Free. (Of course, donations
are accepted.)**

At Duke University you'll find a number of interesting attractions, most notable of
which is Duke University Chapel in the west campus. This 1,800-seat chapel, constructed in the 1930s, was the last of the great collegiate Gothic projects. It features a 5,033-pipe organ with five keyboards and a fifty-bell carillon. Its seventy-
seven intricate stained-glass windows depicting stories from the Bible are also
noteworthy.

Sarah P. Duke Gardens (all ages)

Anderson Street; (919) 684–3698; www.hr.duke.edu/dukegardens/. Hours are 8:00 a.m. to dusk daily. Free.

Here you find fifty-five acres of beautifully kept gardens, both natural and landscaped. There are more than 1,500 kinds of plants along the paths. The walks feature pathways with bridges, grottoes, court lawns, waterfalls, and pavilions. Such a wide variety of plants exists here that you'll find color in bloom practically all year long. In addition, there is an Asiatic Arboretum.

Nasher Museum of Art at Duke University (ages 5 and up)

Located on Campus Drive in the east campus; (919) 684–5135; www.nasher.duke .edu. Hours are 10:00 a.m. to 5:00 p.m. Tuesday, Wednesday, and Friday, 10:00 a.m. to 9:00 p.m. Thursday, 11:00 a.m. to 2:00 p.m. Saturday, and noon to 5:00 p.m. Sunday. $.

Nasher Museum of Art at Duke University is most notable for its fine collection of medieval sculpture, but it is also host to a lovely collection of stained glass and an extensive collection of pre-Columbian exhibits and classical objects. The museum's Chinese jade is quite unusual. American and European paintings, prints, and drawings round out the trip to the museum.

Bennett Place State Historic Site (ages 5 and up)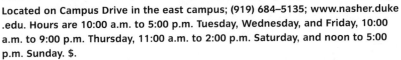

4409 Bennett Memorial Road; (919) 383–4345. Open 10:00 a.m. to 4:00 p.m. Tuesday through Saturday. Free.

Like most major cities in the state, Durham has a rich history. It was at Bennett Place State Historic Site that the Civil War ended. Union general William T. Sherman and Confederate general Joseph E. Johnston met at this farmstead in 1865, seventeen days after Confederate general Robert E. Lee surrendered at Appomattox. Following meetings in Hillsborough, the Durham meeting set up the largest surrender of the war. Although fighting continued in the west, this was the conclusion to the bloody War Between the States. Today the farmhouse and outbuildings have been restored, and the grounds also include a museum and interpretive center. Exhibits concentrate on North Carolina's role in the war, and uniforms, flags, and weapons are on display. A surrender reenactment is presented each April.

Duke Homestead State Historic Site (ages 5 and up)

2828 Duke Homestead Road; (919) 477–5498. Open 9:00 a.m. to 5:00 p.m. Monday through Saturday and 1:00 to 5:00 p.m. Sunday, April through October; 10:00 a.m. to 4:00 p.m. Tuesday through Saturday and 1:00 to 4:00 p.m. Sunday, the rest of the year. Free.

Long before Durham was a medical center, its roots were deeply embedded in the tobacco industry. Much of this history is available for viewing at the Duke Homestead

State Historic Site and Tobacco Museum. The site includes the Duke home, constructed in 1852, plus tobacco barns and two early tobacco factories. The museum chronicles the history of the tobacco industry and production, and cigarette manufacturing. A moving mannequin plants tobacco and helps bring the industry into perspective.

North Carolina Museum of Life and Science
(all ages)
433 Murray Avenue; (919) 220–5429; www.ncmls.org. The center is open 10:00 a.m. to 5:00 p.m. Tuesday through Saturday and noon to 5:00 p.m. Sunday, Memorial Day through Labor Day. $$.

This is a great interactive museum that features a range of exhibits from railroads to aerospace. Included is a display of the *Apollo 15* and *Enos,* the first U.S. spacecraft to orbit Earth. The museum's nature center is the best part of the museum. Here visitors can see a variety of wildlife and learn more about it through hands-on activities. For example, the kids can hold a box turtle or hear a rabbit's snappy heartbeat. There is a farmyard where the kids can pet the animals and a great tropical butterfly house.

Durham Bulls (all ages)
Durham Bulls Athletic Park, Blackwell Street; (919) 768–6000; www.durhambulls.com. $–$$.

One of the most popular attractions for Durham residents are the boys of summer who turn out at the Durham Bulls Athletic Park, the home of the Durham Bulls, a Class AAA baseball affiliate of the Tampa Bay Devil Rays. The Bulls received national attention in 1987 with the release of the movie *Bull Durham,* starring Susan Sarandon, Kevin Costner, and Tim Robbins. Even before the release of the film, area residents helped set attendance records at what is North Carolina's most famous baseball team's stadium.

Wheels Family Fun Park (all ages)
715 Hoover Road; (919) 598–1944. Hours vary according to season. Fees vary by attraction.

Whether a baseball game is on your itinerary or not, you can spend an evening at one of several small amusement parks that Durham has to offer. Wheels Family Fun Park is the largest, with more than eight acres of fun and adventure. The park features the basic amusement park facilities, such as bumper cars, go-karts, and video games, but it also has a skating rink and a miniature golf course.

Where to Eat

Bombay Grille, 2223 East Highway 54; (919) 544–6967. Don't be afraid to try new things; at least that's what I tell my kids. You may have to ask for mild dishes at this Indian restaurant. $$

Bullock's Bar-B-Que, 3330 Quebec Drive; (919) 383–6202. You can check out the pictures of the famous folks who have dined here on what is in the running for the best eastern barbecue in the state. $

Elmo's Diner, 776 Ninth Street; (919) 416–3823. You'll find an Elmo's in Chapel Hill, too, and they pay special attention to kids. You'll find everything from breakfast to burgers, shakes, and malts. $–$$

Foster's Market, 2694 Durham-Chapel Hill Boulevard; (919) 489–3944. Sara Foster opened this as a specialty and takeout food store, but you can also grab a bite on the porch. $

Nikos Taverna, 905 West Main Street; (919) 682–0043. Greek food is served in a historic warehouse in Brightleaf Square. $$

Where to Stay

Brookwood Inn & Suites at Duke University, 2306 Elba Street; (919) 286–3111. This is a very contemporary hotel. Children stay **free.** $$$$

Carolina Duke Motor Inn, 2517 Guess Road; (800) 438–1158. Even if you're a little more budget conscious, you'll still find good service and clean rooms here. $

Millenium Hotel, 2800 Campus Walk Avenue; (919) 383–8575. You could walk to the university from this hotel, but it would be a long one. Still it's a nice place with some efficiencies. $$$

Washington Duke Inn and Golf Club, 3001 Cameron Boulevard; (919) 490–0999. This is a four-star hotel with impeccable service and first-class amenities. Expect to pay for it. $$$$

Wyndham Garden Hotel, 4620 South Miami Boulevard; (800) 972–0264. You'll find very nice rooms and suites here; near the airport. $$$$

For More Information

Durham Convention and Visitors Bureau, (800) 446–8604; www.durham-nc.com.

Raleigh

I-40 brings you in from the east or west, merging into the sometimes confusing road, Interstate 440, which encircles the city.

Raleigh, the state capital, with a population of more than 300,000, has been voted the best place in America to live by both Fortune and Money magazines. It's just as good a place to visit. Raleigh offers all the expected amenities of a big city—the arts, the culture, and the entertainment—and it abounds with great museums and other educational opportunities at the state's largest university and at the government complex. What's more, it has plenty of good old-fashioned Southern hospitality. The city was founded in 1792 and named for Sir Walter Raleigh, who is credited with founding the first English colonies in the Carolinas. While there are big buildings and lots of traffic, one of the first things you'll notice is the abundance of oak trees that add to the city's charm.

State Government Complex (all ages)

Open 8:00 a.m. to 5:00 p.m. Monday through Friday, 9:00 a.m. to 5:00 p.m. Saturday, and 1:00 to 5:00 p.m. Sunday. Free.

A good place to start your visit to Raleigh is downtown. In addition to the state government complex, you'll find museums and more. The State Capitol (919–733–4994) is located in the geographic center of downtown. Built in the late 1830s in Greek Revival style, it houses the governor's office, cabinet offices, legislative chambers, and the state library. The state Legislative Building (919–733–7928) is located across Bicentennial Plaza and is home to the North Carolina General Assembly. Devoted solely to the legislative branch, the General Assembly gives visitors an opportunity to view the legislative process.

North Carolina Museum of Natural Sciences (all ages)

11 West Jones Street; (919) 733–7450; www.naturalsciences.org. Open 9:00 a.m. to 5:00 p.m. Monday through Saturday and noon to 5:00 p.m. Sunday. The first Friday of every month the museum is open until 9:00 p.m. Free, with a charge for some special exhibitions.

The state zoo is one of the best deals for the money, but since the state opened this facility after extensive renovations in April 2000, the Museum of Natural Sciences runs a close second. Visitors here get an opportunity to take a look at the natural world by looking at things that are uniquely North Carolina. Among the most amazing exhibits is a "Prehistoric North Carolina" one that includes Willo, a sixty-six-million-year-old dinosaur with a fossilized heart and the only acrocanthosaurus on display in the world. (You can teach the kids to say akro-cantho-saurus on the way.) Live animals are part of the "Mountains to the Sea" exhibit that presents North Carolina's five distinct habitats. Many of the collections from the old museum once located on Edenton Street are also part of the new facility.

North Carolina Museum of History (all ages)

5 East Edenton Street; (919) 807–7900. Open 9:00 a.m. to 5:00 p.m. Tuesday through Saturday and noon to 5:00 p.m. Sunday. Free.

Mere steps away you'll find the North Carolina Museum of History, which is surprisingly unstuffy and fun for a history museum. The museum is divided into four sections, each depicting a part of North Carolina's history. Included are displays that present a chronological history, the role of women in the state's history, folklife, and sports. Artifacts tell North Carolina's story from the earliest settlements on Roanoke Island as well as the state's role in the Revolutionary and Civil Wars. You'll also find the Capital Area Visitors Center here.

Executive Mansion (ages 5 and up)
200 North Blount Street; (919) 807–7950. Free.

You can take a short walk from the Museum of History to see the Executive Mansion. An impressive mansion built in the Victorian style of architecture, it was constructed largely of handmade bricks and has housed twenty-six families since its completion in 1891. Self-guided tours of the home are permitted on an irregular basis. The Capital Area Visitors Center, located in the North Carolina Museum of History, also conducts guided tours with advance notice. Call for hours or other information.

Historic Homes (ages 5 and up)
The visitor center (919–834–0887) offers walking tours of these attractions and historic homes in the area on Sunday at 2:00 p.m., but you're also welcome to set out on your own. The **Historic Oakwood neighborhood** (919–807–7950) is a 20-block area of Victorian homes built in the late 1800s, bordered by Delson, Edenton, Boundary, and Watauga Streets. Just west of downtown on Hargett Street is the **Joel Lane House** (919–833–3431), which was built in the 1760s and is Raleigh's oldest dwelling. In 1782, representatives of the newly formed legislature selected this site as the capital and purchased 1,000 acres of the Lane plantation to create the city of Raleigh. The furnishings in the home are authentic to the period. Just north of downtown at 1 Mimosa Street you will find **Mordecai Historic Park** (919–857–4364), a former antebellum plantation. Here you can get a glimpse of nineteenth-century life and see the cabin where Andrew Johnson, the nation's seventeenth president, was born. Admission to tour the Lane House and Oakwood is **free,** but there is a fee ($) for the Mordecai tour. Oakwood can be toured at any time. The Lane House is open on an irregular basis, and Mordecai Park is open 10:00 a.m. to 4:00 p.m. Monday through Saturday and from 1:00 to 4:00 p.m. Sunday. Trolley tours ($–$$, **free** for children age six and under) originate from Mordecai Park Saturdays from March through December from 11:00 a.m. to 2:00 p.m.

Exploris (all ages)
201 East Hargett Street; (919) 834–4040; www.exploris.org. Open 9:00 a.m. to 3:00 p.m. Wednesday through Friday, 11:00 a.m. to 5:00 p.m. Saturday, and noon to 5:00 p.m. Sunday. $; free for children under age three.

Simply put, this innovative museum is about the world. The guest becomes a world and time traveler, getting a glimpse of the history of the Berlin Wall before moving on to a study of the life of Anne Frank. With engaging visuals and video and audio technology, Calypso rhythms in Latin America lead to listening to the sounds of the rainforest and learning about the role we can all play in protecting our planet. Exploris is part history museum, part science center, part cultural center, part children's museum. But there's clearly something here for everyone in the family. An IMAX theater is also located here.

Playspace (age 6 months to 7 years)

410 Glenwood Avenue; (919) 832–1212; www.playspacemuseum.com. Open year-round 9:00 a.m. to 5:00 p.m. Tuesday through Saturday and 1:00 to 5:00 p.m. Sunday; from Memorial Day through Labor Day also open Monday 9:00 a.m. to 1:00 p.m. $.

In the Glenwood south area is one of the best spots for young kids—Playspace, a museum that teaches through creative activities and just plain fun. Its hands-on exhibits are designed especially for the development of small children. A special section for infants and toddlers provides an opportunity for Mom and Dad to play, too. For older children, you'll find a water table and a climbing castle. They can learn about the adult world at the child-size town that includes a grocery store, cafe, music room, hospital, and more. A favorite at the museum is the puppet theater.

Pullen Park (all ages)

520 Ashe Avenue; (919) 831–6468. Generally open during daylight hours. Free, with fees for some attractions.

Part of Raleigh's Parks and Recreation Department, Pullen Park offers a train ride through the amusement park, a kiddie boat ride, pedal boats, and a 1912 Dentzel Menagerie Carousel. Of course, you'll find standard park attractions such as tennis courts, softball fields, a swimming pool, and picnic and playground areas. Pullen Park is also home of the TV Land's tribute statue of Andy and Opie Taylor honoring *The Andy Griffith Show.*

North Carolina State University

When you leave downtown, take Hillsborough Street to North Carolina State University; (914) 515–2011; www.ncsu.edu.

With 30,000 students, this is the state's largest institution of higher learning. The university is almost a completely separate town. The campus, noted for its redbrick walkways and buildings, is host to Wolfpack basketball, football, and other sports. In addition, it provides venues for concerts, theater, and the arts. Among the attractions you'll find here are the **NCSU Solar Center** (919–515–3799), a solar demonstration house constructed at Western Boulevard and Gorman Street by the College of Engineering. The Solar Center is open 9:00 a.m. to 5:00 p.m. Monday through Friday and 1:00 to 5:00 p.m. Sunday. Admission is **free.** Another attraction you won't want to miss is the **NCSU J. C. Raulston Arboretum** (919–515–3132), which features 6,000 different kinds of plants from fifty-five countries. Located off Old Hillsborough Street at 4301 Beryl Road, the arboretum also includes a Victorian gazebo and a Japanese garden, with guided tours at 2:00 p.m. Sunday from mid-April to mid-October. Admission is **free.**

North Carolina State Fairgrounds (all ages)
1025 Blue Ridge Road; (919) 821–7400. $–$$.

The best time to visit Raleigh is in the fall, when the North Carolina State Fairgrounds, near the university, come alive with the excitement of the annual state fair. The fair is a traditional festival featuring rides, games, and farm-related events and exhibitions. It is usually held for ten days in the middle of October. When the fair isn't in town, the grounds are host to a flea market on the weekends and a variety of other shows, including livestock and pet shows. Rodeos are also periodically held here, and the fairgrounds are the Raleigh venue for the Ringling Brothers, Barnum and Bailey Circus.

North Carolina Museum of Art (ages 5 and up)
2110 Blue Ridge Road; (919) 839–6262. Guided tours are conducted at 1:30 p.m. daily. Open 9:00 a.m. to 5:00 p.m. Tuesday through Saturday and 10:00 a.m. to 5:00 p.m. Sunday. Free, with a charge for special exhibitions.

North of the university is the North Carolina Museum of Art. It houses the permanent art collection of the state as well as changing exhibits. The museum contains paintings and sculptures dating back 5,000 years that come from as far away as Egypt. Included are works by Raphael, Monet, Botticelli, and others.

Area **Parks**

If you're looking for an opportunity for outdoor recreation, two lakes are within easy driving distance from Raleigh, as are a handful of city and county parks. In Wake Forest, you'll find **Falls Lake State Recreation Area,** located on Creedmoor Road. It is one of the largest recreation facilities in the state and offers camping, hiking, fishing, swimming, a picnic area, playgrounds, boat rentals, and interpretive nature programs. Hours vary according to season. Call (919) 676–1027 for more information.

Southwest of Raleigh is **Jordan Lake Recreation Area,** located on State Park Road. Just take US 64 west out of Raleigh. One of the largest summertime homes of the bald eagle in the eastern United States, Jordan Lake is a great place to study nature. The 15,000-acre recreation area offers a full-service marina as well as opportunities for camping, fishing, and swimming. Hours vary according to season. Call (919) 362–0586 for more information.

Carolina Hurricanes (all ages)

RBC Center, 1400 Edwards Mill Road; (919) 861–2323; www.carolinahurricanes.com. $$$–$$$$.

Hockey fever overtook the city of Raleigh in 2002 as the Carolina Hurricanes slapped their way into the Stanley Cup Finals and then grabbed the Stanley Cup in 2006. The RBC Center has been the home of the 'Canes since October 1999, and it also is home court for North Carolina State's basketball team.

Bullwinkle's (all ages)

1040 Buck Jones Road; (919) 319–7575; www.bullwinkles.com. Open 11:00 a.m. to 9:00 p.m. Monday through Saturday and 11:00 a.m. to 8:00 p.m. Sunday. It's closed Monday and Tuesday in winter. $, fees for activities vary.

Attractions at this massive restaurant and fun center include animatronics, a "liquid fireworks" water show, a 17-foot rock-climbing wall, a gigantic indoor soft-play area, and over forty-five games in the arcade.

Where to Eat

Andy's Pizza, 1302 East Milbrook Road; (919) 872–6797 and 4217 Six Forks Road; (919) 781–9043. The staff makes pizza night even more fun than it already is. $

Angus Barn, 9401 Glenwood Avenue; (919) 787–3535. The Angus Barn is known far and wide for its quality steaks. $$–$$$

Kanki, 4325 Glenwood Avenue; (919) 782–9708 and 4500 Old Wake Forest Road; (919) 876–4157. Food is prepared at your table at this Japanese restaurant. $$$

Where to Stay

Crabtree Summit Hotel, 3908 Arrow Drive; (919) 782–6868. This luxury hotel has all the ambience you could ask for. $$$$

Milner Inn, 1817 Capitol Boulevard, Raleigh; (888) 331–5500. This is a small inn for the budget-minded. $$

The Plantation Inn Resort, 6401 Capital Boulevard; (919) 876–1411. Located near Research Triangle Park, this resort offers top-quality amenities, including two restaurants. $$$$

For More Information

Greater Raleigh Convention and Visitors Bureau, (800) 849–8499; www.visit raleigh.com.

Smithfield

Travel southeast from Raleigh to Interstate 95 and US 70 to find Smithfield.

Ava Gardner Museum (ages 3 and up)
325 East Market Street; (919) 934–5830; www.avagardner.org. Open 9:00 a.m. to 5:00 p.m. Monday through Saturday and 2:00 to 5:00 p.m. Sunday. $–$$.

Your kids might not know exactly who Ava Gardner was (she may be before your time, too, for that matter, but your parents will know), yet they'll probably get a kick out of a visit to the Ava Gardner Museum, located in her hometown of Smithfield. The museum was opened in 1991, a year after the actress died, as a tribute to her. Exhibits include the posters from her fifty-seven films as well as photographs that show her as a child through her years as a seductive leading lady of the 1940s and '50s. You will find other memorabilia from her life at this unique museum, too.

Bentonville Battleground (ages 5 and up)
South of Smithfield on U.S. Highway 701; (919) 594–0789. Open 9:00 a.m. to 5:00 p.m. Monday through Saturday and 1:00 to 5:00 p.m. Sunday, April through October; and 10:00 a.m. to 4:00 p.m. Tuesday through Saturday and 1:00 to 4:00 p.m. Sunday November through March. Free.

This is the site of the largest battle ever fought in the state. The fierce Civil War battle raged for three days, but Union troops eventually beat down Confederate forces, and a month later the war ended in the Carolinas. More than 4,000 men were killed, wounded, or went missing in the battle. Many of them were taken to the farm home of John and Amy Harper, which was turned into a field hospital. The house still stands and is furnished as a field hospital. A section of Union trenches and a cemetery remain as stark reminders of the battle. Other exhibits are on display at the site's visitor center.

Where to Eat

Becky's Log Cabin Restaurant, 2491 US 70 East; (919) 934–1534. You won't find an abundance of places to eat in Smithfield, but this is a good steak house with a neat, rustic atmosphere. $$

Where to Stay

Log Cabin Motel, 2491 US 70 East; (919) 934–1534. This is the home of Becky's Log Cabin Restaurant. Pets are welcome in the sixty-one rooms here. $$

Village Motor Lodge and Restaurant, 198 Mallard Road; (800) 531–0063. A swimming pool, playground, and restaurant make this an okay place to stay. $$

For More Information

Johnston County Visitors Bureau, (800) 441–7829; www.johnstoncounty nc.org.

Kenly

Tobacco Farm Life Museum (ages 5 and up)
U.S. Highway 301, 1.5 miles east of Kenly; (919) 284–3431; www.tobaccofarmlife museum.org. Open 9:30 a.m. to 5:00 p.m. Monday through Saturday and 2:00 to 5:00 p.m. Sunday. $; children age four or younger get in free.

Life on the tobacco farm is the subject on display at the bright Tobacco Farm Life Museum. The exhibits at the museum show how tobacco farming improved the life of the farm families who did it. Here you can visit the Depression era of the 1930s and see artifacts that relate to the farmers' struggles. On display are schoolbooks, medical equipment, and household goods as well as tobacco farming equipment and outbuildings.

Bailey

North of Kenly and east of Raleigh you'll find Bailey.

Country Doctor Museum (all ages)
6629 Vance Street; (919) 235–4165; www.countydoctormuseum.org. Open 10:00 a.m. to 4:00 p.m. Tuesday through Saturday and 2:00 to 5:00 p.m. Sunday. $.

More everyday life from the late nineteenth century is waiting at the Country Doctor Museum, chartered in 1967 in honor of the tradition of the family doctor. It consists of two restored offices of country doctors. It's easy to appreciate how the medical field has progressed when you see the artifacts here. On display are apothecary jars, old stethoscopes, and saws and knives used at battlefield hospitals.

Other Things to See and Do
in the Northern Piedmont

- **Calling All Kids,** Hickory, (828) 328–1113
- **Hickory Dickory Dock,** Hickory, (828) 322–3625
- **Ice Castle,** Newton, (828) 466–1173
- **Mayberry Shazzam Family Entertainment Center,** Pilot Mountain, (336) 368–9900
- **Triangle SportsPlex,** Hillsborough, (919) 644–0339
- **University Lake,** Chapel Hill, (919) 942–8007
- **American Classic Motorcycle Museum,** Asheboro, (336) 629–9564
- **I-85 Golf and Baseball,** Burlington, (336) 578–2391
- **Ice House,** Greensboro, (336) 852–1515
- **Grand Prix,** Greensboro, (336) 664–6222
- **Adventure Landing,** Raleigh, (919) 872–1688
- **Battlezone Laser Adventure,** Raleigh, (919) 847–4263
- **Frankies Fun Park,** Raleigh, (919) 433–7888

The Southern Piedmont

I n North Carolina's Southern Piedmont your family will be treated to some of the state's biggest, best, brightest, tallest, and loudest experiences. At the heart of the region is the state's biggest city, which features major-league sports, the state's largest amusement park, and what is one of the world's best science centers. Not far away you can enjoy down-home fun at the state's largest county fair or visit a small textile community that is set to brighten your Christmas season. The region extends east into the Carolina heartland, where you'll find some of the country's premier golf courses and discover the unusual art of hollerin'.

Jim's
TopPicks in the Southern Piedmont

1. Discovery Place, Charlotte

2. Carowinds, Charlotte

3. Children's Theater of Charlotte

4. Charlotte sports

5. Reed Gold Mine, Stanfield

6. Crowders Mountain State Park, Gastonia

7. Christmastown USA, McAdenville

8. Daniel Stowe Botanical Garden, Belmont

9. Morrow Mountain State Park, Albemarle

10. Lowe's Motor Speedway, Harrisburg

THE SOUTHERN PIEDMONT

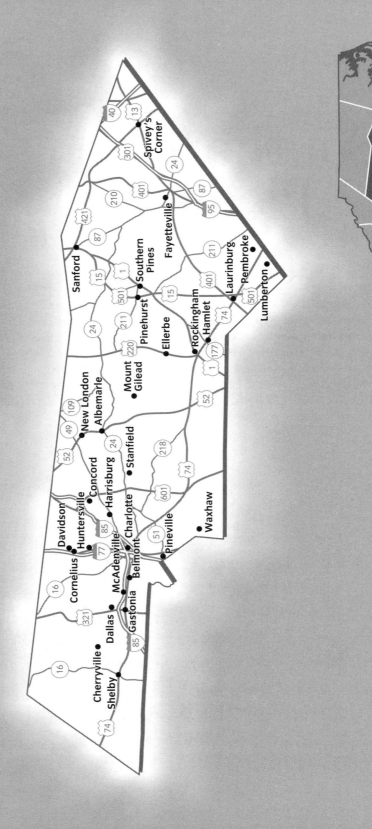

Growth has made travel within some cities difficult, but getting around in this region isn't totally unpleasant. From the north, Interstate 77 bisects Charlotte and intersects with Interstate 85, which runs northeast to Greensboro and southwest into South Carolina. To get to the eastern part of the region from Greensboro, take U.S. Highway 220. From the Triangle Area take U.S. Highway 15/501. U.S. Highway 74 runs along the southern part of the region, and I–95 is a good route to use when traveling the eastern part of the region.

Shelby

Shelby is located along US 74 at the western end of the Southern Piedmont.

Cleveland County Fair (all ages)
1751 East Marion Street (US 74 Business); (704) 487–0651; www.ccfair.net. The fair traditionally runs for ten days from late September through early October. $–$$; an additional fee is charged for many of the attractions, but you can buy combo passes ($$–$$$).

Thousands of people roll into Shelby in the fall for the state's largest county fair which has run continually since 1954. The Cleveland County Fair is a traditional agricultural event featuring carnival rides, games, exhibitions, livestock shows, and contests. Plenty of homegrown food and country crafts will also be on hand for you to buy. During the rest of the year, the fairgrounds host a number of festivals and horse shows.

Where to Eat

Bridges Barbecue, 2000 East Dixon Boulevard; (704) 482–8567. You'll pass this on the main strip in Shelby, so even if you're not hungry when you do stop, take some home for later. $

Satterfields, 4702 East Dixon Boulevard; (704) 734–0400. People come from miles around to eat at this restaurant, which features a variety of selections from pasta to blackened dishes. $$

For More Information
Cleveland County Department of Tourism, (704) 484–8521; www .clevelandcounty.com.

Cherryville

The small town of Cherryville is about a twenty-minute drive through the country northeast of Shelby on Highway 150.

C. Grier Beam Truck Museum (ages 3 and up)
111 North Mountain Street; (704) 435–3072; www.beamtruckmuseum.com. Open 10:00 a.m. to 5:00 p.m. Friday and 10:00 a.m. to 3:00 p.m. Saturday. Free.

There is a small but unique museum in Cherryville. You can check out the old big rigs at the C. Grier Beam Truck Museum, opened in 1982 in a former gas station that once served as the headquarters for Carolina Freight Carriers Corporation. The museum commemorates the history of trucking, and you will see trucks dating back to 1929 and displays that look back at the origin of trucking.

Dallas

Dallas is southeast of Cherryville on Highway 279, just east of U.S. Highway 321.

Gaston County Museum of Art and History (ages 5 and up)
131 West Main Street; (704) 922–7681; www.gastoncountymuseum.org. Open 10:00 a.m. to 5:00 p.m. Tuesday through Friday, noon to 4:00 p.m. Saturday, and 2:00 to 5:00 p.m. every fourth Sunday. Free.

Step back into the 1800s at one of the four-star hotels of the time at the Gaston County Museum of Art and History. Housed in the former Hoffman Hotel, built in 1852, the museum is at the center of the historic district in the former county seat. Since 1984 the museum has been working to renovate the hotel to show how it evolved through several periods. It is now occupied by displays emphasizing the county's textile heritage as well as the largest collection of horse-drawn carriages in North Carolina. You are also likely to see one of many changing art exhibits here or to want to play in the hands-on parlor. In addition, you can get a brochure of information on buildings included in the district's walking tour, or take a short carriage ride offered by various companies ($).

Gastonia

Gastonia is just south of Dallas on US 321.

Crowders Mountain State Park (ages 5 and up)
Find this park by following the signs from US 74; (704) 853–5375. The park generally is open during daylight hours, year-round. Free.

A good place to spend a quiet afternoon hiking or canoeing is at Crowders Mountain State Park. The mountain's stone face, jutting 800 feet above the surrounding area, is an attraction for adventurous mountain climbers. You might even see experienced rappellers taking on the mountain's challenging terrain. You'll find several trails that are easier to climb, and you can fish in the lake or rent a canoe. The park office periodically offers interpretive nature presentations and has a small but engaging nature exhibit hall.

Schiele Museum of Natural History and Planetarium (ages 3 and up) 🎯 👫

1500 East Garrison Boulevard; (704) 866–6900; www.schielemuseum.org. Open 9:00 a.m. to 5:00 p.m. Monday through Saturday and 1:00 to 5:00 p.m. Saturday and Sunday. $; **free** for children under six and on the second Tuesday of each month. Admission fee also charged for programs, special exhibits, and planetarium shows.

Head east on US 74 and right on Garrison Boulevard to the Schiele Museum of Natural History and Planetarium. The museum is continuing its mission of educating Gaston County students, and it has grown to become a staple for the community. Within the museum's walls is North Carolina Hall, showing the six regions of North Carolina during various seasons. Look on top of the cave in one three-dimensional diorama, and you will see a bobcat that wags its tail every few minutes. Look carefully in the cave, and you will see bats on the ceiling. The Hall of Earth and Man presents life as it developed over the last 500 million years. It's almost as if the saber-toothed tiger in one exhibit is actually alive. The museum's space theater presents shows on the arts, history, travel, and ecology, along with more conventional planetarium shows. Outside the museum you will discover more on the "Trail for All Seasons," the Eighteenth Century Backcountry Farm, and the Catawba Indian Village. Interpretive and living-history programs are scheduled at the Schiele Museum throughout the year.

Where to Eat

Rodi, 245 West Garrison Boulevard; (704) 864–7634. Authentic Mediterranean cuisine is served. You'll also find a play area for children and live music for Mom and Dad on weekends. $$

Fish Camps. Gaston County has become more or less famous for its restaurants known as fish camps. They serve, almost exclusively, deep-fried fish along with hush puppies and slaw. Several are located on and near South New Hope Road. Check out one of the following:

Catfish Cove, 1401 Upper Armstrong-Ford Road; (704) 825–3332. $–$$

Graham's Fish Fry, 4539 South New Hope Road; (704) 825–8391. $–$$

Twin Topps, 4547 South New Hope Road; (704) 825–2490. $–$$

Captain's Cap, 3140 Linwood Road; (704) 865–7433; and 670 Park Street, Belmont; (704) 825–4103. With two locations in the area, Captain's Cap also serves calabash-style seafood. $$

Where to Stay

Most of the large chains are represented just off I-85 in Gastonia, making for easy access to the towns located near here, as well as Charlotte.

For More Information

Gaston County Department of Tourism, (800) 849–9994; www.gaston tourism.com.

Christmastown USA

Located between I–85 and US 74 is the town of McAdenville, better known as Christmastown USA. Each December this small textile community turns on more than 350,000 green, red, and white lights on homes, in trees, and around the small lake in the center of town. Speakers play carols, and churches present nativity scenes in one of the state's (and perhaps the nation's) most spectacular Christmas displays. The lights come on in early December and stay on until late in the month from 5:00 to 9:30 p.m. Monday through Friday and 5:00 to 11:00 p.m. Saturday and Sunday. Because the exact dates vary from year to year, call (704) 824–3190.

Belmont

Heading east on US 74 from Gastonia will take you to Belmont, but South New Hope Road is a quicker route to our next stop.

Daniel Stowe Botanical Garden (ages 3 and up)

6500 South New Hope Road; (704) 825–4490; www.dsbg.org. Open 9:00 a.m. to 5:00 p.m. daily and until 6:00 p.m. during daylight savings time. $–$$.

About 110 of the 400 acres of beautiful rolling meadows and woodlands donated to be developed as a garden are now open at this facility, which is quickly developing a reputation as one of the finest gardens in the Southeast. Four themed gardens include walks, fountains, and plaques describing the flora and fauna. Kids shouldn't miss the tunnel fountain, but they better move through it quickly or face getting wet! A half-mile woodland trail is rough but under development. A stained-glass dome tops off the visitor center, which houses a great gift shop for kids and adults and serves as a base for hands-on workshops and other events. An orchid conservatory opens in January 2008.

For More Information

Gaston County Travel and Tourism, (800) 849–9994; www.gaston tourism.org.

Charlotte

The "Queen City" is North Carolina's largest city and is its center for arts, culture, and big-league sports. With a population of a half million, Charlotte became a national financial leader in the late 1980s and early 1990s. This growth only strengthened the financial stability created through Charlotte/Douglas International Airport, which opened the city to the world and made it a transportation hub for the Southeast. But this growth has meant more than additions to the uptown (not downtown) skyline. The city has seen a proverbial boom in the creation of more fun things to see and do.

U.S. National Whitewater Center (all ages, with restrictions) ⚠

820 Hawfield Road; (704) 391–3900, www.usnwc.org. Generally open during daylight hours. $$–$$$$.

On our route to Charlotte, we cross the Catawba River. Since it cuts through the low-lying Piedmont it was never meant for whitewater rafting, at least until 2006. That's when the U.S. National Whitewater Center opened a sprawling, manmade rafting facility just off I-85 in Charlotte. Integrated with miles of biking and hiking trails, the U.S. Olympic Committee has designated the center as an official training site. But there's plenty there for the average family.

The center includes the world's largest manmade recirculating river, which forms a two-hour Class III/IV rafting adventure for ages twelve and above. If you have a younger set, there's whitewater kayaking for ages eight and above and flatwater kayaking for all ages. In addition, there's a climbing center for everyone over age four. And finally, the Eddy Restaurant provides a panoramic view of the facility in addition to selections that range from soup to salmon to steak. Keep in mind when planning, World Cup, Olympic Trials, and other competitions are held here and may limit availability to the public.

Carowinds (all ages) 🎢

Located off I-77 South on the state line, 14523 Carowinds Boulevard; (800) 588–2600. Open 10:00 a.m. to 8:00 p.m. Saturday and Sunday only in mid-March, April, May, September, and through mid-October; open 10:00 a.m. to 8:00 p.m. daily June through late August. $$$$.

This is the state's largest theme park, packed with a day full of fun and adventure for everyone in the family. As you walk through the main gate, you may be greeted by your favorite characters from television and film, past and present. Younger children will adore characters such as the Rugrats, Fred Flintstone, Yogi Bear, Boy Genius Jimmy Neutron, Scooby-Doo, and other characters from Nickelodeon or some other part of TV land. A county fair section has games and rides for all ages, including bumper cars, a carousel, and more.

Some of the rides and attractions for younger guests include the Carolina Gold-rusher, a wooden mine train rollercoaster; Carolina Skytower, an air-conditioned cabin that travels up a 320-foot tower; Ricochet, which takes riders through continuous twists and turns; Rip Roarin' Rapids, a soggy whitewater rafting expedition; and Scooby-Doo's Haunted Mansion. The truly adventurous will want to experience Vortex, a stand-up roller coaster; Top Gun: The Jet Coaster; Drop Zone, which drops visitors 174 feet at more than 50 miles per hour; or even the BORG Assimilator. You can cool off on the Flying Super Saturator just outside Boomerang Bay, which includes several great water slides and more. For a break in the action, you'll want to catch some of the shows at the park, including popular and Christian music concerts in the palladium. **Free** kennels are provided if your pet is with you, and picnic facilities are available if you aren't lured into one of the park's dozens of food stands and restaurants.

Discovery Place (all ages)

301 North Tryon Street; (800) 935–0553; www.discoveryplace.org. Open 9:00 a.m. to 5:00 p.m. Monday through Friday (until 6:00 p.m. in summer), 10:00 a.m. to 5:00 p.m. Saturday, and 1:00 to 5:00 p.m. Sunday (until 6:00 p.m. in summer). IMAX shows are held during operating hours, and during evening hours on weekends. Discovery Place is closed Thanksgiving, Christmas, and Easter. $$–$$$.

Whatever has drawn you to Charlotte, you won't want to miss a chance to see Discovery Place, a national-award-winning, hands-on science and technology center. The complex also includes the Charlotte Observer IMAX Dome Theatre. You can enter a three-story rain forest, explore outer space, or learn about the intricacies of the human body. Best of all, the kids can touch all they want. The center offers an aquarium and tidal pool; the Life Center, which includes a 12-foot-tall heart; and the Science Circus, where you can see explosive chemistry shows and more. The IMAX, considered to be the best motion picture system in the world, is comprised of the largest screen in history and a six-track sound system. Presentations at the IMAX are scheduled throughout the year.

World's Largest **Eyeball**

Discovery Place is home of the world's largest eyeball. The exhibit, which visitors can walk through, explains the parts of the eye in a short audio tour. If a person were large enough to have this eyeball, that person would be 96 feet tall.

A Hoffman **Family Adventure**

My daughter has always been a daredevil. I remember taking one last trip around a theme park at the end of the day when both kids picked the last couple of rides they would go on. Jessica picked the biggest, scariest rollercoaster. Little did her mom know that her plan was to keep her hands in the air the whole ride. She did. And Mom didn't get to hold on either, as she struggled the entire time trying to keep Jessica's hands down.

Uptown Charlotte 🏕️ 🏛️ 🍴 🎵

If you visit Charlotte, make sure to save a couple hours to explore what the marketing pundits like to call uptown, which has become a burgeoning arts center. Frescoes by Ben Long can be found at Bank of America Corporate Center and at TransAmerica Square, both on Tryon Street. Make sure to visit **The Green,** which runs between Tryon and College Streets near the Wachovia Atrium and the Charlotte Convention Center. It's a unique park themed on literature. Bronze works depicting characters from literature, poems on bronze placards written by local schoolchildren, fountains, and hidden speakers that spill out whimsical sounds adorn the park. Bricks also contain fun word puzzles. Trendy restaurants and upscale shops also fill the uptown area. Architectural high points include Founders Hall, with a 10,000-square-foot glass atrium accessible from College Street or through Bank of America Corporate Center on Tryon Street, as well as Wachovia Atrium and Hearst Tower. The **Blumenthal Performing Arts Center** is adjacent to Bank of America Corporate Center and includes two theaters for the Charlotte Symphony, Broadway Lights Series plays, and other presentations. The art deco Hearst Tower is the newest skyscraper to dot the Charlotte skyline and is really cool because the top is actually bigger than the bottom.

Mint Museum of Craft and Design (ages 5 and up)

220 North Tryon Street; (704) 337–2000; www.mintmuseum.org. Open 10:00 a.m. to 5:00 p.m. Tuesday through Saturday and noon to 5:00 p.m. Sunday; closed major holidays. $–$$; free for children ages five and younger and for everyone on Tuesday from 10:00 a.m. to 2:00 p.m.

A huge Chihuly glass chandelier is the centerpiece of this unique museum, which clearly illustrates there's more to craft than you may initially think. Kids and adults will quickly discover new ways of looking at furniture, glass, clay, fiber, metal, and wood through exhibits and activities that focus on creativity, design, materials, process, form, and function.

Big League **Sports**

Charlotte's most exciting addition to its sports entourage came in 1993, when it was awarded an NFL expansion team, the **Carolina Panthers.** Almost immediately the city began construction of the 72,000-seat Bank of America Stadium. A policy of selling privilege seat licenses has made it difficult to get tickets, but the organization has committed to keeping a certain number of single-game seats available for every game. Tickets for single games, on sale in spring when the NFL season schedule is completed, go quickly through Ticketmaster outlets. Call (704) 358-1644 for more information.

In 2004 Bob Johnson, founder of the Black Entertainment Network, bought an NBA franchise for the city to replace the Charlotte Hornets NBA team, which made its way to New Orleans. For a year, the **Charlotte Bobcats** played at the city's old coliseum, while the team, in partnership with the city, built a new state-of-the-art arena in the city's center. Built with the region's rich basketball history and cultural heritage in mind, there are fun things to do at the arena regardless of the event. Exhibits and displays, as well as a kid's interactive center, welcome all. Individual tickets for Bobcats games can be purchased online at www.charlotte bobcatsarena.com; by phone at (800) 495-2295; at the arena's on-site box office; or at the Blumenthal Performing Arts Center ticket outlet, in Founder's Hall in the Bank of America corporate center, 100 North Tryon Street.

Bobcats arena is also home to **The Charlotte Checkers,** an professional hockey affiliate of the New York Rangers and a member of the Eastern Conference Hockey League. Charlotte is known as the birthplace of professional hockey in the South, and the Charlotte Checkers are proud to be part of that history. Following a seventeen-year hiatus from hockey, Charlotte welcomed the Checkers back in 1993. Since their return, the Checkers have made the playoffs nine times—highlighted by an ECHL Championship in 1996. Despite hockey's rough-and-tumble reputation, the organization makes games a great family-oriented event complimented by the state-of-the-art arena. For more information on tickets, contact the Checkers at (704) 342-4423 or visit www.gocheckers.com.

The AAA affiliate of the Chicago White Sox, the **Charlotte Knights,** is ours, even though its home field is in nearby Fort Mill, South Carolina. The stadium is located off I-77 South just across the state line. You can get general admission seats very inexpensively here ($). The park also has a playground and even a miniature golf course. Lots of family fun is offered in the form of post-game fireworks, concerts, and more.

Levine Museum of the New South (ages 5 and up)

200 East Seventh Street; (704) 333–1887; www.museumofthenewsouth.org. Open 10:00 a.m. to 5:00 p.m. Monday through Saturday and noon to 5:00 p.m. Sunday. $; free for children ages five and under.

Focused on history after the Civil War, the Levine's centerpiece exhibit is "From Cotton Fields to Skyscrapers," which illustrates the area's history and how it grew from a primarily farming area to a banking center. Visitors get this story from audio, video, and artifacts from people who actually lived the history from 1865.

Mint Museum of Art (ages 5 and up)

2730 Randolph Road; (704) 337–2000; www.mintmuseum.org. Open 10:00 a.m. to 10:00 p.m. Tuesday, 10:00 a.m. to 5:00 p.m. Wednesday through Saturday, and noon to 5:00 p.m. Sunday. The museum is closed on major holidays. $$; free for children ages eleven or younger. Everyone gets in free 5:00 to 10:00 p.m. each Tuesday.

For culture, a visit to the Mint Museum of Art is a must. Built in 1836 as the first branch of the U.S. Mint, the building in which the museum is housed later served as a Confederate headquarters, a hospital, and an assay office. In 1933 it was moved from its original location uptown and opened as North Carolina's first museum of art three years later. You'll see a complete set of gold coins minted there, American and European paintings, pre-Columbian art, historic costumes, and ancient Chinese ceramics. It holds more than 27,000 items in its collection. You'll also see life-size paintings of King George III and his queen, Charlotte, for whom the city was named. Seeing the queen's carriage will round out your trip to the museum.

Children's Theater of Charlotte (ages 4 and up)

300 East Seventh Street; (704) 973–2828; www.ctcharlotte.org. Prices vary by production.

A really first-class place to take the kids for exposure to performance art is the Children's Theater of Charlotte. The theater is largely dedicated to the arts in education and is heavily involved with the Mecklenburg County school system. Many of the plays are performed by local children; however, the playbill includes several professionally produced productions annually. In the past the theater has presented such gems as *Winnie the Pooh, Treasure Island,* and *Charlotte's Web,* in addition to creative holiday and seasonal productions. It's located in one of newcomers on the Charlotte cultural scene—ImaginOn.

ImaginOn: The Joe and Joan Martin Center (all ages)

300 East Seventh Street; (704) 973–2780; www.imaginon.org. Hours are 9:00 a.m. to 9:00 p.m. Monday through Thursday, 9:00 a.m. to 6:00 p.m. Friday and Saturday, and 1:00 to 6:00 p.m. Sunday. Free, with fees charged for activities and presentations.

Sprawling across a city block, ImaginOn is part library, part theater space—a partnership between the national-award-winning Charlotte-Mecklenburg Public Library system and the Children's Theater of Charlotte. It's fun just to visit this innovative colorful building. But upon exploring you find a cozy section for toddlers and preschool-age children that includes more than 12,000 books and a range of audio/visual materials, computers, games and activities. A "Listening Post" enables children to listen to stories and music. An indoor "garden" with cozy seating and flooring gives babies and toddlers a chance to explore. A separate space for children ages five through twelve includes over 30,000 books, computers with assistance software and skill-building games and activities, an audio/visual alcove with over 3,500 videos, music, and books on CD and CD-ROMS.

Ray's Splash Planet (all ages)
215 North Sycamore Street; (704) 432–4729; www.charmeck.org. Open 9:00 a.m. to 8:00 p.m. Monday through Friday, 9:00 a.m. to 7:00 p.m. Saturday, and 1:00 to 7:00 p.m. Sunday; during summer open until 9:00 p.m. Monday through Friday. $$.

Ray's is a one-of-a-kind indoor water park and a fitness center. The waterpark contains 117,000 gallons of water and a host of adventure. A three-story slide, in the form of a double figure-eight is encircled by The Orbiter, which takes guests on a leisurely ride around the park. Saturation Station features four slides, interactive water play, and a tumble bucket. Moon Beach is a state-of-the-art gradual beach-like entry pool and there are two lanes for lap swimming. The fitness center includes an aerobics and dance room, cardiovascular theater, freeweights, and resistance equipment.

Nature Museum (best for younger children)
1658 Sterling Road; (800) 935–0553. Open 10:00 a.m. to 5:00 p.m. Monday through Saturday and 1:00 to 5:00 p.m. Sunday; closed on Thanksgiving and Christmas. $; free for children under three.

This museum has a number of hands-on exhibits, such as games and push-button displays, to help explain natural history and also features a puppet theater; a butterfly pavilion; an exhibit called Insect Alley; a live animal room that includes owls, snakes, and other nocturnal creatures; and a nature trail. You'll also want to see the talking Grandpa Tree, a mechanical replica of a tree that helps explain some of nature's wonders during special programs that are held nearly every weekend.

Freedom Park (all ages)
1900 East Boulevard; (704) 336–2663. Free.

Before or after you visit the Nature Museum, you can get away from the hustle and bustle of Charlotte traffic at adjacent Freedom Park, one of Charlotte's oldest parks and a longtime favorite for school field trips. Take along a picnic lunch. The kids will be thrilled with a walk around the lake, skating on one of the park's trails, or playing on the park's playground. The park is the site of Festival in the Park, another of Charlotte's big annual celebrations. The festival, held in late September, is a huge arts, crafts, and entertainment event.

Amazing
North Carolina Facts

Charlotte is known as the City of Trees, and one tree you'll see a lot of in this area is the dogwood. The dogwood blossom was chosen as the state flower in 1941.

Charlotte Museum of History/Hezekiah Alexander Homesite
(ages 5 and up) 🏛️ 🎫

3500 Shamrock Drive; (704) 568–1774; www.charlottemuseum.org. Open 10:00 a.m. to 5:00 p.m. Tuesday through Saturday (and Monday in summer), and 1:00 to 5:00 p.m. Sunday. $–$$; free for children ages five and under. Every Sunday is a free family day.

Like most towns in the Old North State, Charlotte has a rich historical heritage. To get a glimpse of this history, a good place to start is at the Charlotte Museum of History and Hezekiah Alexander Homesite. Built in 1774, the home is the oldest dwelling in Mecklenburg County. The 5,000-square-foot stone house includes a museum with exhibits that concentrate on the history of the city. In the two-story springhouse you'll see a hand-hewn log kitchen with a working stone fireplace. Tours are offered daily at 1:15 and 3:15 p.m. Docents dressed in eighteenth-century costumes lead visitors through the buildings and grounds, discussing artifacts and furnishings found in the buildings and illustrating the everyday lives of the Alexanders.

A 36,000-square-foot museum building includes an extensive exhibits program that tells the story of Charlotte-Mecklenburg from the eighteenth to the twentieth century. A changing exhibit space is located on the second floor. The American Freedom Bell, a seven-ton ground-level bell guests can ring themselves in honor of those who fight for the freedom of America, is also on display. It acts as a permanent reminder that Charlotte was the location of the first official declaration of freedom from British rule.

Where to Eat

All of Charlotte's top hotels have top restaurants plus there are top chains such as the Cheesecake Factory, Ruth's Chris, and Carrabba's, and you won't have any trouble finding something to satisfy everyone in the family. Here are some of our favorites:

Baoding, 4722 Sharon Road; (704) 552–8899. Baoding is not only a great Chinese restaurant, it's also the name of the city in China that is Charlotte's sister city. $$

Fuel Pizza Cafe, 500 South College Street (704–370–2755); 101 South Boulevard (704–335–7375); 1501 Central Avenue (704–376–3835); and 214 North Tryon Street (704–350–1680). After running around Charlotte all day you can gas up at this filling station–themed pizza chain. $

Lupie's Café, 2718 Monroe Road; (704) 374–1232. It doesn't look like it, but Lupie's has great burgers and homestyle meals. You won't regret stopping here. $

Mert's Heart & Soul, 214 North College Street; (704) 342–4222. Comfort food is served here in an atmosphere of southern blues. $$

The Open Kitchen, 1318 West Morehead Street; (704) 375–7449. This is a classic Italian place where you'll feel right at home. $–$$

Pike's Soda Shop, 1930 Camden Road; (704) 372–0092. Old fashioned soda shop fare is served at Pike's. $$

Price's Chicken Coop, 1614 Camden Road; (704) 333–9866. The Chicken Coop is carry-out only but don't miss this treat. $

The Ranch House, 5614 Wilkinson Boulevard; (704) 399–5411. This is a basic steak house, but it is very good. $$$

Rock Bottom Restaurant & Brewery, 401 North Tryon Street; (704) 334–2739. Rock Bottom turns into a young-adult hangout at night, but by day and early evening it serves a great selection of burgers, sandwiches, and full entrees. $$

Where to Stay

While you can find economical accommodations in the Charlotte area along the interstates leading into the city, expect to pay top dollar for accommodations in the city, especially uptown. Here are some of the city's top places to stay:

Ballantyne Resort, 10000 Ballantyne Commons Parkway; (704) 248-4000. Ballantyne Resort is a luxury resort located in South Charlotte. $$$$

The Dunhill Hotel, 237 North Tryon Street; (704) 332–4141. Listed on the National Register of Historic Places, this uptown hotel offers first-class treatment. $$$$

Morehead Inn, 1122 East Morehead; (704) 376–3357. This is a historic bed-and-breakfast that will accommodate children. $$$$

OMNI Charlotte Hotel, 132 East Trade Street; (800) 843–6664. If you want to splurge uptown, this AAA Four-Diamond hotel will do nicely. $$$$

The Park Hotel, 2200 Rexford Road; (704) 364–8220. If the Westin isn't the city's best hotel, the Park is. Even though it is quite large, it's still very comfortable. $$$$

Plaza Hotel on Carowinds, 225 Carowinds Boulvevard, Fort Mill, South Carolina; (803) 548–2400. If you are planning a Carowinds trip you can find several chains on the North Carolina side. On the South Carolina side you find The Plaza Hotel. $$$$

The Westin Hotel, 601 South College Street; (704) 375–2600. This is one of Charlotte's largest, and possibly best, hotels. You should expect top-notch service from the staff here, as you would at any Westin. $$$$

Huntersville, Davidson, **and Cornelius**

While you're in the Charlotte area, plan to spend some time exploring the towns along I-77, north of the city, as well as Lake Norman, the largest artificial lake in North Carolina. Built by Duke Power Company to accommodate its hydroelectric and nuclear power plants, Lake Norman is a big draw for boating and fishing enthusiasts from across the state. Ten public access areas around the 32,500-acre lake are perfect for camping, swimming, and fishing. Duke Power has also established a 1,400-acre public park north of Huntersville. You'll find a variety of large hotels in the Lake Norman area, and Lake Norman Rentals in Mooresville (800–408–5997) can help you find larger places for a vacation stay. For more information contact the Lake Norman Convention and Visitors Bureau, (704) 987–3300, or www.lakenormancvb.org.

For More Information

Charlotte Convention and Visitors Bureau, (800) 722–1994; www.visit charlotte.com.

Main Street Charlotte, (800) 231–4636.

Huntersville

Scottish Heritage Center at Rural Hill Plantation

4431 Neck Road; (704) 875–3113; www.ruralhillplantation.org. Open 9:00 a.m. to 5:00 p.m. Monday through Saturday. $; special events have special times and prices.

Rural Hill Plantation is home away from home for area Scots. It's the historic homestead of Major John and Violet (Wilson) Davidson, who saw Rural Hill grow to become one of the most prosperous plantations in the Carolina's piedmont. They raised ten children who continued their legacy. The original home has not survived, but a reproduction stands instead. Original remnants include a smoke house, ash house, well house, barn, chicken shed, and granary. Two of the last remaining one-room schoolhouses in Mecklenburg County—one for white and one for African American children—are also located on the Rural Hill property.

The plantation hosts several fun events throughout the year such as the Sheep Dog Trials in November, the Amazing Maize Maze, a 1760 Carolina Thanksgiving, and the Loch Norman Games each April. World-class athletes compete in various competitions, including the caper toss, and there are contests in bagpipe, fiddle, harp, and

Scottish dance. More than ninety Scottish and Scots-Irish clans and organizations bring their banners to demonstrate their support and share family genealogy and heritage exhibits with visitors.

Latta Plantation Nature Center (ages 5 and up)

5225 Sample Road; (704) 875–1391; www.lattaplantation.org. The park is open during daylight hours, and facilities are free. The Latta house (704-875-2312) is open 10:00 a.m. to 5:00 p.m. Tuesday through Saturday and noon to 5:00 p.m. Sunday, April through September. $; free for children ages five and under.

A good place to visit in Huntersville is Latta Plantation, a nineteenth-century cotton plantation located in the Latta Park Nature Preserve. The 1,090-acre park borders Mountain Island Lake and includes an interpretive center, equestrian center, and hiking and horse trails. In addition, the park presents living-history tours of the James Latta house on the first and third Thursday of each month. The two-story Federal-style house, built in 1800, is elaborately decorated to match the intricate detail of the architecture.

Carolina Raptor Center (all ages)

600 Sample Road; (704) 875–6521; www.carolinaraptorcenter.org. Open from 10:00 a.m. to 5:00 p.m. Tuesday through Saturday and noon to 5:00 p.m. on Sunday. $–$$; children under five and under are admitted free.

Also located in the Latta Park Nature Preserve, the center opened in 1980 as a haven for injured eagles, hawks, and other birds of prey. Today, it is a sprawling center that combines fun and education. After the birds have been rehabilitated, some are released into the wild, while others are put on display in a natural wooded area and used for educational demonstrations. A 25,000-foot outdoor eagle aviary gives visitors an opportunity to see these remarkable birds of prey up close—closer than ever possible in the wild.

Duke Energy's Energy Explorium (ages 5 and up)

1339 Hagers Ferry Road; (704) 875–5600; www.dukeenergy.com. Open 9:00 a.m. to 5:00 p.m. Monday through Friday and noon to 5:00 p.m. Saturday and Sunday. Free.

The explorium presents hands-on exhibits where you can throw the switches on model nuclear and coal-fired plants. You can power a television by converting your body's energy on a treadmill, play computer games, and figure out how much energy you get for a dollar. You can also burn off some energy on a mile-long nature trail.

Carolina Renaissance Festival (ages 5 and up)

16445 Poplar Tent Road; (704) 896–5544. Open weekends from 10:00 a.m. to 5:30 p.m. late September to early November. $$–$$$; children under five get in free.

The Carolina Renaissance Festival is quickly becoming one of the area's biggest attractions. Sixteenth-century Europe is re-created during weekends in the fall. Don't be surprised to find yourself at the edge of a jousting contest or in the middle of a sword fight. You can enjoy the antics of the court jester and see knights dressed in full armor. Finding a feast fit for a king, complete with big turkey legs, won't be any problem, either. And when you finish eating, you can browse through acres of shops and galleries.

Where to Eat

Acropolis Cafe & Grille, 20659 Catawba Avenue, Cornelius; (704) 894–0191. Sandwiches, salads, and Greek specialties are offered here. $

Big Al's Pub and Grubberia, 8301 Magnolia Estates Drive; (704) 987–6582. Big Al can whip up everything from burgers and sandwiches to Italian dishes in a very casual atmosphere. $–$$

Buzzy & Bear's Grill, 9709-B Sam Furr Road; (704) 895–2692. If you can't tell by the name, this is a fun place to get brats or a hot dog. Buzzy & Bear, the owners, might even show up. $

Fuddruckers, 16625 Statesville Road; (704) 896–8390. This chain serves huge burgers and the like. Fix them up anyway you like at the dressing bar. $

Where to Stay

Davidson Village Inn, 117 Depot Street, Davidson; (704) 892–8044. Kids stay **free** at this inn, near the very picturesque Davidson College. $$$$

Pineville

Pineville is southeast of Charlotte off Highway 16.

James K. Polk Memorial (ages 5 and up)
308 South Polk Street; (704) 889–7145. Open 9:00 a.m. to 5:00 p.m. Tuesday through Saturday and 1:00 to 5:00 p.m. Sunday, April through October. The rest of the year, open until 4:00 p.m. Sunday. Free.

The birthplace and childhood home of the eleventh president of the United States, the James K. Polk Memorial features exhibits on his life and times. You can see an audiovisual display here as well as take a guided tour of the home. The reconstructed house is typical of those during Polk's childhood. The kitchen and house are authentically furnished with period pieces from the early 1800s. The Mecklenburg Chapter of the Daughters of the American Revolution erected a stone monument for our eleventh president at the site in 1904. Picnic facilities are available.

Zuma Fun Center (all ages)

10400 Cadillac Street; (704) 552–7888; www.zumafuncenters.com. Open noon to 9:00 p.m. Monday through Thursday, noon to midnight Friday, 10:00 to midnight Saturday, and noon to 9:00 p.m. Sunday.

To give the kids a treat for lunch or dinner, Zuma Fun Center is always a big hit. The amusement center/restaurant offers delicious pizza and a chance to let the kids run off some steam. Everyone in the family might want to ride go-karts or bumper boats or even play a round of miniature golf. Younger children can play in Harry's Clubhouse, a play park with rides designed especially for them, and older kids can brush up on their batting at the cages.

Waxhaw

Take Highway 16 south from Pineville to reach Waxhaw.

Listen and Remember (ages 5 and up)

Waxhaw Ampitheater, 3115 Little Tom Starnes Road; (704) 843–2300 or (704) 764–7159. The play is performed each Friday and Saturday in June. $–$$.

Waxhaw is an area rich in Native American history. That history is presented each June in *Listen and Remember.* The musical drama, which was locally written, is a production of the Waxhaw Historical Festival and Drama Association. It has been revised over its thirty-plus years in production. The outdoor performance leads you through history, beginning with settlers moving in on local Native American territories, to the Revolutionary War, to the life of Andrew Jackson, the seventh president of the United States, who was born near here.

Museum of the Alphabet (ages 5 and up)

6409 Davis Road; (704) 843–6000. Open 9:00 a.m. to noon and 1:00 to 3:30 p.m. Monday through Saturday. Admission is free, but donations are accepted.

Where in the world did words come from? That question is answered at the Museum of the Alphabet, an unusual but enticing collection of exhibits that trace the early origins of written communication from ancient times through the development of the Roman alphabet to our English alphabet today. You can also see a working model of the first printing press, displays on alphabets of foreign languages, and descriptions of the systems of alphabets created for the hearing- and sight-impaired.

Amazing
North Carolina Facts

A historical marker on Highway 75 says that Andrew Jackson was born in Union County in North Carolina, but most encyclopedias and historical accounts say he was born in Waxhaw, South Carolina. The place of Jackson's birth has been debated since 1815, with a total of four states and Ireland claiming his birth.

Cane Creek Park (all ages)

5213 Harkey Road; (704) 843–3919; www.co.umon.nc.us. The park generally is open during daylight hours, daily during the summer and only on weekends the rest of the year. $; other fees vary by activity.

To enjoy outdoor recreation for a day, or even a weekend, try Cane Creek Park. The park offers you an opportunity to wet a line at the trophy bass lake, rent a paddle-boat, take a swim in cool, clear water, or even play a round of miniature golf. Cane Creek also offers three campgrounds to accommodate tents or recreational vehicles, with prices ranging from $10 to $29 per night. You can also enjoy miles of scenic hiking trails or splashing around in a canoe or rowboat. The park also offers sports equipment rental.

Harrisburg

You can get to Harrisburg via I-85 from Charlotte, or you can also reach it from the Lake Norman area.

Lowe's Motor Speedway (ages 7 and up)

555 Concord Parkway South; (704) 455–3200 for ticket information or (704) 455–3204 for more information on tours; www.lowesmotorspeedway.com. Tours ($, children ages two and under free) are held 9:00 a.m. to 5:00 p.m. Monday through Saturday and noon to 5:00 p.m. Sunday, except when racing events are scheduled.

Thousands of NASCAR fans from across the country flock here each May and October to watch their favorite drivers negotiate speeds up to 200 miles per hour at one of the country's premier racing facilities. The Coca-Cola 600, held each Memorial Day weekend, draws a huge crowd—second only in size to the Indianapolis 500, which is held the same day. As crowds roll in by recreational vehicle, truck, and car, the entire area lights up with races and activities all month long. A family-oriented event in downtown Charlotte called **Speed Street** takes place three days before the race and includes NASCAR simulators, music, food, and other activities. Racing excitement also picks up in October, culminating in the running of the UAW-GM Quality 500. If you plan on getting a ticket to one of the major races, be aware that these cars are very loud. Even the adults will need earplugs, and the noise is likely to bother children who are sensitive to it.

In addition to these major sporting events, Lowe's Motor Speedway hosts the Legends Car Summer Shootout ($–$$$) each Tuesday during the summer. Legends cars are small replicas of 1937 and 1940 Fords and Chevrolets. Games, other spectator events, activities, and entertainment from the world's fastest mascot, Lug Nut, are part of the show.

Other events held at the speedway include a regular schedule of events at the short dirt track, auto shows, motorcycle racing, go-kart racing, and tours of this spectacular facility. On these tours, you visit the garages, pits, and winner's circle. When the track is not in use, you can take a trip around the track through the Richard Petty Driving School. Finally, pick out a gift at the gift shop for the Nextel Cup fan in your life.

Backing Up Classics (ages 5 and up)

4545 Highway 29, Concord; (704) 788–9500; www.backingupclassics.com. The facility is usually open seven days a week, from 8:00 a.m. to 6:00 p.m. Monday through Friday, 8:00 a.m. to 1:00 p.m. Saturday, and 10:00 a.m. to 5:00 p.m. Sunday, but hours may vary according to activity at the speedway. $$–$$$.

Next to the speedway near the border of Harrisburg and the city of Concord, you can visit Backing Up Classics. Step back into the 1950s at this unique museum that presents classic cars and dragsters from years gone by. You will also see memorabilia and cars from the sport of racing. The gift shop features a huge selection of unique 1950s and race-related souvenirs and gifts.

Concord

Concord is just a hop, skip, and jump from Harrisburg on either U.S. Highway 49 or Highway 29.

Concord Mills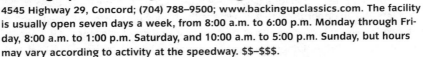

8111 Concord Mills Boulevard; (704) 979–5000; www.concordmills.com. Open 10:00 a.m. to 9:30 p.m. Monday through Saturday and 11:00 a.m. to 7:00 p.m. Sunday.

This sprawling center offers more than just shopping. In addition to 200 stores, it includes a NASCAR simulator, a huge game room, an indoor amusement park for younger children, a Build-a-Bear Workshop, and restaurants. It has a twenty-four-screen movie theater and a Bass Outdoor Pro Shop that features an outdoor RV center. There is also a NASCAR Speedpark featuring an array of rides, go-karts, bumper boats, mini-golf, and more. Of course, you'll find standard mall fare including a food court, outlet stores, and specialty shops.

Frank Liske Park & Soccer Complex (all ages) ⊙ △ 🚌 🏛

4001 Stough Road; (704) 920–2700. Open generally during daylight hours. Free; fees charged for some activities.

Located near the center of the County, this park has just about everything one would hope to find at a park. Fishing is allowed in the ten-acre lake and paddleboats are available for rent. Guests can play a round of miniature golf and there are plenty of playgrounds, picnic shelters, and walking and fitness trails.

Where to Eat

Troutmans' Bar-B-Q, with five locations, has established quite a reputation in the area. The locations and their respective phones numbers are 362 Church Street North (704–786–5213); 1875 Highway 601 (704–786–9714); 1096 Highway 29 North (704–786–6317); 8335 West Franklin Street, Mount Pleasant (704–436–9806); and 530 South Cannon Boulevard, Kannapolis (704–938–6001). $

Where to Stay

Colonial Inn, 1325 Highway 29 North; (704) 782–2146. Decorated in colonial fashion, this small inn is great for a quiet stay in a convenient location. $$$

Mayfair Motel, 1516 Highway 29 North; (704) 786–1175. This affordable motel has a playground in addition to a pool and refrigerators in some rooms. $$

Stanfield

Stanfield is east of Charlotte on Highway 24/27.

Reed Gold Mine (ages 3 and up) 🏛

9621 Reed Mine Road; (704) 721–4653; www.ah.dcr.state.nc.us/sections/hs/reed/reed.htm. Open 9:00 a.m. to 5:00 p.m. Tuesday through Saturday, April through October; 10:00 a.m. to 4:00 p.m. Tuesday through Saturday and 1:00 to 4:00 p.m. Sunday, November through March. The museum is free, and the panning area is open on a seasonal basis for a nominal fee.

Some say there could still be gold in Stanfield. You can try to find some of it as you pan for gold at Reed Gold Mine, off Highway 200. The brown highway signs may confuse you, so from Concord, take U.S. Highway 601, then turn south onto Highway 200. Here you will experience the country's first gold rush, which started with the discovery of a nugget (big enough to be used as a doorstop) near here in 1799. North Carolina remained the leader of gold production until the California gold rush in 1848. Today visitors at the site can see a film on more of this history, exhibits on the mining process, and the tools the miners used, as well as the underground tunnels of the nation's first gold mine.

Amazing
North Carolina Facts

At the age of twelve, Conrad Reed discovered a seventeen-pound gold nugget in Little Meadow Creek, and it was, in fact, used as a doorstop for three years. When it was identified as gold, Conrad's father, John, opened the mine for business.

For More Information

Cabarrus County Convention and Visitors Bureau, (800) 848–3740; www.cabarruscvb.com.

Albemarle

From the Reed Gold Mine, Highway 24/27 will take you to the historic town of Albe-marle, near the border of the Uwharrie National Forest.

While this isn't a famous tourist area, Albemarle offers a handful of attractions, mainly ample opportunity to enjoy the outdoors. But first take a trip to the historic downtown area, which served as a cultural and commercial haven for the rural area in the late 1800s and early 1900s. The Stanly County Chamber of Commerce (704–982–8116) can provide you with a walking map of the downtown area, where you'll see many charms from the late nineteenth and early twentieth centuries. You can get a glimpse of the art deco style of architecture of the 1920s at the Albemarle Opera House or at the Alameda Theater, where silent films once played. Both are located near East Main Street.

Morrow Mountain State Park (all ages)

State Road 1719; (704) 982–4402. The park opens at 8:00 a.m. and generally closes at dusk. Admission to the park is free, but there are fees for some activities.

North of downtown you'll find Morrow Mountain State Park, which offers the beauti-ful crystal-clear waters of the adjacent Lake Tillery. The landscape of this area, located in the heart of the foothills, is interesting. Because they were formed by vol-canic eruptions thousands of years ago, the hills have resisted erosion and main-tained a rugged appearance against a beautiful backdrop of green in the spring and summer. You'll find a number of trails in the park, ranging in length from a half mile to 6 miles. A small natural-history museum, located at the center of the park, explains the development of the region and includes exhibits on the wildlife and the vegetation that occupy the area. A family camping area can accommodate tents and recreational vehicles year-round, but there are no facility hookups. Water, showers, and toilets are available nearby. If you want to stay for a week, you can rent one of six cabins in the park, from April through October. In addition to the natural bounty, the park also has a swimming pool and boat and canoe rentals.

For More Information

Stanly County Convention and Visitors Bureau, (800) 650–1476; www.stanlycvb.com.

New London

Take U.S. Highway 52 north to New London from Albemarle.

Cotton Patch Gold Mine

41697 Gurley Road; (704) 463–5797; www.cottonpatchgoldmine.com. Open 9:00 a.m. to 5:00 p.m. Tuesday through Sunday. $–$$.

More camping facilities and a shot at striking it rich are available north of Albemarle at the Cotton Patch Gold Mine, located just off US 52 at Highway 740. The campground accommodates tent camping as well as full facility hookups for recreational vehicles, in addition to restrooms and showers. You can pan for gold and other minerals here with buckets of dirt that are provided.

Mount Gilead

Head southeast from Albemarle on Highway 73 to Mount Gilead.

Town Creek Indian Mound (ages 5 and up)

Located off Highway 73; (910) 439–6802. Open 9:00 a.m. to 4:00 p.m. Tuesday through Saturday and 1:00 to 4:00 p.m. Sunday. Free.

You'll find the Town Creek Indian Mound, a ceremonial center for the Creek Indian Nation that occupied the area as early as 1450, in Mount Gilead. The site, which served as a meeting place for religious ceremonies, and even for executions of enemies 300 years ago, has been rebuilt nearly to completion over the past fifty years. The earthen mound—a sort of stage—is encircled by a wall constructed of logs, bound together by cane, and several other structures made of dirt, sticks, and thatch. Presentations are held to explain the structure, the history of the Native Americans, and the research that has been done in the area.

Where to Stay

Cardinal Pines Plantation Inn, 1570 Lilly's Bridge Road; (800) 711–1134. This is a very small, historic bed-and-breakfast that would be suitable only for quieter children. $$

Ellerbe

From Mount Gilead, head southeast onto Highway 73 and turn south on US 220.

Runners from all over the Southeast come to the small town of Ellerbe each April for one of the state's most demanding marathons. The 26-mile course, which is extremely hilly, has enjoyed increasing success over the past several years.

Rankin Museum of American Heritage and Natural History (ages 5 and up) 🔾🄻

131 East Church Street; (910) 652–6378; www.rankinmuseum.com. Open 10:00 a.m. to 4:00 p.m. Tuesday through Friday and 2:00 to 5:00 p.m. Saturday and Sunday. $.

The Rankin Museum is a heralded collection that offers you an opportunity to travel back in time all over the world. This diverse collection of exhibits and artifacts is used to explain the heritage of North America, South America, Central America, and Africa. Here you'll see displays such as a fierce polar bear, a Central American jaguar, and a host of moose, elk, and caribou. In addition, the museum features displays on Native American life and a fine mineral collection.

Rockingham

US 220 south from Ellerbe is the route to Rockingham.

Rockingham Dragway (ages 3 and up) 🔾

2152 Highway 1; (910) 582–3400; www.rockinghamdragway.com. Prices vary by race.

Although it lost status as a hub for NASCAR racing in 2004, high-speed action is still here in Rockingham. The Rockingham Dragway is host to IHRA Drag Racing Action. In addition, the racetrack holds sports car, motorcycle, and go-kart races as well as auto shows and other events throughout the year.

Hamlet

US 74 will take you southeast out of Rockingham to Hamlet.

National Railroad Museum (ages 5 and up)
**2 Main Street; (910) 582–3317; www.micropublishing.com/railroad/. Open 10:00 a.m. to
5:00 p.m. Saturday and 1:00 to 5:00 p.m. Sunday. Free.**

This museum is located in the old Seaboard Air Line Railway depot, built in 1900. The
kids will love the extravagant model train layout that features the Orange Blossom
Special and the Silver Meteor. The exhibit is designed as the system appeared in the
early twentieth century. The museum also includes artifacts, photographs, and maps
preserving the railway's heritage, which was once crucial to the area, including the
Railroad Hall of Fame.

Southern Pines

To get from Hamlet to Southern Pines, take U.S. Highway 1 North.

Weymouth Woods Nature Preserve (ages 3 and up)
**1024 North Fort Bragg Road; (910) 692–2167. Open 9:00 a.m. to 6:00 p.m. Monday
through Friday (until 7:00 p.m. during daylight savings time) and noon to 5:00 p.m.
Sunday. Free.**

The Weymouth Woods Nature Preserve, south of Southern Pines, offers an introspec-
tive look at the natural features of the area. Here you will find 900 acres of wildflowers, wildlife, and peaceful rolling streams. The preserve includes more than 4 miles of
hiking trails, a beaver pond, and a nature museum. At the museum you can see how

Golf Capital of the World

Known as the Golf Capital of the World, Pinehurst/Southern Pines and
the surrounding area offer the best amenities for those who play golf, and
much more. In addition to world-class golf competition, the area also
supports tennis competitions and equestrian events throughout the year.
International cycling teams have also begun training here. You'll find
more than forty championship golf courses in the area, not to mention
dozens of plush resorts. Pinehurst Number Two was the site of the 1999
and 2005 U.S. Open Championship.

the area evolved and listen to a night-sounds display that highlights the nocturnal wildlife of the Sandhills region. Each Sunday in the spring and summer a nature study program is presented by a naturalist.

For More Information

Even the worst hotels and restaurants in the Pinehurst/Southern Pines area are very nice. Unless the children play golf, a trip here isn't going to be much fun. If they are learning how to play, a trip here is a must. So for more information and a **free** guide, contact the **Convention and Visitors Bureau for the Village of Pinehurst/Southern Pines/ Aberdeen Area,** (910) 692–0619; www.homeofgolf.com.

Sanford

North of Pinehurst and Southern Pines, you'll find Sanford on US 1.

House in the Horseshoe (ages 5 and up) 🏛

324 Alston House Road; (910) 947–2051. Open 10:00 a.m. to 4:00 p.m. Tuesday through Saturday (until 5:00 p.m. April through September). Free.

You'll want to see the House in the Horseshoe, about 10 miles west of Sanford in a bend in the Deep River. Built in 1772, this cotton plantation home features a gabled roof and big Flemish Bond chimneys. Bullet holes in some of the walls are evidence of the Revolutionary War battles fought on the grounds. One of those battles is re-created each August.

Laurinburg

To get here, travel south on US 15/501 from the Southern Pines area or east on US 74 from Hamlet.

Indian Museum of the Carolinas (ages 5 and up)

607 Turnpike Road; (910) 276–5880. Open 10:00 a.m. to noon and 1:00 to 4:00 p.m. Wednesday and Thursday, and 1:00 to 4:00 p.m. Sunday. Free.

The town of Laurinburg has a rich Native American heritage and offers a visit to the Indian Museum of the Carolinas. It features dozens of exhibits on Carolina Native American life, including many examples of art and some 200,000 archaeological artifacts. Included are weapons, jewelry, costumes, and a dugout canoe.

Pembroke

The town of Pembroke is located east of Laurinburg and just north off US 74.

Strike at the Wind (ages 5 and up)
The play is presented from early July to early September each year at the Lakeside Amphitheater, located off Highway 711, 638 Terry Sanford Drive; (910) 522–6111. $–$$.

Robeson County, located to the south of the Southern Pines area, is home to 26,000 Lumbee Indians, who were recognized neither by the Cherokee Nation nor as U.S. citizens before the Civil War. Each summer relive the Lumbee struggle to overcome this oppression during *Strike at the Wind,* a wonderful but sobering outdoor drama. The play depicts the life of the leader of the Lumbee, Henry Berry Lowrie, and his people in their struggles during the Civil War. Lowrie was crucial in the Lumbee efforts to free themselves from slavery and eventually win voting rights.

Lumberton

From Pembroke take US 74 East to I-95 North to Lumberton.

While Lumberton is the county seat, you won't find a lot to do here. There are some nice, affordable hotels if you're passing through and a couple of attractions that you might want to catch, such as the play in Pembroke.

Exploration Station (ages 1 to 11)
104 North Chestnut Street; (910) 738–1114; www.explorationkids.com. Open 10:00 a.m. to 5:00 p.m. Tuesday, Wednesday, and Friday; 10:00 a.m. to 8:00 p.m. Thursday; and 10:00 to 4:00 p.m. Saturday. $

Kids play doctor in a make believe hospital where they can examine X-rays or look after babies. They can milk a cow or watch ducks cascade down a waterfall. In all there are eleven interactive exhibit areas, including a farmhouse, bank, schoolroom, general store, the hospital, and others. The center also includes a play area designed specifically for infants. Exploration Station also presents special programs in the form of tea parties and more.

Amazing North Carolina Facts

The pine tree was selected as the state tree in 1963.

Robeson Planetarium—Science & Technology Center (ages 5 and up)
Highway 72/711; (910) 671–6015; www.robesonsky.com. Open 8:00 a.m. to 5:00 p.m. daily. Free.

This is a small science museum that has multimedia astronomy shows and exhibits largely related to space science. When NASA telecasts from space, the center is connected. The facility is actually part of the Robeson County school system but it does offer some public programs.

Where to Eat

Chuckles Pizza, 123 Farm Brook Drive; (910) 671–1700. You can get burgers and sandwiches in addition to pizza here. $

John's, 4880 Kahn Drive; (910) 738–4709. This is a nice place for having such a simple name. John's has a good children's menu and varied American cuisine. $$

Redwood Motor Lodge, 4800 Kahn Drive; (910) 739–4304. This economical hotel has forty rooms, a playground, a pool, and pets are welcome. $$

Sleepy Bear's Family Campground, 465 Kenric Road; (910) 739–4372. With a name like that, who could resist? The campground offers tent and trailer sites, a playground, a pool, and more. $

Where to Stay

Since this is near the I-95 corridor, you'll find a lot of national franchise accommodations, but for local flavor try some of these:

For More Information

Lumberton Area Chamber of Commerce, (800) 359–6971; www.lumberton-nc.com.

Fayetteville

Fort Bragg Military Base (ages 5 and up)
You can call the base for general information at (910) 396–5401; www.bragg.army.mil; or visit the information center on Randolph Street and Bragg Boulevard; open 8:30 a.m. to 4:30 p.m. Monday through Friday and 9:00 a.m. to 4:00 p.m. Saturday and Sunday. Free.

More than 200 years of history are presented at Fort Bragg in Fayetteville, one of the largest military bases in the world. Home to 130,000 active military personnel and their families, including the famous 82nd Airborne Division, U.S. Special Operations, and the U.S. Army Parachute Team, the sprawling base is open to the public. (Nearby Pope Air Force Base is not open to the public.) You can tour the 200 square miles of the military reservation to see both contemporary military life and the history of the United States' involvement in war. Daily parachute drops are an exciting attraction for visitors. Call (910) 396–6366 for information on drop schedules.

82nd Airborne Division Museum (all ages)
Building C-6841, Ardennes Street, Fort Bragg; (910) 432–3443. Open 10:00 a.m. to 4:30 p.m. Tuesday through Saturday. **Free.**

This fascinating museum is the first thing you'll want to see at Fort Bragg. It features thousands of artifacts from this internationally famous division. Items on display include helmets, weapons, parachutes, aircraft, and more from World War I to Operation Desert Storm. A film on the division's history is also presented.

The John F. Kennedy Special Warfare Museum (all ages)
Ardennes and Marion Streets, Fort Bragg; (910) 432–4272. Open 10:00 a.m. to 4:00 p.m. Tuesday through Sunday. **Free.**

This museum features exhibits on unconventional forms of warfare, including displays on the Green Berets and Special Operation Units. You'll also see military art and cultural items from around the world, mostly from the Vietnam War era.

Airborne and Special Operations Museum (all ages)
100 Bragg Boulevard; (910) 483–3003; www.asomf.org. Open 10:00 a.m. to 5:00 p.m. Tuesday through Saturday and noon to 5:00 p.m. Sunday. Museum admission **free;** admission to theater and simulator $–$$; children eight and under **free** when accompanied by paying adult.

This has quickly become one of the area's premier attractions. This state-of-the-art facility houses exhibits and programs that highlight the honor, courage, duty, and heroic feats of this unique sector of our armed forces from 1940 to today. A large-screen theater features specially produced movies showing these forces in action. A twenty-four-seat simulator allows riders to experience a helicopter attack, parachute jump, and off-road pursuit. You'll also find a memorial garden, parade area, and unit memorials.

In Memory

While touring Fort Bragg, you'll come across a number of memorials to those who gave their lives in various wars. At the JFK Chapel you'll see stained-glass windows memorializing the Green Berets, plus a monument that the late actor John Wayne designed and donated to the base. Some of the tombstones at the Fort Bragg Cemetery date back to 1918.

History in Fayetteville

When you're done exploring Fort Bragg, you and your family will want to check out the many more attractions that await you in Fayetteville. Fayetteville has played key roles during defining moments in America's history. Named after the Revolutionary War hero Marquis de Lafayette, the legislature met here in 1789 to ratify the U.S. Constitution. During the Civil War, General Sherman's Union troops burned the N.C. Arsenal, a munitions center for the Confederacy located here. Today, many structures have been painstakingly preserved in four historic districts: Downtown Historic District, Haymount Historic District, Liberty Point National Register District, and Market House Square National Register, all of which can be seen on a self-guided tour. Some examples of what you'll see on the tour include Cool Spring Tavern. Built in 1788, it is the oldest structure in the city. The tavern housed the delegates who ratified the U.S. Constitution. At Liberty Point on June 20, 1775, patriots signed a petition declaring independence from Great Britain. The building at this site is the oldest known commercial structure in Fayetteville, constructed between 1791 and 1800. The First Presbyterian Church was rebuilt in 1832. The building's most significant feature is a wooden truss roof, the only one of its kind in the state. If you have an appetite for history, you can get a brochure for the self-guided tour of the city's historical homes and buildings at the **Fayetteville Area Convention and Visitors Bureau,** 515 Ramsey Street, (800) 255–8217; www.visitfayettevillenc.com.

First Presbyterian Church (all ages)

Located at the corner of Bow and Ann Streets; (910) 483–0121. Open 8:00 a.m. to 4:30 p.m. Monday through Friday. Sunday services are held at 8:30 and 10:55 a.m. Free.

This 1816 church is a brilliant example of Southern Colonial architecture and features a wooden truss roof. Inside you'll see lovely whale-oil chandeliers, communion silver, and handmade wrought-iron locks.

Museum of the Cape Fear Historical Complex (ages 5 and up)
801 Arsenal Avenue; (910) 486–1330; http://ncmuseumofhistory.org/osm/mcf.html.
Open 10:00 a.m. to 5:00 p.m. Tuesday through Saturday and 1:00 to 5:00 p.m. Sunday.
Free.

A division of the North Carolina Museum of History, the Museum of the Cape Fear
Historical Complex collects, preserves, and interprets the cultural history of southern
North Carolina from prehistory to the present. It includes three facilities. The
museum presents traditional museum exhibits that chronicle the early history of
southeastern North Carolina from Native American culture and European settlement,
to industrial influences, to the Civil War. **Arsenal Park** commemorates the day Sherman came to Fayetteville. A U.S. Arsenal, commissioned in Fayetteville in 1836, was
taken over by the Confederacy when the Civil War broke out and was seized by Sherman in March 1865. The site also includes the restored 1897 **Victorian** residence
built by E. A. and Josephine Poe.

Fascinate-U Children's Museum (all ages)
116 Green Street; (910) 829–9171. Open 9:00 a.m. to 5:00 p.m. Tuesday through Friday,
10:00 a.m. to 5:00 p.m. Saturday, and noon to 5:00 p.m. Sunday. $.

This is one of a growing number of centers in North Carolina that exist purely for children. The museum features a variety of interactive exhibits that let children discover
the world around them.

Where to Eat

Haymont Grill and Steakhouse, 1304
Morganton Road; (910) 484–0261. This
is a pleasant casual restaurant that
serves American, Greek, and Italian
dishes. $

Where to Stay

Clarion Prince Charles Hotel, 450 Hay
Street; (910) 433–4444. Reminiscent of
an Italian palazzo, this 1925 eight-story
landmark features Palladian windows
and doors, marble floors and staircases,

and massive columns. It's listed in Historic Hotels of America. $$$$

Deluxe Inn, 2123 Cedar Creek Road;
(910) 484–2666. This is a good place for
an overnight stop, and pets are allowed.
$$

For More Information

**Fayetteville Area Convention & Visi-
tors Bureau,** (800) 255–8217; www.visit
fayettevillenc.com.

Spivey's Corner

From Fayetteville, take I-95 North to U.S. Highway 13 East to arrive at the home of the National Hollerin' Contest.

National Hollerin' Contest (all ages)

Midway High School, 15375 Spivey's Corner Highway; (910) 567–2600; www.hollerin contest.com. $; preschool children get in free. Third Saturday in June, from 11:00 a.m. to 7:00 p.m.

That's right! The best windpipes in the country show up here for this annual event, held the third Saturday of June. Since 1969 the contest has featured the lost art of hog callin'—also an early way of communicating with folks living on neighboring farms. Now the event gets national attention, with winners regularly appearing on *The Late Show With David Letterman* and other talk shows. In addition to being entertained by the champion hollerers, you'll find crafts, gospel and country music, and plenty of food. Other contests include whistlin', conch shell and fox horn blowin', junior hollerin', and ladies callin'.

Other Things to See and Do
in the Southern Piedmont

- **The Climbing Place,** Fayetteville, (910) 486–9638

- **Fun, Fun, Fun,** Fayetteville, (910) 864–1307

- **Fort Bragg Riding Stables,** Fayetteville, (910) 396–4510

- **Jumbbas Ranch,** Fayetteville, (910) 484–2798

- **Adams Stage Lines,** Concord, (704) 537–5556

- **Ken Schrader's Seekonk Grand Prix,** Concord, (704) 795–7106

- **NASCAR Speedpark,** Concord, (704) 979–6770

- **Hendrick Motorsports Museum,** Harrisburg, (704) 455–3400

- **LaserQuest,** Charlotte, (704) 567–6707

- **Ice House,** Pineville, (704) 889–9000

- **Adventure Landing,** Gastonia, (704) 866–4242

The Southern Coast

Grab a blanket and the sunscreen. Plan to relax, play in the surf and sand, enjoy fresh seafood, or take a boat ride. North Carolina's Southern Coast is full of southern-facing beaches that make for calm waters and warm winds. This region is comprised of the Coastal Plain, the southern tip of the Outer Banks, Cape Lookout National Seashore, and the South Brunswick Islands—a series of small barrier islands.

While many of these islands, and the communities on them, don't offer an immense number of tourist attractions, you're likely to find that they are great places to set up housekeeping at a cottage for a week and take any number of day trips. In addition, you will find some of the best golf courses in the Carolinas, a unique

Jim's
TopPicks on the Southern Coast

1. USS *North Carolina* battleship, Wilmington

2. Riverboat rides on Cape Fear

3. North Carolina Aquarium at Kure Beach

4. Wild ponies of Carrot Island

5. Camping at Carolina Beach State Park, Carolina Beach

6. Bald Head Island

7. Calabash restaurants

8. Southport Fourth of July Celebration

9. Museum of Coastal Carolina, Ocean Isle Beach

10. Waiting for loggerheads

THE SOUTHERN COAST

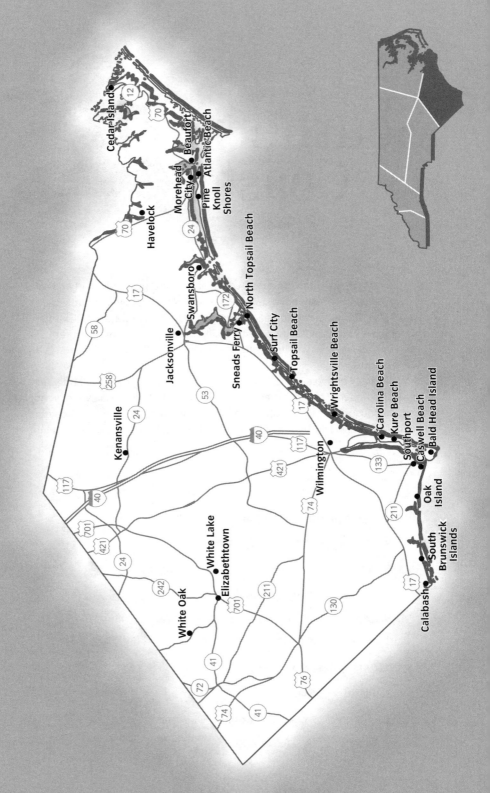

community that features seafood restaurants and two of the state's educational aquariums. Here you can also learn a lot about history, from the eighteenth century to World War II.

Your adventure on the Southern Coast begins in the Bladen Lakes area, where you'll find a beach long before you get to the coast. The best route to take from the Charlotte area is U.S. Highway 74. From Raleigh Interstate 40 is a speedy route right into Wilmington. U.S. Highway 17 runs the length of the coast, but it goes through many towns, so travel is generally slow. Use it to move from town to town and stick to the major highways for longer travel.

White Oak

Harmony Hall (ages 5 and up) 🏛
1615 River Road; (910) 866–4844. Open 10:00 a.m. to 4:00 p.m. Saturday and Sunday afternoons with live demonstrations of broom making, soap making, and black-smithing from 2:00 until 4:00 p.m. Free, but donations are accepted.

As you head into this area, the first stop you will want to make is at Harmony Hall, located in White Oak. Built in the 1760s, Harmony Hall is one of the oldest plantations in North Carolina and was once home to the state's first constitutionally elected governor, Richard Caswell. During the Revolutionary War, British general Charles Cornwallis commandeered the home. A period reenactment is held and wagon rides are offered during the annual Harmony Hall Reunion Picnic the first Saturday in May. Several other historic buildings, including a chapel, schoolhouse, and log home, have been moved to the property.

Elizabethtown

Turnbull Creek State Forest (ages 3 and up)
4470 Sweet Home Church Road; (910) 588–4161; www.dfr.state.nc.us/esf/tcesf.htm. Open 9:00 a.m. to 5:00 p.m. Monday through Friday and 11:00 a.m. to 5:00 p.m. Saturday mid-March through mid-November. Free.

Turnbull Creek State Forest, located north of Elizabethtown, was founded in 1986 and is still under development. Visitors to the park can take one of several trails, including the fire control trail, where you can explore the park's fire-fighting equipment and scout plane. The forest caters mainly to schools in the area, but some of the educational programs may be available from the rangers at the forest office. Picnic facilities are available as well.

Jones Lake State Park (all ages)
113 Jones Lake Drive; (910) 588–4550. Generally open during daylight hours. Free.

This wonderful park in Turnbull Creek State Forest offers recreational activities within its 2,200 acres. Here you can camp, fish, hike, and swim. Interestingly, the park includes one of two natural lakes known as Carolina bays. There are hundreds of thousands of these bays, named for the bay trees found growing around them, in the southeast. But most are smaller than 500 feet in length. The Jones Lake bay, however, is approximately 8,000 feet long. The lake comprises 224 acres and nearby Salters Lake, also in the park, is 315 acres. What's more interesting is that their formation is a mystery. Scientists have long theorized about the origin of the Carolina bays. Many hypotheses have been proposed, including underground springs, wind and wave action, dissolution of subsurface minerals, and meteor showers. So far, no single explanation has gained universal acceptance.

Troy Hole Battleground (all ages)
Located in a ravine that runs from downtown Elizabethtown to the Cape Fear River; (910) 862–2066.

Another good place for a picnic is historic Troy Hole Battleground. The park includes a playground, picnic facilities, and the opportunity to learn more about the battle that took place on the grounds. In 1781, seventy patriots defeated a Tory force of more than 400 men by sending a spy, Sallie Salter, into their camp on the pretense of selling eggs. They then launched a carefully planned midnight attack.

White Lake

Take U.S. Highway 701 north from Elizabethtown to get here.

Before heading off to the coast, you might want to consider this beautiful area for your family's annual vacation. Billed as The Nation's Safest Beach, White Lake offers all the amenities of a beach vacation, but it's not on the coast. The lake is the largest of seven lakes known as the **Bladen Lakes,** which were formed by meteors that crashed into Earth more than 100,000 years ago. White Lake offers crystal-clear waters with a lovely, white-sand bottom, along with amusement rides, arcades, restaurants, and other commercial entertainment and activities. The cool fresh water is safer for kids because of the absence of tides, currents, and unexpected depressions that are found at coastal beaches.

The area offers more than a dozen accommodations that include hotels, motels, cottages, and campgrounds. **Goldston's Beach,** one of the oldest recreation areas on the beach, was developed by local entrepreneurs, beginning at the turn of the twentieth century. It offers accommodations in apartments, cottages, and a motel. A bathhouse is available at the beach, as is a sandwich shop for a quick lunch. The kids will probably want to head to the arcade, too, or to one of the piers to get in a little fishing. For more information call the resort at (910) 862–4064.

Where to Stay

Brisson's Cottages and Apartments, 1770 White Lake Drive; (910) 862–2495. This company offers rooms, cottages, and efficiencies. $$$

Lasley's Motel, 1930 White Lake Drive; (910) 862–3473. You'll find more of the same on the waterfront. $$$

Melwood Court, 1994 White Lake Drive; (910) 862–2416. This establishment is a little larger than the others in the area. $$$

For More Information

Town of White Lake, (910) 862–4800; www.whitelakenc.com.

Calabash

Take US 701 south out of White Lake to Highway 130. Then take Highway 17 south to Calabash.

Now we can head to the coast. If you haven't discovered it before, a visit to Calabash, located in the southeast corner of the state on US 17, is sure to become a family tradition every time you come to this part of the coast. This small fishing community is the southernmost town in North Carolina and has become famous for the Calabash style of cooking seafood. Fish, shrimp, and other goodies are deep-fried to a golden brown and are usually served with hush puppies and coleslaw. Once, more than thirty family-style restaurants lined the streets of this quaint village, where fresh local seafood is delivered daily. In 1989, Calabash merged with the Carolina Shores golfing community, which includes not only some of the best courses in the Carolinas but a wide variety of specialty shops as well. Today the number of restaurants is dwindling because of competition from other restaurants in South Carolina's bustling Myrtle Beach tourist area, but it's still a great place to get your seafood dinner.

South Brunswick Islands

Begin your trek up the coast by heading north on US 17. Here on the South Brunswick Islands, you'll find three similar communities: Sunset Beach, Ocean Isle Beach, and Holden Beach.

Sunset Beach

Accessible only by a unique one-lane pontoon bridge, you'll quickly learn where this laid-back island just off the coast got its name. You'll feel almost secluded if you decide you want to rent one of the large cottages situated behind the tall sand dunes on Sunset Beach. This little island, only 3 miles long, is the southernmost of the three communities.

Ingram Planetarium (ages 3 and up)

7625 High Market Street in The Village at Sunset Resort; (910) 575–0033. Open 3:00 to 8:00 p.m. Tuesday through Sunday. $–$$.

Ingram Planetarium opened in summer 2002 as part of a collaboration with the nearby Museum of Coastal Carolina. It shows traditional planetarium programs on a 40-foot dome in its ninety-seat theater. The center also includes a few space-related exhibits, brainteasers, puzzles, and other hands-on activities.

Where to Stay

Sunset Properties, 419 Sunset Boulevard South; (910) 579–9900; www.sunset beachnc.com. Four hundred cottages are offered by this agency.

Sea Trail Plantation & Golf Resort, 211 Clubhouse Road; (888) 229–5747. This is the largest resort on Sunset Beach, offering everything from efficiencies to villas on the golf course. $$$$

Ocean Isle Beach

This island is located just north of Sunset Beach.

Ocean Isle Beach provides more surf, sand, and sunshine. Here you can enjoy 7 miles of beaches and fish from the surf or pier. To get out on the ocean and try your fishing luck in deeper water, drop by Ocean Isle Fishing Center on the Causeway (910–575–3474). It offers full- and half-day fishing trips. If you'd like to try your hand at crabbing, it probably can be done just outside your back door. Everything you need is here on this island, including restaurants, specialty shops, a miniature golf course, and a water slide.

Museum of Coastal Carolina (ages 3 and up)

21 East Second Street; (910) 579–1016. Open 10:00 a.m. to 8:00 p.m. Monday and Thursday; 10:00 a.m. to 5:00 p.m. all other days in summer. Hours are limited the rest of the year. $.

Whether you are at Ocean Isle for a day or a week, make it a point to stop by the Museum of Coastal Carolina. You don't have to get wet to see the spectacular sites of local ocean life. Wall and floor murals and actual specimens from the sea in the reef room give you a feeling of actually being in the water. The museum includes shark jaws, a huge seashell collection, dioramas of coastal animal life, and Civil War artifacts. The museum also has a turtlewatch program and hosts outdoor concerts in the summer.

Where to Stay

Brick Landing Plantation, 1900 Goose Creek Road Southwest; (800) 438–3006. Brick Landing offers condos and villas. $$$$

Islander Inn, 57 West First Street; (888) 325– 4753; www.islanderinn.com. The Islander Inn offers oceanfront accommodations, featuring a heated indoor pool, Jacuzzi, and an outdoor pool overlooking the beach. A complimentary continental breakfast is included. $$$$

The Winds Clarion Inn and Suites, 310 East First Street; (800) 334–3581. This is a very nice resort hotel with a lovely subtropical garden. $$$$

Here's a list of Realtors at Ocean Isle:

Cooke Realtors, 1 Causeway Drive; (800) 622–3224.

East Coast Realty Vacations, 20 East Second Street; (866) 263–7263.

McMillan Real Estate, 7122 Beach Drive; (866) 579–9100.

Ocean Isle Beach Realty, 15 Causeway Drive; (800) 374–7361.

R. H. McClure Realty, Inc., 24 Causeway Drive; (800) 332–5476.

Sand Dollar Realty, 102 Causeway Drive; (800) 457–7263.

Sloane Realty, 16 Causeway Drive; (800) 843–6044.

Williamson Realty, 119 Causeway Drive; (800) 727–9222.

For More Information

You can call the town of Ocean Isle Beach at (800) 248–2504 to get information on accommodations or visit www.oceanislebeach.com.

Holden Beach

Holden Beach is easily accessible from US 74 if you're coming from the west.

If beautiful sunsets and seclusion aren't enough to keep the kids entertained, give the largest and northernmost of the Brunswick Islands a try. The 11 miles of beach have long been a favorite haunt of those who live to fish, but the area has grown to be more family oriented. It now includes amusements, arcades, and other commercial attractions.

Festival By the Sea (all ages)

Holden Beach's biggest annual event attracts people with its arts and crafts, parade, games, and entertainment. The festival kicks off the last Friday of October with a Halloween carnival for children and continues Saturday with road races, volleyball, sand-sculpture contests, and kite-flying contests. A street dance is also traditionally held that night. Gospel singing is the center of attention on Sunday as the festival continues until dark. Call (910) 754–6644 for more information.

Where to Stay

Here's a complete list of Holden Beach Realtors:

Alan Holden Vacations, 128 Ocean Boulevard West; (800) 720–2200; www.holden-beach.com.

Coastal Vacation Resorts, Inc., 131 Ocean Boulevard West; (910) 842–8000.

Craig Realty, 3262 Holden Beach Road Southwest; (888) 746–2777.

Hobbs Realty Vacations, 114 Ocean Boulevard West; (910) 842–2002.

For More Information

Call the town hall of Holden Beach at (910) 842–6488 for more information.

You can call the **South Brunswick Islands Chamber of Commerce** at (800) 426–6644 for information on accommodations and golf packages.

Oak Island

Highway 211 will give you access to Oak Island.

Formerly the towns of Long Beach and Yaupon Beach, the Town of Oak Island offers an unusual fifty-two public beach accesses (most with parking), two public boat ramps, several areas to put in canoes and kayaks, and an extensive sidewalk system for biking and walking. Here you'll find parks and playgrounds and youth-friendly facilities such as the newly completed skateboard park. It also includes mainland areas where you'll find a large grocery, department stores, and fast-food restaurants. You'll love the calm surf offered on the southern-facing islands. Here you'll be able to swim along 9 miles of beach. There is also a big arcade that includes a swimming pool as well as video games and billiard tables.

Oak Island Nature Center & Register Park

End of Fifty-second Street; (910) 278–5518. Hours vary. Free.

Overlooking the marsh and Intracoastal Waterway, the Oak Island Nature Center offers a wide range of educational activities for children and adults alike. The Talking Trees Walking Trail introduces visitors to the dogwood, red cedar, southern magnolia, and black gum. Visitors also meet a ferret, prairie dog, hedgehog, guinea pig, rabbit, gecko, and moon crab in a small animal exhibit. The center also has a large touch tank with marine creatures native to the island community. Restrooms and picnic facilities are also located here.

A Hoffman **Family Adventure**

For a number of years my brother and his family have rented a large house on what used to be called Long Beach on Oak Island and always invite an assortment of extended family members and friends to share the week with them. We've been lucky enough to make the trip for a few days on a couple of occasions.

One of the fondest memories that I have of these trips is sitting quietly in the dark on the beachfront deck waiting to spot one of the famed loggerhead turtles that visit this part of the coast during the summer. We never actually saw one of the 200- to 500-pound creatures visit, but we awoke one morning to find one had left one hundred or more eggs that looked like Ping-Pong balls next to our boardwalk. These amazing creatures come from their feeding grounds hundreds of miles away, as far as Cuba or the Dominican Republic in some cases, year after year to nest. Some researchers believe the turtles return to the same place where they hatched. So far they've been able to substantiate only that the adults do return to the same beach.

Where to Stay

Blue Water Point Motel & Marina, 5710 West Fifty-seventh Place; (910) 278–1230; www.bluewaterpointmotel.com. $$$$

Island Resort and Inn, 500 Ocean Drive; (910) 278–5644; www.islandresortandinn.com. $$$-$$$$

Ocean Crest Motel, 1411 East Beach Drive; (910) 278–3333; www.ocean-crest-motel.com. Ocean Crest is one of a few hotels located on the island. $$$

Here are Oak Island's realty companies:

Better Beach Rentals, 8601 East Oak Island Drive; (877) 441–0009; www.betterbeachrentals.com.

Century 21/Dorothy Essey & Associates, 6102 East Oak Island Drive, Long Beach; (877) 410–2121.

Coastal Vacation Resorts-Oak Island, 5618 East Oak Island Drive; (888) 703–5469; www.coastalvacationresortsoakisland.com

Margaret Rudd & Associates, 210 Country Club Drive; (800) 733–5213.

Oak Island Accommodations, 300 Country Club Drive; (800) 243–8132; www.rentalsatthebeach.com.

Caswell Beach 〰️🔺🦀

The second community on Oak Island is Caswell Beach. In addition to the gentle tides along the 4 miles of beach, here you will find the **Oak Island Lighthouse,** the nation's most modern, which opened in 1958. Also located on this beach is the Oak Island Coast Guard Station and **Fort Caswell.** Built in 1826, the fort is now owned by the North Carolina Baptist Assembly. The Civil War stone-and-earthen fort was abandoned in 1865 during a violent naval bombardment north of here. Today you can tour what remains of the fort and bunkers. For more information call (910) 278–9501.

For More Information

Southport–Oak Island Chamber of Commerce at (800) 457–6964; www.oakislandnc.com.

Southport

To get to Southport, take Highway 133 north from Oak Island to Highway 211 and head east.

Southport is located at the junction of the Cape Fear River, the Intracoastal Waterway, and the Atlantic Ocean. If your family enjoys sailing and deep-sea fishing, this is the place to go. But this port city, which is more than 200 years old, offers much more. You'll want to spend some time exploring the more than a dozen antiques shops beneath huge old live oaks and take advantage of some of the exquisite dining available in the village. The town is becoming famous for the **Southport Fourth of July Celebration,** which has become one of the state's largest annual celebrations, featuring games, contests, food, and, of course, fireworks.

Amazing North Carolina Facts

Southport was originally incorporated in 1792 as Smithville, but citizens in 1887 voted to change its name to Southport with the goal of attracting a port. Their plans went awry when the port was established in the City of Wilmington to the north.

Progress Energy Visitors Center (ages 3 and up)
8520 River Road Southeast; (910) 457–6041. **Hours vary. Free.**

A good educational afternoon trip is only about 2 miles north of town on Highway 87. Take along a picnic lunch when you visit the Progress Energy Visitors Center. You'll want to allow about an hour to see the thirty hands-on displays on energy, electricity production, energy conservation, and nuclear power.

Orton Plantation Gardens (ages 5 and up)
9149 Orton Road Southeast, Winnabow; (910) 371–6851; www.ortongardens.com. Open daily 8:00 a.m. to 6:00 p.m. March through August and 10:00 a.m. to 5:00 p.m. September through November. $–$$; free for those five and under.

Take Highway 87 North to Highway 133, and you'll find two other interesting attractions to round out your day trip. First check out Orton Plantation Gardens, just off Highway 133. The plantation is surrounded by what once were rice fields that have now been converted into colorful gardens, bordered by live oak trees.

Brunswick Town State Historic Site (ages 5 and up)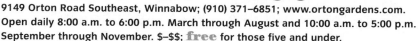
8884 St. Phillips Road Southeast, Winnabow; (910) 371–6613. Open 10:00 a.m. to 4:00 p.m. Monday through Saturday and 1:00 to 5:00 p.m. Sunday, April through October; 10:00 a.m. to 4:00 p.m. Tuesday through Saturday and 1:00 to 4:00 p.m. Sunday, November through March. Free.

After you visit Orton Plantation Gardens, head to the Brunswick Town State Historic Site, just a few minutes away. Brunswick Town was the first capital of the colony of North Carolina and was a leading seaport during most of the eighteenth century. When you visit the museum at the site, you will see various artifacts and exhibits excavated from the remains of the original buildings, which were burned to the ground by the British in 1776. You'll also see the earthworks of Fort Anderson, built to help keep the Cape Fear River open for Civil War blockade runners, who shipped supplies to Confederate forces. It fell in 1865 during a fierce battle that also collapsed several other area forts. Markers have been erected to explain the history of the area.

N.C. Maritime Museum at Southport (all ages)
116 North Howe Street; (910) 457–0003. Open 9:00 a.m. to 5:00 p.m. Tuesday through Saturday. $.

A branch of the N.C. Maritime Museum at Beaufort, this museum houses a collection of memorabilia pertaining to the vast nautical history of Southport, the Lower Cape Fear, and southeastern North Carolina. It includes a 2,000-year-old 54-inch Indian canoe fragment, Civil War Blockade exhibits, including a 200-pound torpedo and an extensive collection of delicate ship models. The River Pilots, Rescues and Aids to Navigation section offers a variety of nautical instruments.

Where to Stay

The Captain's Bridge, 113 North Howe Street; (910) 457–6401; www.thecaptains bridge.com. This is one of the city's newest hotels located near the waterfront.

River Oaks Motel, 512 North Howe Street; (910) 457–1100. This motel will suit you if you're planning to be out and about a lot and don't want to spend a lot on lodging. $$

Riverside Motel, 103 West Bay Street; (910) 457–6986. Riverside is a very small motel that is, of course, on the waterfront. $$$

Sea Breeze, 608 West Street; (910) 457–5263. The Sea Breeze is the largest of the accommodations in Southport, with rooms and efficiencies. $$$

Brunswick Coast Properties, 611 North Howe Street; (910) 448–0189; www.brunswickcoastproperties.com.

For More Information

NC Brunswick Islands, (800) 795–7263; www.ncbrunswick.com.

Bald Head Island

Bald Head Island is one of North Carolina's most exclusive and beautiful vacation resorts. You won't find any cars or even a bridge to this natural and historical area. To get here you must take a private yacht or catch the ferry ($$–$$$) at Indigo Plantation and Marina (910–457–5003), off West Ninth Street in Southport. Security is provided at the twenty-four-hour parking lot ($) at the marina. Daily trips to the island are made on the hour, 8:00 a.m. to 6:00 p.m., except noon. Return trips to the mainland are made on the half hour, 8:30 a.m. to 6:30 p.m., except 11:30 a.m. Day trip packages ($$$$) are also available, and some are **free** for children under three. Call (910) 457–5003 for details.

Old Baldy (all ages)

(910) 799–4640. Hours vary, so call ahead to see when it's open. Free.

In addition to fine dining, shopping, and relaxing by the pool or on the beach, you won't have any trouble finding ways to spend your time on this island of "sea oats, sand castles, and sunsets." "Old Baldy," North Carolina's oldest lighthouse, built in 1817, marks the west side of Bald Head Island. Although its function was replaced by the Oak Island Lighthouse in 1935, the 110-foot tower is open for climbing. The Old Baldy Foundation, formed in 1985 and charged with maintaining the lighthouse, also operates a museum in a replica of the lighthouse keeper's cottage.

Bald Head Island Club (all ages)
South Bald Head Wynd; (910) 457–7300. Fees vary by activity.

Most rental accommodation packages on the island include a temporary member-
ship to the Bald Head Island Club, which offers fine dining, live entertainment, a clubhouse, and a host of recreational facilities. Here you can enjoy the swimming pool, a
challenging golf course, tennis courts, and croquet greenswards. Coaching for young
and old alike is available for all these activities. The club offers a range of dining experiences, including elegant evening dining, a lunch grill, a cafe for casual dining, and a
poolside delicatessen.

Island Passage
North Bald Head Wynd; (910) 457–4944. Seasonal hours.

This store offers a selection of sportswear and accessories. You can also get help in
planning a number of different activities, such as clamming, crabbing, cycling, and
canoe trips. Equipment for these adventures—as well as beach umbrellas, chairs, or
even an extra golf cart—is available for rent.

Shoals Club (all ages)
Located near Cape Fear Point; (910) 454–4888; www.shoalsclub.com. Seasonal hours.

Just like it used to be, the Shoals Club is a place for families to enjoy seaside pastimes
just as they did at the pavilions of old. The oceanfront club includes dining areas, a
lounge, fitness room, shower and locker facilities, swimming pools, and direct beach
access. Parents lounging on the porch can watch their children swimming in the pool
below. Towel service is offered at the pool, and chairs and umbrellas are available to
take to the beach as well. Regular poolside cookouts and buffets bring even more
dining options, along with a chance to enjoy live music, sunsets, and socializing with
fellow members and vacationers. The Shoals Club recreation department organizes a
range of recreation and social activities for all ages that include outdoor adventures,
pool games, beach volleyball, and ice cream socials for teens. The Common at Cape
Fear Station provides a place for children's day camps and teen gatherings.

Holidays on **Bald Head**

You might want to plan your trip to Bald Head Island around one of the
many special events planned throughout the year, beginning with the
Easter sunrise service at "Old Baldy" and the annual Easter egg hunt.
Your family can hunt for Blackbeard's buried treasure on Memorial Day.
Or you can come out for the golf cart parade, sand castle competition,
and family Olympic games on the July 4th weekend. Special celebrations
are held on most other holidays, too.

Bald Head Island Conservancy (all ages)
7000 Federal Road; (910) 457–0089. Some programs require a small fee.

The conservancy sponsors workshops for young people, including canoe trips, turtle walks, beach sweeps, and conservation programs, but its biggest task is the preservation of the endangered loggerhead turtle. More than 30 percent of all the loggerhead turtle nesting sites recorded on the North Carolina coast are on this island. The Sea Turtle Nest Protection Project is responsible for monitoring the nesting of these endangered turtles and holds special programs about them.

Where to Stay

Accommodations on Bald Head Island include two bed-and-breakfast inns, several condominiums, and homes ($$$$). Whichever you choose, you'll find yourself on a vacation of luxury. All rental accommodations on the island come with fully equipped kitchens, washers and dryers, and one four-passenger golf cart.

Bald Head Island Limited, (800) 515-1038.

Bald Head Island Limited, (800) 432-7368.

Bald Head Island Rentals, (800) 680-8322.

Marsh Harbour Inn, (800) 680-8322; www.marshharbourinn.com. While many of the rooms here accommodate couples, Marsh Harbour welcomes small families, too. $$$$

Marsh Harbour Inn, (800) 432-7368.

Old Baldy Associates, Inc., (910) 457-5551.

Theodosia's, (800) 656-1812; www.theodosias.com. Located on the harbor, Theodosia's also has accommodations for small families for weekend excursions. $$$$

For More Information

Bald Head Island Information Center, (800) 234–2441; www.baldhead island.com.

Pleasure Island

You're sure to enjoy yourself on Pleasure Island. Its two communities are Kure Beach and Carolina Beach. From the north the island is accessible by car over the U.S. Highway 421 bridge. From the south, you'll have to take the toll ferry ($$) from Southport to Fort Fisher. Crossings begin at 8:00 a.m. and end at 7:00 p.m., year-round. They are less frequent in winter.

Kure Beach

Kure Beach features a dozen charming hotels, motels, and inns. You can also rent one of the many available cottages. The beaches here are generally uncrowded, but several areas have lifeguards on duty. In addition, the pier, the oldest on the Atlantic coast, is conveniently located in the middle of town.

North Carolina Aquarium (all ages)

900 Loggerhead Road; (910) 458–8257; www.ncaquariums
.com. Open 9:00 a.m. to 5:00 p.m. daily. $$; free for children ages five and under.

Right away you'll find plenty to do here on Pleasure Island.
The first attraction you'll come to is the North Carolina Aquarium, one of three such aquariums on the North Carolina coast.
The aquarium is sure to draw your kids into the world of
ocean life. Here they'll see a shark tank that includes a
gigantic whale shark, where they can ask questions of
one of the divers while he's in the tank. Visitors also
get a chance to pick up a number of sea creatures
at the touch pool. This aquarium also features a
stingray exhibit, a turtle exhibit, a life-size whale
sculpture, and an alligator pond. There are
special educational programs including
films and presentations at the aquarium,
in addition to special field trips.

Fort Fisher State Historic Site (ages 5 and up)

1000 South Fort Fisher Boulevard; (910) 458–5538. Open 9:00 a.m. to
5:00 p.m. Monday through Saturday and 1:00 to 5:00 p.m. Sunday, April through October; 10:00 a.m. to 4:00 p.m. Tuesday through Saturday and 1:00 to 4:00 p.m. Sunday,
the rest of the year. Free.

Fort Fisher was one of the Confederacy's last major strongholds during the Civil War.
The site includes a monument commemorating the largest land–sea battle of the
war, which was fought in January 1865. Also at the earthen fort is a reconstructed
gun emplacement, and you can walk along an interpretive history trail. The fort's
museum features displays on the Confederate defense system, dioramas, an audiovisual show, and war artifacts. Picnic facilities are also available.

Where to Eat

Big Daddy's, 206 K Avenue; (910)
458–8622. Big Daddy offers steaks,
seafood, and more. $$

Jack Mackerel's Island Grill, 113 K
Avenue; (910) 458–7668. You'll find fun
island food and decor here. $$

Where to Stay

Admiral's Quarters Motel, 129 South
Fort Fisher Boulevard; (910) 458–5050.
This is a small motel with rooms and efficiencies near the pier by the ocean. $$

Blue Marlin Apartments and Cottages, 309 North Fort Fisher Boulevard;
(910) 458–5752. The Blue Marlin is a
nicely kept facility by the ocean. $$–$$$

Kure Keys Motel, 310 Fort Fisher Boulevard; (910) 458–5277. This is a very pretty oceanfront hotel. $$$

Palm Air Cottages, 133 Fort Fisher Boulevard; (910) 458–5269. Cottages have screened porches, plus there's a pool and picnic area. It is, however, one block from the beach. $$$

Sand Dunes Motel, 123 Fort Fisher Boulevard South; (800) 535–4984. You'll find clean rooms and efficiencies here as well as an oceanfront pool, which is a nice amenity. You can use their grills for cookouts, too. $$

Seven Seas Inn, 130 Fort Fisher Boulevard; (910) 458-8122. This is a pretty motel with rooms and efficiencies, oceanfront pool, covered gazebos, and a picnic area with grills. $$$$

For long-term rentals, try one of the following:

Beach Front Vacations, Inc, 129 Fort Fisher Boulevard South; (800) 535–4984; www.beachfrontvacationsinc.com.

Island Realty, 325 Fort Fisher Boulevard North; (910) 458–8800.

For More Information

Town of Kure Beach, (910) 458–8434; www.visitkure.com.

Carolina Beach

Carolina Beach is just north of Kure Beach on Highway 421.

Carolina Beach offers a number of amenities for a fun-filled beach vacation, and it's about a twenty-minute drive south of Wilmington down Highway 421. It's full of a variety of natural areas but offers the thrill of water slides and amusement rides, too.

Jubilee Amusement Park (all ages)

1000 North Lake Park Boulevard; (910) 458–9017; www.jubileepark.com. **Hours vary according to weather and season. Fees vary by activity.**

The Jubilee Amusement Park, located on Highway 421 immediately after you cross the bridge from the north, offers dozens of exciting rides, including a Ferris wheel, a merry-go-round, go-karts, and water slides.

Carolina Beach State Park

Located at State Road 1628 and Dow Road; (910) 458–7770. Campsite rental ($) available.

You'll find plenty of hotels, motels, and cottages for rent at Carolina Beach, but you can also camp at Carolina Beach State Park, located on the waterway on the west side of the island. You can fish here, but no swimming is allowed, although public beach access is only a few minutes away. The park is one of the world's few natural habitats of the Venus flytrap, a unique carnivorous plant that traps and dissolves insects that land on its leaves. There are several nature trails in the park, and markers will help you guide your family through them. Picnic facilities are available during daylight hours. Paddleboats and kayaks are also available for rent at the park lake.

Amazing
North Carolina Facts

The rare Venus flytrap is merely the most interesting of six different species of insect-eating plants you and the kids can see at Carolina Beach State Park. The Venus flytrap possesses a nervous system that is similar to that of a mammal. Charles Darwin pronounced it "the most wonderful plant in the world."

Where to Eat

The Ocean Grill, 1211 South Lake Park Boulevard; (910) 458–2000. Once this was the Carolina Beach Pier. Now a tiki bar is located on the ocean just beyond this good restaurant. $$

Squigley's Ice Cream & Treats, 208 South Lake Park Boulevard; (910) 458–8779. This fun ice cream parlor serves more flavors than you can imagine.

Where to Stay

Atlantic Towers, 1615 South Lake Park Boulevard; (800) 232–2440. This is an eleven-story tower of condos. It has a video game room and pool. $$$$

Golden Sands Motel, 1211 South Lake Park Boulevard; (888) 458–8334; www.goldensandscarolinabeach.com.

Here is a list of larger Carolina Beach Realtors:

Atlantic Shores Real Estate, 9 South Lake Park Boulevard, Suite A3; (800) 289–0028; www.atlanticshoresrealty.com.

Beach Girls Realty, 245 North Lake Park Boulevard; (910) 458-5611.

Beacon House Cottages, 714 Carolina Beach Avenue North; (877) 232–2666; www.beaconhouseinnb-b.com.

Bowman & Associates Real Estate, 1420 South Lake Park Boulevard; (866) 458–6363; www.annbowman.com.

Bryant Real Estate, 1401 North Lake Park Boulevard; (800) 994–5222; www.bryantre.com.

Bullard Realty, 1404 South Lake Park Boulevard; (800) 327–5863.

Cabana Suites, 222 Carolina Beach Avenue, North; (800) 333-8499.

Carolina Beach Realty, 1009 B-3 North Lake Park Boulevard; (910) 458–4444.

Century 21 Castle Realty, 1006 South Lake Park Boulevard; (800) 360–8225; www.century21castlerealty.com.

Coast Walk Vacation Rentals, 607 North Lake Park Boulevard; (910) 458–0868.

Gardner Realty, P.O. Box 2125, Carolina Beach, 28428; (910) 458–8503.

North Pier Ocean Villas, 1800 Canal Drive; (800) 476–1589 www.northpiervillas.com.

United Beach Vacations, Inc., 1001 North Lake Park Boulevard; (910) 458–9073.

Walker Realty, 501 North Lake Park Boulevard; (910) 458–3388.

Wilmington

Wilmington is the largest and fastest-growing city on North Carolina's coast and offers dozens of attractions for people of all ages. From the large historic downtown district to the Intracoastal Waterway, the city is full of arts, recreation, and just plain fun, whether you are here for a day or for a week. The Wilmington area has been home to many famous people, including NBA superstar Michael Jordan, television journalists David Brinkley and Charles Kuralt, singer Sammy Davis Jr., and more. The city has come to be known as "Hollywood East." Hundreds of feature films and television shows have been made in the area, including *Firestarter, Ironweed, Muppets in Manhattan, I Know What You Did Last Summer, Dawson's Creek,* and *One Tree Hill.* Tours are available at the EUE/Screen Gems Studios the largest studio east of Hollywood. And if you're lucky, you might find yourself with a chance to be an extra or to meet a star from the "other Hollywood."

Tregembo Animal Park (all ages)
5811 Carolina Beach Road; (910) 392–3604; www.tregemboanimalpark.com. Open 10:00 a.m. to 5:00 p.m. daily. $–$$; children under two are admitted free.

About 10 miles north of Carolina Beach you can treat your kids to a trip to the Tregembo Animal Park. The zoo includes more than seventy different animals in five acres of forestlike surroundings. You'll see zebra, baboons, monkeys, exotic birds, a Siberian tiger, and a camel. The zoo has a gift shop and plenty of concessions as well. Two small museums feature mounted animals, fossils, arrowheads, and World War II memorabilia.

EUE/Screen Gems Studios (all ages)
1223 North Twenty-third Street; (910) 343–3500; www.screengemsstudio.com. Tours offered on weekends and occasionally on weekdays depending on production schedules. $$$.

Take a tour of the largest full-service motion picture facility in the United States east of California. Since 1984, EUE/Screen Gems Studios has turned out hundreds of films, television shows, and commercials. Nine sound stages and support services can accommodate virtually any imaginable production. The tour on foot includes a visit to *Dawson's Creek* and *One Tree Hill* sets.

USS *North Carolina* (ages 3 and up)
Located at US 17/74 and 76/421; (910) 251–5797; www.battleshipnc.com. Open daily from 8:00 a.m. to 8:00 p.m., mid-May to mid-September and 8:00 a.m. to 5:00 p.m. the rest of the year. $–$$; free for children five and under.

The most popular tourist attraction in Wilmington is the USS *North Carolina,* located across the Cape Fear River just west of downtown. Known as "The Showboat," the battleship was commissioned in 1941, served in all twelve major Pacific naval campaigns in World War II, and earned fifteen battle stars. It was the most powerful battleship in the world at the time. In 1961 the ship was carefully restored, and today it stands majestically as a memorial in honor of the nearly 10,000 North Carolinians who gave their lives during the war. You will probably want to spend at least two hours exploring the ship's nine decks, including the mess deck and galley, sick bay, and engine room. The kids will be amazed at the size of the 16-inch guns that trim the deck. They certainly will want to take a peek through the captain's periscope for a view of downtown. A look at the barbershop and living quarters provides an interesting perspective on military life in the 1940s. Signs, pictures, and push-button tapes will guide you through the ship. A picnic area and snack bar are located nearby.

Greenfield Park and Gardens (ages 5 and up) 🏃 🚣

1510 Third Street; (910) 341–7855. The park generally is open daily during daylight hours. Free.

If you make it to Wilmington in the spring or summer, take the 5-mile scenic drive around Greenfield Park and Gardens, located south of the USS *North Carolina* on US 421. Greenfield Lake is the recreation center of the 180-acre park, but spend a little time cruising through the cypress and dogwood trees. In the spring the park comes alive with color as azaleas and roses begin to bloom. At the lake you can bring along a picnic lunch, rent a canoe or paddleboat, or take a hike down the 4-mile walking trail.

Rides on **the River**

Captain J. N. Maffitt Cruises, located at Riverfront Park at the corner of Market and Water Streets, offers taxi rides to the USS *North Carolina* memorial ($). Rides run every half hour, except 11:30 a.m. and 3:30 p.m. You can also catch a boat there for an informative sight-seeing cruise on the Cape Fear River. *Henrietta III* cruises depart from Water and Dock Streets April through December. This narrated tour ($–$$) takes you about 8 miles down the river. It's a good way to get a look at the historic buildings and learn about the importance of the port town. Tours are offered at 2:30 p.m. Tuesday through Sunday. An additional 11:00 a.m. cruise is offered during the summer. Call Cape Fear Riverboats at (800) 676–0162 or visit www.cfrboats.com for more information.

Moores Creek National Battlefield (ages 5 and up)

200 Moores Creek Road; (910) 283–5591. Open 9:00 a.m. to 5:00 p.m. daily. Free.

Another educational afternoon trip to take if you're staying in Wilmington is to the Moores Creek National Battlefield, a thirty-minute drive north on Highway 210, off US 421. This site commemorates the first Revolutionary War battle fought in North Carolina in February 1776. Markers and monuments lead you through a self-guiding trail and help explain the battle. A visitor center includes a small museum with photos, an audiovisual program, and war memorabilia. The site is also a nice place for a picnic.

Downtown Wilmington

Before you take on downtown Wilmington, you'll want to get hold of a guide map at the visitor center at the corner of Third and Princess Streets or by calling (800) 222–4757. You can either take a riverfront walking tour or see most of downtown during a driving tour in a single day. Trolley tours are available by calling (910) 763–4483.

Wilmington Railroad Museum (ages 5 and up)

501 Nutt Street; (910) 763–2634; www.wilmingtonrailroadmuseum.org. Open 10:00 a.m. to 5:00 p.m. Monday through Saturday and 1:00 to 5:00 p.m. Sunday, April through October. It's closed Monday the rest of the year. $; free for children under age two.

All aboard for the Wilmington Railroad Museum, where you'll find that the railroad is almost as important as the river is in this port town. The museum features dozens of exhibits from the railroads, dating back to 1840, and model railroad displays. You can board a steam locomotive and a caboose outside the museum. There's also an interactive children's Thomas the Tank Engine play area.

Cotton Exchange (all ages)

321 North Front Street; (910) 343–9896. Most shops are open 10:00 a.m. to 5:30 p.m. Monday through Saturday and 1:00 to 5:00 p.m. Sunday.

You can walk from the Wilmington Railroad Museum down Front Street to the Cotton Exchange, which features more than thirty unique restaurants and shops in well-preserved, century-old buildings. The shops once served as warehouses for the former cotton company, but now you'll find specialty shops, clothing stores, and antiques.

Bellamy Mansion (ages 8 and up)

503 Market Street; (910) 251–3700; www.bellamymansion.org. Tours are on the hour from 10:00 a.m. to 5:00 p.m. Tuesday through Saturday and 1:00 to 5:00 p.m. Sunday. $$.

Bellamy is one of the most significant historic homes in North Carolina. It's an excellent example of antebellum architecture that was built by free and enslaved black artisans for John Dillard Bellamy, a nineteenth-century physician, planter, and business leader. After the fall of Fort Fisher in 1865, Federal troops commandeered the house as their headquarters. Today it is a museum that focuses on history and the design arts as well as historic preservation.

Burgin Wright House (ages 5 and up)
224 Market Street; (910) 762–0570. Open 10:00 a.m. to 4:00 p.m. Tuesday through Saturday, except July 4, Thanksgiving, Christmas, and New Year's. $–$$.

Built in 1770, this three-story home is an example of the gentleman's town house of the times. Its huge foundation is constructed of stone from the city's old jailhouse. As you walk through the home, you'll see a collection of lovely eighteenth-century furniture and decorations.

The Zebulon Latimer House (ages 5 and up)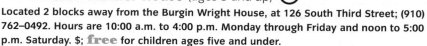
Located 2 blocks away from the Burgin Wright House, at 126 South Third Street; (910) 762–0492. Hours are 10:00 a.m. to 4:00 p.m. Monday through Friday and noon to 5:00 p.m. Saturday. $; free for children ages five and under.

The furniture in this 1852 home is the original furniture that belonged to this prominent merchant and his family. While it isn't the oldest home in the area, it is unique because of its Italianate Revival construction. The house is headquarters for the Lower Cape Fear Historical Society, which conducts tours of the homes in the historic district.

Cameron Art Museum (ages 5 and up)
3201 South Seventeenth Street; (910) 395–5999; www.cameronartmuseum.com. Open 10:00 a.m. to 5:00 p.m. Tuesday through Sunday with extended hours until 9:00 p.m. on Friday. $–$$; free for children ages four and under.

Your next stop is a cultural one, and just a few blocks down Orange Street. Cameron Art Museum is a complex of three distinctive buildings dating back to the early 1800s. The museum's main attraction is a collection of three centuries of work by North Carolina artists. You can peruse collections of paintings, Jugtown pottery, and sculpture, all of which were created in the state. In addition, the museum attracts collections from all over the world. The joy is that you never know what you'll find here from trip to trip.

Children's Museum of Wilmington (ages 1 to 11)
116 Orange Street; (910) 254–3534; www.playwilmington.org. Open 10:00 a.m. to 5:00 p.m. Monday through Friday, 10:00 a.m. to 6:00 p.m. Saturday, and 1:00 to 6:00 p.m. Sunday. $; free for infants under age 1.

This hands-on playspace features new state-of-the art exhibit areas themed on a three-ring circus, a pirate ship and port area, and international diner and grocery. Other features include a toddler area, animal adventures, an art room, and a science lab.

Cape Fear Serpentarium (all ages)

20 Orange Street; (910) 762–1669; www.capefearserpentarium.com. Open 11:00 a.m. to 5:00 p.m. Monday through Friday and 11:00 a.m. to 6:00 p.m. Saturday and Sunday. $$.

If you think this attraction sounds a little creepy, you're right. The Cape Fear Serpentarium houses the world's largest collection of bushmasters as well as other reptiles from all over the world. Here you'll see snakes, crocodiles, dragons, and more. It also includes **The Africa Museum** that displays a fantastic collection of African tribal artifacts, including a real voodoo witch doctor's ceremonial costume, tribal swords, spears, and ritual objects.

Ghost Walk of Old Wilmington (ages 6 and up)

Riverfront at Market & Water Streets; (910) 794–1866; www.hauntedwilmington.com. Offered at 6:30 p.m. Tuesday through Saturday in November and March, and Thursday through Saturday, December through February, and at 8:30 p.m. nightly during daylight saving time. $$$.

Offered by actors who fancy themselves ghost hunters, the ghost walk takes participants on a journey into the depths of Old Wilmington. From creepy alleyways to the windy riverfront, you'll hear tales of pirates and cut-throats who once terrorized this port city. Homes and landmarks, beneath centuries-old live oaks with Spanish moss dangling from their limbs bring dismal accounts of poor lost souls.

Cape Fear Museum of History and Science (ages 5 and up)

814 Market Street; (910) 341–7450; www.capefearmuseum.com. Open 9:00 a.m. to 5:00 p.m. Tuesday through Saturday (also open Monday from Memorial Day through Labor Day) and 1:00 to 5:00 p.m. Sunday. $; kids ages two or younger get in free.

Another one of Wilmington's big draws for families is the Cape Fear Museum. A 21-foot scale replica of the Wilmington waterfront and a 31-foot diorama are only two of the hundreds of exhibits at this special museum. The museum tells the story of the region from prehistoric times to the present in Waves and Currents: The Lower Cape Fear Story, a 600-square-foot exhibit that shows the development of this part of the coast. You'll also discover special interactive programs for children, videos, the Michael Jordan Discovery Gallery, and more. Many of the programs offered at the museum change from time to time, but you can call for more information.

Where to Eat

Chris's Restaurant, 853 South Seventeenth Street; (910) 763–1791. Greek and Italian are on the menu here. $$

Elijah's, located in Chandler's Wharf at 2 Ann Street; (910) 343–1448. This is one of Wilmington's better casual restaurants, featuring seafood and more standard American cuisine. $$

Hollywood East Cinema Grill, 4402 Shipyard Boulevard; (910) 792–1084; www.hollywoodeastcinemagrill.com. Simple fare, sandwiches, burgers, and such is offered along with fairly current films. $

Middle & McDaniel Restaurant & Creamery, 614 South College Road; (910) 793–9994. Family-style seafood, salads, and homestyle meals are offered here, but save room for dessert. $

Paddy's Hollow, located in the Cotton Exchange at 321 North Front Street; (910) 762–4354. With its cobblestone walk and antique brick this friendly restaurant has more turn-of-the-century atmosphere than you can imagine. $$

The Pilot House, located in Chandler's Wharf at 2 Ann Street; (910) 343–0200. This is another casual restaurant over-looking the Cape Fear River. It serves good, Southern-style food. $$

Wilson's Restaurant, 4925 New Centre Drive; (910) 793–0999; www.wilsons restaurant.com. Wilson's is more than a restaurant, offering live music, a game room, and more.

Where to Stay

You might find deciding where to stay in Wilmington a little more difficult than it is for the rest of the coast. There are simply a lot of choices. But skipping the chain hotels, here are a few possibilities:

The Carolinian Inn, 2916 Market Street; (800) 528-1234; www.thecarolinianinn .com. Featuring sixty rooms, this inn will provide a comfortable stay. $$$

Graystone Inn, 100 South Third Street; (910) 763–2000. One of the most highly recommended B&Bs in the city, the four-star inn welcomes children over the age of twelve. $$$$

The Greentree Inn, 5025 Market Street; (910) 799–6001. Children stay **free** at this inn, which is within walking distance of the beach and restaurants. It, of course, has a pool, too. $$–$$$

Wrightsville Beach

Wrightsville Beach is a family community that has become a popular meeting place for reunions or extended-family vacations. It's quieter than most, and a beautiful 5-mile stretch of white beach has been well preserved. The area offers fine hotels, motels, apartments, and cottages. The village also offers a number of delightful restaurants and shops. Johnny Mercer's Pier and several marinas will give you the opportunity for fishing, but if you come here you'll probably be charmed into just relaxing.

Airlie Gardens (ages 5 and up)

300 Airlie Road; (910) 798–7700; www.airliegardens.org. Open 9:00 a.m. to 5:00 p.m. daily with some extended hours for events and peak seasons. $$; children ages nine or younger get in **free.**

If you're heading from Wilmington to Wrightsville Beach, take an hour or so to visit Airlie Gardens, located just off US 74/76. The 5-mile scenic drive features extensive azalea and camellia plantings, truly a sight to behold during the month of April. You will also see a variety of rare evergreen trees, stately live oaks, well-kept lawns, and lakes as you make your journey through the park.

Where to Eat

Blockade Runner, 275 Wynick Boulevard; (910) 256–2251. You can order off the menu, but the Blockade Runner is known for its buffets. $$

The Oceanic Restaurant, 703 South Lumina Avenue; (910) 256–5551. Great views are afforded at this oceanfront restaurant. Prime rib and seafood are the specialties. $$

South Beach Grill, 100 South Lumina Avenue; (910) 256–4646. Enjoy a great burger on the patio for lunch or visit in the evening for unique, eclectic, regional cuisine for dinner. $–$$

Where to Stay

Back on the beach in Wrightsville, your accommodation choice should probably be a cottage from one of the local Realtors:

Bryant Real Estate, 1001 Lumina Avenue; (910) 256–3764.

Intracoastal Realty, 605 Causeway Drive; (800) 822–4588.

Laney Real Estate, 803-G South College Road, Wilmington; (800) 733–1428; www.laneyrealestate.com.

Here are some other choices if you choose not to rent:

Blockade Runner Resort, 275 Waynick Boulevard; (800) 541–1161; www .blockade-runner.com. This popular resort has all waterfront rooms and several water activities on site. $$$$

The Harbor Inn, 701 Causeway Drive; (888) 507–9402. Although it's not on the beach, this is a nice place with a pool, access to the beach, and a short dock for fishing or watching the boats come in. $$$

One South Lumina, 1 South Lumina Avenue; (800) 421–3255. This beachfront hotel is within walking distance to stores and other amenities and offers large rooms and suites. $$$–$$$$

Station 1, 95 South Lumina Avenue; (800) 635–1408. Leasing a condo or town house here gives you access to tennis and basketball courts, a pool, and a barbecue pit. $$–$$$

Surf Suites, 711 South Lumina Avenue; (910) 256–2275. All forty-six rooms here have kitchens, and it's AAA approved. $$$$

Waterway Lodge, 7246 Wrightsville Avenue; (800) 677–3771. Bike rentals are available from this pet-friendly lodge. Rooms and condos are offered, and kids under twelve stay **free.** $$$$

For More Information

Cape Fear Coast Convention and Visitors Bureau, (800) 222–4757; www.cape-fear.nc.us.

Topsail Island

From Wilmington, take US 17 north to Highway 50 to reach Topsail Island.

You'll find that the beaches on Topsail Island are still largely uncrowded, but you'll also discover many other fun things to do on this island, located midway between Jacksonville and Wilmington. The island got its name from merchant sailors who frequently saw pirates hiding in the marshes on the west side of the island. Tall foliage hid the ships, but the sailors could see the tops of the sails, hence the name Topsail (pronounced topsil) Island.

Surf City

Surf City is the commercial center of Topsail Island, but the beauty of the beaches has been well preserved. One of the last swinging bridges in North Carolina will take you across the Intracoastal Waterway.

Loggerhead **Turtle Exhibit**

While visiting much of North Carolina's coast, you may be surprised to wake up one morning to find that a loggerhead turtle has visited your beachfront cottage and nested there. The Topsail Turtle Project has been established to help protect this endangered species, which nests along Topsail Island's 26 miles of beach from May through August. Volunteers and the Topsail Kiwanis Club have established a Loggerhead Turtle Exhibit at the Surf City town hall, on Highway 210. The exhibit explains the life cycle of the turtle and includes nesting replicas and photographs. You'll also learn how to help preserve the reptile at the **Karen Beasley Sea Turtle Rescue and Rehabilitation Center,** 822 Carolina Avenue, Topsail Beach, where you will actually come face to face with injured turtles. The exhibit is open 8:00 a.m. to 5:00 p.m. daily. Call (910) 328–1000 for more information.

Topsail Island Trading Company
201 New River Drive, Surf City; (910) 328–1905.

You'll find an interesting blend of gifts, beach supplies, and other goodies. Captain Ed, an entertaining mannequin playing the piano, will greet you and the kids. You'll want to try one of the more than thirty flavors of fudge and a big glass of freshly squeezed lemonade. The shop also stocks a healthy supply of North Carolina–made products from crafts to confections. Here you can also arrange a relaxing boat tour of the Intracoastal Waterway. *Kristy's Kruiser II,* a 33-foot pontoon boat, is ready to take you on forty-five- or ninety-minute tours ($$$), where you're likely to see osprey, pelicans, egrets, and porpoises in their natural habitats. Children under age two ride **free.** Trips leave at 2:00, 4:00, 6:00, and 8:00 p.m. Call (910) 328–8687 for more information on boat tours.

Where to Eat

Max's Pizza, 602 Roland Avenue #A; (910) 328–2158. We list Max's because it's usually easy to get everybody to go along with having pizza. $

Mollie's Casual Dining, 107 North Shore Drive; (910) 328–0505. For a casual dinner, breakfast, or lunch head to Mollie's. $

Southside Seafood Restaurant, 209 North New River Drive; (910) 328–0803. You will need to dress a little for Southside, but unlike some other area seafood restaurants many dishes here are made from local catches. $$–$$$

Where to Stay

Here is a list of Surf City Realtors:

A Beach Place Realty, 106 North Topsail Drive; (910) 328–2522.

Access Realty, 513 Roland Avenue; (910) 328–4888.

Anchor Real Estate, 205-D Roland Avenue; (910) 328–5011.

Beach Properties, 302 North New River Drive; (800) 753–2975.

Bryson and Associates, 809 Roland Avenue; (800) 326–0747.

Century 21 Action, 518 Roland Avenue; (910) 328–2511.

Island Real Estate, 405 Roland Avenue; (800) 622–6886.

Topsail Realty, Inc., 712 South Anderson Boulevard, Topsail Beach; (910) 328–5241.

Ward Realty Corp., 116 South Topsail Drive; (910) 328–3221.

Topsail Beach

Topsail Beach is the southernmost community on Topsail Island. It's accessible only from the north via Highway 50.

Topsail Beach is the least crowded area on the island, but there are two fishing piers and a quaint shopping district. Stop in at **Island Treasures,** a different sort of souvenir shop in a rustic building on the south end. It's a good place to browse for gifts or for the kids to pick up a game or water toy. The shop also features a Christmas corner and North Carolina art, pottery, and porcelain.

Topsail Island Museum (all ages)
720 Channel Boulevard; (910) 328–1038. Open 2:00 to 4:00 p.m. Tuesday Thursday, Friday, and Saturday, April through October. **Free.**

In the community center you can visit the Topsail Island Museum where Operation Bumblebee, a U.S. missile project from the 1940s, and the history of the island are explained. Videotapes, operation displays, and World War II artifacts help depict this island's history.

Where to Eat

Breezeway Restaurant, 636 Channel Boulevard; (910) 328–7751. Breezeway offers mainly seafood but has other items as well. Check out the seafood lasagna. $$

Where to Stay

Breezeway Motel and Restaurant, 636 Channel Boulevard; (910) 328–7751. This is the home of the famous restaurant by the same name. $$

Sea Path Realty, 920 South Anderson Avenue; (910) 328–4201.

Topsail Motel, 1195 North Anderson Boulevard; (910) 328–3381. Your private front porch is practically on the beach here. $$$

Amazing
North Carolina Facts

In the 1940s Topsail Beach played a significant role in the origination of the U.S. space program. Tall, white concrete structures, used as observation towers during Operation Bumblebee, still stand. Operation Bumblebee was a secret U.S. Navy project that resulted in the development of the ramjet and technology that allowed human beings to break the sound barrier. These findings also led to the development of the U.S. space program and other advances in technology. The former test launchpad has been converted into a patio, and in 1993 the building where the test rockets were assembled was converted into the town's community center and a museum.

North Topsail Beach

Head north from Surf City on Highway 210, and you'll find North Topsail Beach.

This community is noted for natural diversity. It was once a separate island, but time slowly turned the sea into land. Now you'll find picturesque marshes home to egrets, herons, and other graceful creatures, against a backdrop of dense maritime forests. Just minutes away are beautiful sand dunes and roomy beaches.

Where to Stay

Villa Capriani, 790 New River Inlet Road; (800) 934–2400. This is a very picturesque facility, offering villas with an array of amenities. Several pools and tennis courts are on the premises. $$$$

For More Information

The Greater Topsail Area Chamber of Commerce & Tourism, (800) 626–2780; www.topsailcoc.com.

Pender United Tourism, (800) 626–2780; www.visitpender.com.

Jacksonville

From Sneads Ferry take Highway 172 north to Highway 24.

Camp Lejeune (all ages)

Jacksonville is home to Camp Lejeune, a 110,000-acre U.S. Marine Corps base. There aren't any formal tourist attractions on the base, but you can get a glimpse of how the Marines live and work by visiting the site. You'll need to present a valid driver's license, automobile registration, and proof of insurance at the information center on Highway 24 to be admitted onto the base. You'll want to take the kids to the **Beirut Memorial,** located just east of the camp on US 17. The large granite memorial was built in honor of the 273 American Marines, sailors, and soldiers who were killed in

Shrimp **Festival**

The town of Sneads Ferry, located on the mainland on Highway 172, is home to the annual **Sneads Ferry Shrimp Festival.** Since 1971 the community has sponsored this two-day event, usually held the second weekend in August. Here the whole family will enjoy a parade, carnival, arts and crafts, historical displays, and, of course, lots of fresh shrimp. Call (910) 327–4911 for more information.

the 1983 attack on the U.S. barracks in Lebanon. Along Lejeune Boulevard, each Bradford pear tree represents the loss of one life from U.S. involvement in Lebanon and in the 1983 U.S.-led invasion of Grenada. For more information about the base's self-guided tour, call (910) 451–7426.

Where to Stay

The Liberty Inn, 1723 Lejeune Boulevard; (910) 353–3336. This is a pretty inn and surprisingly inexpensive, with rooms and efficiencies plus the added bonus of a game room. $$

Triangle Motor Inn, 246 South Wilmington Highway; (910) 455–4923. This is an older but updated facility. $$

For More Information

Onslow County Tourism, (800) 932–2144; www.onslowcountytourism.com.

Swansboro

From Jacksonville take Highway 24 east to get to the Swansboro area.

Worthy Is the Lamb (ages 5 and up)
Across the bridge from Swansboro at the Crystal Coast Amphitheater, 246 Amphitheater Drive; (800) 662–5960; www.worthyisthelamb.org. Performances are held roughly June through August at 8:30 p.m. Thursday, Friday, and Saturday and in September at 8:00 p.m. Friday and Saturday. $$–$$$; children under five are free but might have trouble sitting through the production.

For a moving, unforgettable experience, take the kids to see *Worthy Is the Lamb,* presented each summer at the Crystal Coast Amphitheater. The two-hour play is an inspirational, musical drama that documents the life of Christ, from his mission to his crucifixion and resurrection. The spectacular set, a replica of the city of Jerusalem, is placed in front of a gorgeous, natural backdrop—the scenic White Oak River, representing the Sea of Galilee.

Bear Island and Hammocks Beach State Park (ages 3 and up)
1572 Hammocks Beach Road; (910) 326–4881. **Access via ferry from dock off Highway 24, about 4 miles south of Swansboro. Ferry leaves every half hour from 9:30 a.m. to 5:30 p.m. daily. $.**

Also located a short drive and ferry ride from Swansboro is Bear Island and Hammocks Beach State Park. This isn't an expedition for softies. Bear Island's 892 acres constitute a naturally preserved area with huge shifting sand dunes, a maritime forest, and marshlands. A primitive family camping area is available, or you can bring supplies for a picnic and take a swim from the unspoiled beaches. If you want to take in the natural beauty of the island, the interpretive displays at the ferry dock will get you started on one of the nature trails.

Where to Eat

Church Street Deli and Coffee House, 105 Church Street; (910) 326–7572. Of course the kids aren't old enough to start a coffee habit, but they can get hand-dipped ice cream here. $

Paddy's, 108-A West Corbett Avenue; (910) 326–8800. This Irish-style pub is fun for children and adults. $

Yana's Ye Olde Drug Store and Restaurant, 119 Front Street; (910) 326–5501. Play a tune on the jukebox and check out the pictures of stars from the 1950s on the walls. Yana offers a lot of variety for breakfast and lunch. $

Pine Knoll Shores

From Swansboro take Highway 24 to Highway 58 and cross Bogue Sound.

Theodore Roosevelt Natural Area (ages 3 and up)
1 Roosevelt Drive. Open 9:00 a.m. to 5:00 p.m. Monday through Saturday and 1:00 to 5:00 p.m. Sunday. Free.

Just across the bridge from Swansboro is a long, slender island with tons of fun waiting. This small community is home to the Theodore Roosevelt Natural Area and the North Carolina Aquarium, one of three located along North Carolina's coast. The area is dedicated primarily to preservation, but you'll also find a hiking trail and observation towers.

North Carolina Aquarium (all ages)
1 Roosevelt Drive; (252) 247–4003; www.ncaquariums .com. Open 9:00 a.m. to 5:00 p.m. daily; closed Thanksgiving, Christmas, and New Year's Day. $; free for children under six.

At the aquarium you'll dive deep into a sea of exhibits, programs, and a live, hands-on display. This aquarium features live loggerhead turtles, colorful fish tanks, and

an open tank where the kids can pick up crabs and other sea creatures. It's okay—they won't hurt you. The aquarium also sponsors presentations on-site and at various locations throughout the area. In the Living Shipwreck exhibit divers answer questions. Visitors get a chance to meet ocean creatures, alligators, and others face to face. Outside, the aquarium has two nature trails, a marsh overlook where you can bird watch, a fossil hunt, a beautiful bronze sculpture, and a reflecting pool.

Where to Stay

Atlantis Lodge, 123 Salter Path Road; (800) 682–7057. Oceanfront suites with efficiency kitchens are offered at the pet-friendly location. It includes a waterfall pool and lounge with pool and table tennis.

Atlantic Beach

From Pine Knoll Shores, take Highway 58 to Atlantic Beach.

Atlantic Beach is a little more popular than some of the other beach communities on the southern coast. It's a good central location for active families looking to fill their vacation with day trips and other adventures. Atlantic Beach is host to a sand-sculpture contest, usually held the first weekend in May, and the Carolina Kite Fest in October.

Fort Macon State Park (ages 3 and up)

Located at the east end of Highway 58; (252) 726–3775; www.ils.unc.edu/parkproject /visit. The park, including picnic facilities and bathhouse, is open generally during daylight hours. Free.

Fort Macon State Park is one of the most popular attractions here. The fort is a massive, five-sided fortress constructed in 1826 to protect the region against foreign attacks. It was seized from Union forces at the start of the Civil War and changed hands several times over the course of the war. Fort Macon served as a federal prison for nearly a decade after the Civil War and was garrisoned for use during World War II. Rangers present programs on a daily basis during vacation seasons, including a deafening musket-firing demonstration. They also conduct tours of the fort, or you can tour it yourself with the help of push-button tapes and mannequin displays. Some parts of the fort, including the commandant's quarters, have been restored to their wartime condition.

Where to Stay

Here are Atlantic Beach's larger realty companies:

Atlantic Beach Realty, #14 Causeway Shopping Center; (800) 786–7368.

Atlantic Sun Properties, 205 Atlantic Beach Causeway; (252) 808–2786.

Bluewater GMAC Vacation Rentals, 311-C Atlantic Beach Causeway; (866) 467–3105.

Cannon & Gruber Realtors, 509 Atlantic Beach Causeway; (800) 317–2866.

Century 21 Coastal Properties, 610 Atlantic Beach Causeway; (800) 849–1995

Coldwell-Banker Spectrum Properties, 515 Atlantic Beach Causeway; (800) 334–6390.

Ocean Resorts, 2111 West Fort Macon Road; (800) 682–3702.

Realty World-First Coast Realty, 407 Atlantic Beach Causeway; (800) 972–8899.

Sunny Shores, 520 Salter Path Road; (800) 626–3113.

Tetterton Management Group, 513 Morehead Avenue; (252) 247–3101.

Whispering Sands Realty, 212 West Fort Macon Road; (252) 247–3429.

Your other choices, if you choose not to rent, include:

Atlantic Beach Villas, 715 West Fort Macon Road; (800) 438–6493. One- to three-bedroom condos with both indoor and outdoor pools, a private boardwalk to the beach, and recreation room are offered here.

Beach Vacation Properties, 1904 East Fort Macon Road; (800) 334–2667. This is a well-known establishment with lots of amenities, such as a game room, a restaurant, a playground, laundry facilities, and more. $$$$

Bogue Shores Suites, 1918 West Fort Macon Road; (800) 613-5043. Bogue Shores Suites is located soundside and will accommodate small families. $$$.

Oceanana Family Resort, 700 East Fort Macon Road; (252) 726–4111. More homey than fancy, the resort features two- and three-bedroom apartments, a **free** breakfast of fruit and pastries served by the pool daily, and occasional watermelon parties. You can relax on the oceanfront lawn while the kids play on the playground. $$$

Seahawk Motor Lodge, 105 Salter Path Road; (800) 682–6898. This is a small, very nice facility with rooms, cottages, and horseback-riding packages. $$$

Seafood Galore

The lovely waterfront community of Morehead City is the host of the **North Carolina Seafood Festival,** held the first weekend in October. Here you'll be treated to seafood galore and can enjoy the flounder-flinging contest, as well as live entertainment and plenty of games and activities for the kids. Activities are held mainly on the waterfront, but the county abounds with events, including sailboat and road races, and tennis and golf tournaments. Call (252) 726–6273 for more information.

Morehead City

Just north of Atlantic Beach across the bridge on U.S. Highway 70 on the mainland, you come to Morehead City.

Carteret County Museum of History and Art (ages 5 and up)
100 Wallace Drive; (252) 247–7533. Open 1:00 to 4:00 p.m. Tuesday through Saturday. Free.

Any time of year, be sure to see the Carteret County Museum of History and Art in Morehead City. The museum is a potpourri of changing exhibits, ranging from native artifacts to vintage clothing to war items to shells, and more.

The Crystal Coast Jamboree (all ages)
1311 Arendell Street; (866) 580–7469; www.crystalcoastjamboree.com. Schedule varies according to season. $$$–$$$$.

The jamboree presents a fun, Vegas-style variety show appropriate for the entire family. Song, dance, and performance from a variety of eras and genres creates a show and atmosphere that's fun for everyone.

Where to Eat

Anchor Inn Restaurant and Lounge, 2806 Arendell Street; (252) 726–2156. Located in the Best Western, this restaurant is a good place to get seafood and much more, including pasta and steak. $$

Mrs. Willis' Restaurant and Lounge, 3002 Bridges Street; (252) 726–3741.

This is an old local favorite with lots of homemade specialties served in a rustic atmosphere. $

Where to Stay

Morehead City is a great town for day trips while staying on the nearby coast. Accommodations at Atlantic Beach are more likely to suit families, but if you prefer more picturesque, quiet surroundings, here are a couple of suggestions:

Debra W. Ball Real Estate, Inc., 224 Brandywine Boulevard; (252) 808–2255.

Morehead Motor Inn, 3300 Arendell Street; (252) 726–5141.

For More Information

Carteret County Tourism Development Bureau, (800) 622–6278; www.nccoastchamber.com.

Beaufort

US 70 crosses the Beaufort Inlet from Morehead City to Beaufort.

Historic Beaufort (ages 5 and up)

Bus trips depart from Beaufort Historic Site, 138 Turner Street; (252) 728–5225; www.historicbeaufort.com. Tours are at 11:00 a.m. and 1:30 p.m. Monday, Wednesday, and Friday and at 11:00 a.m. Saturday from April through October. $$.

You'll want to spend some leisurely hours strolling the boardwalk in this picturesque waterfront town, or catch the big red double-decker bus for a tour of Historic Beaufort-by-the-Sea. Historic Beaufort Bus Tours will take you on a one-hour tour of North Carolina's third-oldest town, narrated by a guide dressed in eighteenth-century clothes.

Beaufort Historic Site (all ages)

138 Turner Street; (252) 728–5225. Guided tours are held at 10:00 and 11:30 a.m. and at 1:00 and 3:00 p.m. Monday through Saturday. $–$$; children under six are free.

If you can't catch a bus tour, guided tours and living-history demonstrations are offered at the Beaufort Historic Site. You'll see weavers working on antique looms and more. The site includes four homes built around the turn of the nineteenth century: The courthouse was built in 1796; the county jail was built in 1829; and the apothecary and doctor's office were built about 1859 and remained in use until as late as 1933. All buildings have been totally restored, and you'll see many authentic pieces of furniture and tools used at the time.

North Carolina Maritime Museum (ages 3 and up)

315 Front Street; (252) 728–7317. Open 9:00 a.m. to 5:00 p.m. Monday through Friday, 10:00 a.m. to 5:00 p.m. Saturday, and 1:00 to 5:00 p.m. Sunday; closed New Year's Day, Thanksgiving, and Christmas. Free.

The skill of the seafarers of yesteryear comes alive at the North Carolina Maritime Museum. The museum features full-size watercraft and displays that help you discover many of the mysteries of the sea. One exhibit highlights artifacts recovered from the shipwreck believed to be the former flagship of Blackbeard the pirate, the *Queen Anne's Revenge*. Artifacts, recovered from 25 feet of water by state underwater archaeologists with the aid of the museum, are being housed and conserved and prepared for exhibit here. At the **Harvey W. Watercraft Center,** located across the street, you can see how these wooden boats were made as skilled craftsworkers construct them in front of you. The museum also sponsors special programs throughout the year, including the Strange Seafood Exhibition and trips on a research vessel, where you can actually help collect and identify marine life. No admission is charged to the museum, but call ahead for information on special events and trips.

Mystery Harbour Cruise Ship (ages 5 and up)
Located on Front Street; (252) 728–2527. The narrated voyages are held three times daily from April through October. Call for departure times or other information. $$.

Beware! Stay alert at all times on board the *Mystery Harbour Cruise Ship*. You never know when a pirate might come aboard the vessel as you tour the harbor near Beaufort. The ninety-minute cruise begins at Front Street and takes you past historic places, Blackbeard's house, and the natural sites on the nearby islands. The mystery ship also provides great half-day fishing trips ($$–$$$) that are ideal for children and beginners. Fishing on calm waters means seasickness won't be a problem, and all equipment is provided for you. Fishing trips begin at 8:00 a.m. and end at noon.

Carrot Island Ferry Adventures (ages 5 and up)
Located on Orange Street; (252) 728–7555. Ferries leave every thirty minutes from 9:00 a.m. to 5:00 p.m. daily. $–$$.

Sometimes you can see the wild ponies of Carrot Island and Shackelford Banks grazing the shoreline from the Beaufort waterfront, but for a better look and to learn more you'll want to catch the ferry from Harpoon Willie's on Orange Street. Not only will you see the ponies, but you can also swim in the crystal-clear waters and hunt for shells along the white, sandy beach. The **Rachel Carson Estuarine Reserve,** which spans this chain of islands, offers occasional two-and-a-half-hour guided tours, including a Kid's Island Adventure. These point out various aspects of nature and maritime heritage and are conducted in addition to the ferry trips.

Cedar Island

The ferry to the Outer Banks leaves from the town of Cedar Island on the island of the same name. (It's about a forty-five-minute drive from Beaufort to Cedar Island. Take US 70 north to Highway 12, which crosses a bridge onto the island.) You'll want to be sure to call ahead and make reservations for this and all other toll ferries you plan to use. Reservations can be made up to thirty days in advance. For a complete ferry schedule or to make reservations, call (800) 773–1094. If you don't make reservations, the wait can be hours long. The trip to the Outer Banks is more than two hours, so be sure to have something for the kids to do.

Outer Banks/Cedar Island Stables (all ages)
120 Driftwood Drive; (252) 225–1185. $$$$.

If you have some time before you hop the ferry, you can spend it on horseback before you leave. Outer Banks/Cedar Island Stables offers horseback rides for children and adults, experts and novices. Experienced parents can lead their children on a half-hour beach ride.

Havelock

Heading back to the west from Beaufort on Highway 101, you come to Havelock.

Croatan National Forest (ages 5 and up)
Off US 70; (252) 638–5628. Sites and trails in the forest are generally open during daylight hours April through October. All facilities are free except camping sites ($).

Havelock is home to Cherry Point Marine Corps Air Station and is largely a retirement community. But you'll also find the 157,000-acre national forest bordering the Neuse River, which is home to deer, black bear, eagles, the endangered red-cockaded woodpecker, and a host of other creatures. The forest has a nice family campground, and you can hike, fish, and swim here. It's also home to the carnivorous Venus flytrap and several other rare plants.

Kenansville

Traveling from Havelock to Kenansville takes about two hours via US 17 from either Highway 58 or US 70. Take US 17 to Jacksonville and then U.S. Highway 258 to Highway 24 and head west.

Kenansville is located west of the Croatan National Forest in North Carolina's heartland, which includes more farmland than anything else.

Cowan Museum (ages 5 and up)
411 South Main Street; (910) 296–2149; www.cowanmuseum.com. Open 10:00 a.m. to 4:00 p.m. Tuesday through Saturday and 2:00 to 4:00 p.m. Sunday. Free.

You won't find a lot to do between Havelock and the small town of Kenansville, but the Cowan Museum makes for a good stop while you're on the road. Built in 1848, the Cowan Museum offers an interesting perspective on early American life. Hundreds of items, from tools to sewing machines, fill the museum's displays. Also on the grounds are a classic one-room schoolhouse and a blacksmith's shop.

Liberty Hall (ages 5 and up) 🏛
409 South Main Street; (910) 296–2175. Interpreters provide guided tours of the grounds 10:00 a.m. to 4:00 p.m. Tuesday through Saturday and 2:00 to 4:00 p.m. Sunday. $; children age five or under get in free.

Also on Highway 24 you'll find Liberty Hall, a plantation built for the Kenan family in the early 1800s. Here you can explore the main house, a restored example of antebellum architecture, where you will see two dining rooms (one for winter, one for summer), a wine cellar, and bedrooms, all of which have been fully furnished. You can also see the attached kitchen, carriage house, and smokehouse.

Other Things to See and Do
on the Southern Coast

- **Docksiders Gifts and Shells,** Topsail Island, (910) 328–1421
- **Patio Playground,** Topsail Island, (910) 328–6491
- **Spinnaker Surf and Sport,** Topsail Island, (910) 328–2311
- **Jungle Rapids,** Wrightsville Beach, (910) 791–0666
- **Springbrook Farms Trolley and Carriage Tours,** Wilmington, (910) 251–8889
- **Adventure Tours,** Wilmington, (910) 763–1785
- **Climb On,** Wilmington, (910) 794–8722
- **Carolina Beach Jungle Mini-Golf and Batting Cages,** Carolina Beach, (910) 458–8888
- **Blackbeard's Lair,** Surf City, (252) 328–4200
- **Professor Hackers Lost Treasure Golf & Raceway,** Atlantic Beach, (252) 247–3024

The
Northern
Coast

North Carolina's Northern Coast offers much more than the thrill of riding waves in the surf, an abundance of sunshine, and all the other amenities that come with a beach vacation. Here you'll also find rich history, intertwined with the present. The inland towns offer tours of majestic old homes and museums, while the islands in the area offer evidence of the early settlers' trials as they first began to settle the mysterious New World. At the turn of the twentieth century, coastal winds lured two brothers from Ohio to learn to fly. They are memorialized on Hatteras Island.

But don't forget to take advantage of the natural aspects of this area, where the land works in fragile balance with the sea. That sometimes angry sea once threat-

Jim's
TopPicks on the Northern Coast

1. Cape Hatteras Lighthouse, Buxton

2. Wright Brothers National Memorial, Kill Devil Hills

3. Jockey's Ridge State Park, Nags Head

4. *The Lost Colony,* Manteo

5. *Elizabeth II* State Historic Site, Manteo

6. Wild mustangs of Corolla

7. North Carolina Aquarium on Roanoke Island

8. Taking a ride on a ferry

9. Fishing from Nags Head Pier

10. Driving up Highway 12

THE NORTHERN COAST

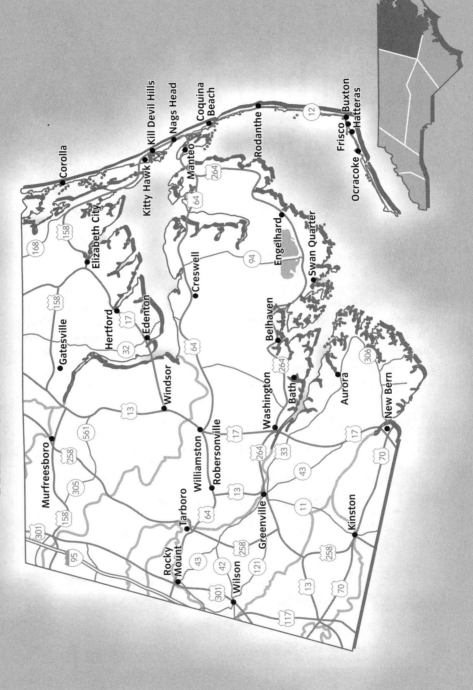

ened America's tallest lighthouse in this land of lighthouses. There is also a lot to learn about the ocean and the creatures that live in and around it. You'll find ample opportunity to observe nature and work with it through fishing and the educational programs available along the coast.

From Raleigh, U.S. Highway 64 is probably the easiest and most direct route to the Manteo and Nags Head areas. U.S. Highway 264 will give you a little different picture and is a more direct route to the Ocracoke area. Once you're here, finding your way around won't be much of a problem. U.S. Highway 17 runs the length of the coastal plain inland. Highway 12 runs through the 75 miles of Cape Hatteras National Seashore, which includes Ocracoke, Hatteras, and Bodie Islands.

Kinston

We'll start in the southern part of the Northern Coast region, at the intersection of U.S. Highways 17 and 258, where you'll find Kinston.

CSS *Neuse* State Historic Site (ages 3 and up) 🏛

2612 West Vernon Avenue (US 70 Business); (252) 522–2091. Open 9:00 a.m. to 5:00 p.m. Monday through Saturday and 1:00 to 5:00 p.m. Sunday, April through October; 10:00 a.m. to 4:00 p.m. Tuesday through Saturday and 1:00 to 4:00 p.m. Sunday, November through March. Free.

Part of North Carolina's Civil War heritage is told in Kinston, even though it's less than a heroic epic. In Kinston you will find the CSS *Neuse* State Historic Site. The *Neuse*, known as "the gunboat" locally, is a 158-foot ironclad ship that looks somewhat like a river barge. The Confederate Navy began construction of the boat in 1862, but it would never be completed. In March 1865, the Confederacy launched the boat in a hasty attempt to improve its faltering chances in the Civil War, but on March 12 the crew set fire to the ship and sank it to keep it from being captured by the enemy. A museum has been created on the grounds where the boat rests to tell about its history and the role this river town played in the Civil War. The museum includes a slide show and artifacts from the vessel.

Also on the site is the **Governor Caswell Memorial,** dedicated to Richard Caswell, the first governor of the independent state of North Carolina. He served in that post for six years and headed the committee that wrote the state constitution. You can see a sound and light show depicting the governor's life and visit his grave at the site.

Health & Science Museum (all ages)

403 West Caswell Street; (252) 939–3302; www.neusewaypark.com. Open 9:30 a.m. to 5:00 p.m. Tuesday through Saturday and 1:00 to 5:00 p.m. Sunday. Free.

Kinston's Health & Science Museum at Neuseway Park includes a small planetarium as well as science exhibits. A giant Operation Game (you remember the guy with the red lightbulb nose, don't you?), a kid-sized replica of Lenoir Memorial Hospital, and giant replicas of the mouth, stomach, and intestines, big enough to crawl through, aim to teach kids about health. Other exhibits such as a bubble machine and giant pendulum give insight into physics.

The Exchange Nature Center (all ages)

401 West Caswell Street; (252) 939–3367. www.neusewaypark.com. Open 9:30 a.m. to 5:00 p.m. Tuesday through Saturday and 1:00 to 5:00 p.m. Sunday. Free.

In addition to wildlife exhibits, this facility includes a fishing pond with piers and canoe rentals. There's also a campground with RV and tent sites. It's also part of Neuseway Park.

Caswell No. 1 Fire Station Museum (all ages)

118 South Queen Street; (252) 527–1566 or (252) 522–4676. Open 10:00 a.m. to 4:00 p.m. Tuesday, Thursday, and Saturday. Free.

In 1895, a fire nearly destroyed the downtown Kinston area, so the city responded by building this fire station. It's now a museum that includes a 1922 American LeFrance Pumper and a collection of helmets, nozzles, ladders, fire extinguishers, and other memorabilia.

Where to Stay

WestParke Inn & Suites, 4774 US 70 West; (252) 527–1500. The Westparke has a heated pool and offers a continental breakfast. $$$

For More Information

Kinston Convention and Visitors Bureau, (800) 869–0032; www.visit kinston.com.

Kinston-Lenoir County Chamber of Commerce, (252) 527–1131; www .kinstonchamber.com.

New Bern

East of Kinston on US 70 at the junction with US 17 is where you'll find New Bern.

New Bern is the picture of Southern hospitality, located on the scenic Trent and Neuse Rivers. Settled in 1710 by German and Swiss colonists, it is North Carolina's second-oldest city and the state's first capital.

Tryon Palace Historic Site and Gardens (ages 5 and up)
610 Pollock Street; (800) 767–1560; www.tryonpalace.org. Open 9:00 a.m. to 5:00 p.m. Tuesday through Saturday and 1:00 to 5:00 p.m. Sunday. Two-and-a-half-hour tours begin every half hour. $$–$$$.

The city features more than 150 historical landmarks, including Tryon Palace Historic Site and Gardens. Guided tours of the luxurious restored home of British Royal Governor William Tryon, built in 1770, are available from costumed guides. You and your children not only will see the antiques and furniture that adorn the home but also will enjoy the demonstrations of cloth making, candle making, blacksmithing, and more.

Also part of the complex is the **Dixon-Stevenson House,** built in 1828 and decorated with furniture and antiques from the Federal and Empire periods. The **John Wright Stanly House,** built in 1783, also is part of the complex. The home has been furnished with pieces from that period, and the gardens have been designed like eighteenth-century English gardens. You can take a trolley tour ($$–$$$) of New Bern's Historic District from Tryon Palace for an additional fee, or you can get a **free** walking map here and continue to explore the city on your own.

A Day at the Farm (all ages)
183 Woodrow McCoy Road, Cove City; (252) 514–9494.

This historic dairy farm comes complete with old dairy barns, milking equipment, and period antiques. If it's fall, check out the pumpkin patch. Other times of the year, visit the peanut patch, fish and duck pond, farm animals, and the playground, or take a hayride.

Fireman's Museum (ages 5 and up)
410 Hancock Street; (252) 636–4087. Open 10:00 a.m. to 4:00 p.m. Monday through Saturday. $.

The Fireman's Museum features Civil War relics in addition to an extensive collection of early fire-fighting equipment. Original photographs have been preserved for the museum's displays, and you also will be able to view old steam pumpers and other fire-fighting equipment used in the nineteenth century.

Where to Eat

Cow Cafe, 319 Middle Street; (252) 672–9269. Ice cream is made on the premises. Plus the kids can play in the barnyard and meet MooAnnie, who plays the keyboard. $

The Chelsea Restaurant, 335 Middle Street; (252) 637–5469. The Chelsea building was initially used by Caleb Bradham, inventor of Pepsi-Cola, as his second drug store. $$

Aurora

From New Bern take Highway 55 east to Highway 306 and head north to the small town of Aurora.

Aurora Fossil Museum (ages 3 and up)
400 Main Street; (252) 322–4238. Summer hours are 9:00 a.m. to 4:30 p.m. Monday through Saturday and 1:30 to 4:30 p.m. Sunday. Free.

This museum tells the story of the coastal plain from the birth of the Atlantic Ocean to the present and features an unusual exhibit of life in the ocean fifteen million years ago. Here you can view dozens of fossils from the Miocene and Pliocene epochs and even give fossil finding a shot yourself at a mound across the street.

Where to Stay

Many of the accommodations in New Bern are B&Bs geared toward couples. You'll also find a few chain franchises, and a couple other choices.

BridgePointe Hotel & Marina, 101 Howell Road; (877) 283–7713. Located on the Neuse and Trent Rivers across from Historic Downtown New Bern, the BridgePointe is near all the local attractions. $$$

Vacation Resorts International, 1141 Broad Creek Road; (800) 625–4874. This organization offers 120 waterfront condos with a lot of amenities, such as golf and tennis privileges, bike rentals, and a playground on premises. $$$$

For More Information

Craven County Convention & Visitors Bureau, (800) 437–5767; www.visitnewbern.com.

Greenville

At Aurora, Highway 306 merges with Highway 33, which will take you west to Greenville, one of the largest cities in the coastal region.

Here you will find plenty to do, whether your family is into the arts, history, or the outdoors. In Pitt County, you'll find more than twenty parks, six art galleries, a number of museums, and dozens of points of historical interest.

River Park North (all ages)

1000 Mumford Road; (252) 329–5461. Generally open during daylight hours. Free.

One of the highlights you'll want to catch in Greenville is River Park North on the Tar River. Here you can fish, hike, and picnic year-round, and paddleboats are available on Saturday and Sunday when the weather is nice. You can also borrow a rod and reel here.

Adventures in Health Children's Museum (all ages)

1000 Mumford Road; (252) 752–7231. Open 1:00 to 5:00 p.m. Tuesday through Sunday, November through February; 1:00 to 6:00 p.m., March through October. Free.

While at River Park North, stop in at the Adventures in Health Children's Museum, a hands-on exhibit that focuses on anatomy and physiology. For example, one exhibit, designed to teach about stress, puts you in a cubicle with flashing lights and then your stress level is tested. A second cubicle has been designed to help relax you and bring your stress level back down. Designed to promote healthy lifestyle choices, the museum also dedicates some time to safety and emergency preparedness.

Greenville Museum of Art (ages 5 and up)

802 South Evans Street; (252) 758–1946; www.gmoa.org. Open 10:00 a.m. to 4:30 p.m. Tuesday through Friday and 1:00 to 4:00 p.m. Saturday and Sunday. Free.

The Greenville Museum of Art holds permanent collections and maintains space for traveling exhibitions. The Commons Gallery features works of North Carolina artists, which makes up about half of the museum's collection. The Francis Speight and Sarah Blakeslee Gallery is a permanent exhibition of works by the two who called Greenville home. In the Look & Learn Gallery, two- and three-dimensional art from the museum's Education Collection engage young visitors in various activities.

The Walter L. Stasavich Science and Nature Center (all ages)

1000 Mumford Road; (252) 329–4560. Open year-round 9:30 a.m. to 5:00 p.m. Tuesday through Saturday and 1:00 to 5:00 p.m. Sunday. $.

River Park North is also home to another museum, The Walter L. Stasavich Science and Nature Center. Here the kids will love looking at the displays of African animals, colorful butterflies, and huge mammals. The live reptile display and turtle touch tank are also big draws.

Where to Eat

Chico's Mexican Restaurant, 521 Cotanche Street; (252) 757–1666. This is a fun Mexican restaurant near East Carolina University. There is great selection on both the adult and children's menus. $

Christine, 207 Southwest Greenville Boulevard; (252) 355–9500. Offering continental cuisine, this is one of the city's nicer offerings. $$$

Where to Stay

If you aren't headed to the beach, Greenville is a good central location from which to explore this area, especially the aspects that relate to history. Here are a couple choices for accommodations; unfortunately, none have pools, which you have to find at the larger places.

East Carolina Inn, 3900 Stantonsburg Road; (252) 752–2122. This inn offers nice accommodations. $$$

University Inn, 3304 South Memorial Drive; (252) 756–7084. This is another small, nice hotel. $$$

For More Information

Greenville–Pitt County Convention & Visitors Bureau, (800) 537–5564; www.visitgreenvillenc.com.

Washington

From Greenville, catch US 264 east to the city of Washington.

"The Original Washington," named in 1775 for the George who would become the first president of the United States in 1789, might prove the perfect quiet stopping point before or after a trip to the beach. Many of the buildings on the waterfront have been renovated but aren't open to the public. A number of them have been converted into shops and restaurants if you're interested in a quiet day of shopping. The city of Washington provides a map of its historic district for walking tours.

Whichard's Beach Marina Campground (all ages)
3660 Whichard Beach Road; (252) 946–0011.

While many of the bed-and-breakfast inns here have minimum age requirements for children, Whichard's Beach Marina Campground offers adventure for the whole family. Located a mile south of town on US 17 along the Pamlico River, the campground offers beaches, a marina, a game room, a water slide, and more.

For More Information

Washington Visitor Center, 138 South Market Street; (800) 546–0162; www .visitwashingtonnc.com.

Bath

Bath is just a few miles east of Washington on Highway 92.

Historic Bath (ages 5 and up)

Tours of the town and homes are conducted April through October, 9:00 a.m. to 5:00 p.m. Monday through Saturday and 1:00 to 5:00 p.m. Sunday. Historic Bath is open the rest of the year 10:00 a.m. to 4:00 p.m. Tuesday through Saturday and 1:00 to 4:00 p.m. Sunday. $. You can get more information on Historic Bath at the visitor center on Carteret Street or call (252) 923–3971.

This is North Carolina's first town, settled in the late seventeenth century and incorporated in 1705. Here you can tour the Palmer-Marsh House, which features one of Santa Claus's favorite stopping points—a 17-foot-wide chimney. The Van Der Veer House, built in 1795, features a gambrel roof and houses trinkets and other items that highlight the town's three centuries of history. Saint Thomas Church, the oldest church in North Carolina, is also part of the historic district. It has walls that are more than 2 feet thick. A nice place for a picnic is on the waterfront, located nearby on Front Street. The Bonner House—nestled among elm, walnut, cedar, and dogwood trees—is one of the best remaining examples of early nineteenth-century Carolina architecture and is available to tour.

Goose Creek State Park

Located just west of Bath on Highway 92; (252) 923–2191. The park is open during daylight hours. Free. Fees are charged for camping and boat rental.

Goose Creek State Park, located along the Pamlico River, offers primitive camping, hiking, fishing, swimming, other outdoor activities, and nature programs. Two board-walks let you actually walk out into the swamp and marsh, where oak trees are draped with Spanish moss.

Belhaven

To reach Belhaven from Bath, head east on Highway 99.

Belhaven Memorial Museum (ages 3 and up)

201 East Main Street; (252) 943–3055. Open 1:00 to 5:00 p.m. daily except Wednesday. Free.

Do your kids collect things? If they do, they will get a kick out of the Belhaven Memorial Museum. Located in Belhaven city hall, this museum grew out of a collection begun by Mrs. Eva Blount Way at the turn of the twentieth century. It started with her collection of 30,000 buttons but has grown to include coins, shells, war memorabilia, tools, and more.

Where to Eat

River Forest Manor, 600 East Main Street; (252) 943–2151. This restaurant has gained some notoriety in the area. It serves a great dinner smorgasbord. $$

Swan Quarter

Continuing east from Belhaven on US 264 takes you to Swan Quarter.

Swan Quarter Wildlife Refuge (all ages)

38 Mattamuskeet Road, Highway 94; (252) 926–4021. The refuge is open year-round during daylight hours. Free.

This refuge consists of 16,500 acres of salt marsh and woodlands bordering Pamlico Sound. Fishing is allowed at Bell Island from a 1,100-foot pier, but you and the kids might be more interested in just sitting back and watching. The refuge is host to a number of migratory birds that can be seen here, including terns, black ducks, brown pelicans, and loons.

Engelhard

Continue east on US 264 to find Engelhard.

Mattamuskeet National Wildlife Refuge (all ages)

Highway 94, Swan Quarter; (252) 926–4021. The refuge is generally open during daylight hours. Free.

A more popular stopping point is the Mattamuskeet National Wildlife Refuge, farther east on US 264 near Engelhard. The 50,000-acre refuge includes Lake Mattamuskeet, the largest natural lake in North Carolina. It is 18 miles long and 5 to 6 miles wide but averages only 2 feet in depth. The refuge provides protection for migratory birds, such as ducks, geese, tundra swans, and occasionally a bald eagle. Fishing and crabbing are allowed at the lake and adjacent canals during the spring, summer, and fall. During the winter the refuge is home to birds that migrate from as far away as Canada.

Where to Stay

Mattamuskeet Campground, Route 1,
Fairfield; (252) 926–0911. Has sites with
trailer hookups and for tents. $

Ocracoke

Now we'll jump across the Pamlico Sound to the Outer Banks, starting with Ocracoke Island.

You can get to the village of Ocracoke by ferry from Swan Quarter or Cedar Island. Crossing time is more than two hours, and the cost is $10 for the average vehicle. Reservations are highly recommended; without them waits can be very long.

At Ocracoke, Highway 12 runs up the length of the island. Although it is quiet in Ocracoke, your family will love this charming village on the southern tip of the island. The island, which is 16 miles long, is home to just 700 people, many of whom still carry an Elizabethan accent in terms like "hoigh toid" for "high tide." It is so charming here, in fact, it barely seems to change from visit to visit. In 2007 Ocracoke was named America's Best Beach in the annual survey by Dr. Beach.

By the time you get to Ocracoke Village you'll find the narrow streets—lined with countless shops, ice cream stands, restaurants, and inns—fairly crowded during the summer months. But don't worry about the crowds; you'll find plenty of room to stretch out north of the village. Before you get to Ocracoke you will want to have a walking map, available on the ferries and at the National Park Service Visitor Centers located at the ferry docks. You'll find more than a dozen hotels, several bed-and-breakfast inns, and rental cottages that are available.

Ferries

Reservations for toll ferries are recommended and can be made up to thirty days in advance. For a complete ferry schedule or to make reservations, call (800) 773–1094. The ferries on longer routes such as these are fairly comfortable and include air-conditioned lounges, complete with snack machines. The kids will probably want to spend some time on the sun deck to take in spectacular views of the islands and the shrimpers who will be hard at work.

Ocracoke Lighthouse (all ages)
Lighthouse Road; (252) 928–4531. Free.

If you don't plan to spend some time taking in the history of this island, you'll miss a lot of the charm it has to offer. You'll want to see the Ocracoke Lighthouse, west of the village. Hike if the weather is nice because parking is extremely limited on the small street. Built in 1823, the lighthouse is the state's oldest still in operation. Its beam that shines at night can be seen from 14 miles away, but it's not open for climbing.

Teach's Hole (all ages)
West end of Highway 12; (252) 928–1718; www.teachshole.com. Open 10:00 a.m. to 5:00 p.m. Monday through Saturday. Free.

Teach's Hole is a pirate specialty shop that includes an exhibit about one of the island's most famous visitors—Edward Teach, also known as Blackbeard the Pirate. A self-guided tour depicts the escapades of the swashbuckler and his companions.

Banker Ponies (all ages)
North of Ocracoke Village on Highway 12 are the Banker Ponies. These horses ran wild on the island until the late 1950s, when they were penned at their current home. The small horses are descendants of horses brought to the New World by Spanish explorers as early as the sixteenth century and can be viewed and photographed from an observation deck just off the highway.

Bikes, Tours, **and More**

A fun way to see the village and most of the island is by bicycle. **The Slushy Stand** (252–928–1878), on the corner of Highway 12 and Silver Lake Road, provides more than just a quick snack. Here you can rent bikes for adults and children ($–$$$). If you're ready to hit the beach, you can also rent umbrellas, chairs, and boogie boards. You can also call Ride the Wind Surf Shop (252–928–6311) or Restless Native Boat Rentals (252–928–1421). Austin Boat Tours (252–928–4361) can help you plan your trip. It provides family activities, guided tours, and more. Active families will find a lot to do on Ocracoke Island. **Schooner Windfall Sailing Tours** (252–928–7245) is ready to get you out on the water. If wetting a line is more your pace, here are the local fishing charters: **Anchorage Marina** (252–928–6661), **Capt. David Nagel "Drum Stick"** (800–825–5351), **"Miss Kathleen"** (252–928–4841), **"Rascal" Sportfishing** (252–928–6111), and **Tarheel Charters** (252–928–9966).

Amazing
North Carolina Facts

Blackbeard was killed in a battle near Ocracoke by the British Royal Navy in 1718. Some say his treasure is still buried on the coast. Expeditions to find this treasure have even been conducted as far south as Topsail Island.

Where to Eat

Because of the tourist nature of the area even the pubs in Ocracoke are kid-friendly, so while it may look like a place for adults to party, most pubs treat children well.

Back Porch, 110 Back Road; (252) 928–6401. This is one of the better seafood places on the island. It has a children's menu and basket-size portions in case there are any other light eaters in the family. $$–$$$

Captain Ben's Restaurant, Highway 12; (252) 928–4741. Captain Ben offers a more budget-minded selection of seafood, plus other American dishes. $–$$

Howard's Pub and Raw Bar, Highway 12; (252) 928–4441. This is one of the kid-friendlier places, offering an array of burgers, chicken, and pizza as well as oysters. It has checkers and other assorted games and mind benders for you to play while waiting for your meal. $

Pony Island Restaurant, Highway 12; (252) 928–5701. This is one of the few restaurants on the island that tends to be family-style in both price and atmosphere. $$

Where to Stay

In case I haven't made it clear, you're not going to find a lot of places to stay along the Northern Coast, at least not until you get to Ocracoke. Then the decision gets very difficult.

Anchorage Inn & Marina, Highway 12; (252) 928–1101. Located on Silver Lake, this is a pet-friendly place with rooms and some efficiencies. There is a small cafe, too. $$–$$$

Beachcomber Campground, Highway 12; reservations for this oceanfront campground, 3 miles from the village, can be made through Ticketmaster outlets, or call (252) 928–4031. The campground gets you away from the hustle and bustle of tourists and is very scenic and nicely kept. $

Blackbeard's Lodge, 111 Back Road; (800) 892–5314; www.blackbeards lodge.com. This is Ocracoke's oldest hotel with thirty-eight rooms and apartments. $$$

Bluff Shoal Motel, Highway 12; (252) 928–4301. This is a very small motel located on the harbor with very reasonable prices but few amenities. $$–$$$

Boyette Realty, (800) 928–4261; www.boyetterealty.com.

The Castle on Silver Lake, Silver Lake Road; (800) 471–8848. Very nice rooms and condos with piers are waiting here at this inn that offers bikes and a game room. $$$$

Darlene Doshier at Sun Realty, (252) 921–0225, www.sunrealtyouterbanks .com.

Edward's of Ocracoke, State Road 1343; (252) 928–4801. Edward's is a small, homey facility. It has bikes for rent on-site. $$–$$$

Harborside Motel and Shop, Highway 12; (252) 928–3111. As the name indicates, this motel is indeed on the har-

bor. It, too, is a small facility with just fourteen rooms and four efficiencies. $$$

Ocracoke Island Realty, Highway 12; (252) 928–6261. This is one of three large realty companies that handle rental of a number of cottages on the island, as well as several condos.

For More Information

Ocracoke Civic and Business Association, (252) 928–6711; www.ocracoke village.com.

Hatteras

The free Ocracoke ferry takes you across Ocracoke Inlet to Hatteras Island, the central island in the Outer Banks. Highway 12 continues up the length of the island.

By the time you get to the northern portion of Ocracoke Island, where the Cape Hatteras National Seashore begins, you'll find that the major attractions here are the sun, sand, and unspoiled beauty. You will also find an ample supply of shops where you can buy a cheap T-shirt or grab a snack. The seashore is more undeveloped than any other portion of the Atlantic Coast, but a visit to any one of the villages here provides ample opportunity for educational and adventurous day trips. Hatteras Village,

Graveyard of **the Atlantic**

Off the coast of Hatteras Island are the dangerous Diamond Shoals, a bank of shifting sand ridges beneath the sea. They have been blamed for helping to sink more than 600 ships in the area, earning Hatteras the nickname "Graveyard of the Atlantic." Some of the sunken ships are visible from shore, depending on tides and the shifting sand. Much of Hatteras Island is untamed and uncrowded. You might want to take some time for a quiet walk on the beach or just take in the scenery.

the southernmost community on Hatteras Island, is home to a renowned charter fishing fleet, and home to the Graveyard of the Atlantic Museum, where the remnants of the original Fresnel lens that once shone bright atop the Cape Hatteras Lighthouse is now displayed.

Camping Ⓐ

Four camping areas are available along the Cape Hatteras National Seashore on a first-come, first-served basis, except for the one on Ocracoke, where reservations are recommended. All of these National Park Service facilities have showers, restrooms, tables, drinking water, and grills, but no utility hookups. Campgrounds are located at Oregon Inlet, Cape Point in Buxton, Frisco, and on Ocracoke Island. You can get more information on the entire Cape Hatteras National Seashore by calling (252) 473–2111.

Fishing

With the Gulf Stream only about 30 miles from the islands, fishing is ideal offshore from Hatteras, a quiet community on the southern tip of Hatteras Island. Fishing charters are available from a number of fishing centers in the area. Charters are only for experienced anglers as they go for yellowfin tuna, dolphin, and king mackerel on offshore tours. By chartering a small boat in the sound and hiring a guide, you can go for trout, flounder, and striped bass in one of the sounds. Or you might try your luck fishing from the pier located a few miles north of the village or at one of the other seven piers located along the Hatteras seashore. Trout, blues, mullet, and flounder are just a few of the possibilities when fishing from a pier in Hatteras.

Call the North Carolina Division of Marine Fisheries at (800) 682–2632 for information on regulations or the Dare County Tourist Bureau Fishing Line (I think that's a pun!) at (800) 682–6262 for what's good for catching at any particular time.

Where to Eat

Breakwater Restaurant, 57896 Highway 12, Oden's Dock; (252) 986–2733. Open for dinner only, this is a nice new restaurant that features unusual seafood dishes, beef, and other American cuisine. $$$

Captain Jack's, Highway 12; (252) 986–2250. This site boasts local fresh deep-sea and sound-caught seafood—and steaks, too. $$$

Fish Tales, Hatteras Village; (252) 986–6516. This spot is less elegant and serves everything from omelets to fresh local seafood. $$

Hatterasman Drive-In, Highway 12, (252) 986–1001. Come here for a change of pace. Fish tacos, burgers, sushi, burritos, seafood, smoothies, and desserts are offered. $

Sonny's Waterfront Restaurant, Highway 12; (252) 986–2922. Like many restaurants in the area, seafood is the specialty, especially the buffet, but Sonny's serves pasta, steak, and chicken, too. $$

Where to Stay

Breakwater Inn, 57896 Highway 12; (252) 986–2565. Pets are permitted here, and the motel has a pool and efficiencies. $$–$$$

Hatteras Marlin Motel, 57753 Highway 12; (252) 986–2141. A wide selection of rooms, suites, and efficiencies is available here. $$–$$$$

Hatteras Realty, Highway 12 South; (252) 995–5466. You'll have to rent by the week here, but the facilities are very nice and affordable when making arrangements that way. $$$

Sea Gull Motel, Highway 12; (252) 986–2550. This waterfront motel has a pool and efficiencies, rooms, and cottages. $$$

Here is a list of companies that have rental locations here and other places on the Outer Banks.

Colony Realty Corp., (800) 962–5256; www.hatterasvacations.com.

Dolphin Realty Inc., (800) 338–4775; www.dolphin-realty.com.

Midgett Realty, (800) 527–2903; www.midgettrealty.com.

Outer Beaches Realty, Inc., (888) 627–3650; www.outerbeaches.com.

Sun Realty, (800) 334–4745; www.sunrealtync.com.

Surf or Sound Realty, (800) 237–1138; www.surforsound.com/obvb.

Frisco

Push on north up Highway 12 just a little farther, and you come to another of the island's tiny villages, Frisco.

Frisco Native American Museum and Natural History Center
(ages 3 and up)
Highway 12; (252) 995–4440; www.nativeamericanmuseum.org. Open 11:00 a.m. to 5:00 p.m. Tuesday through Sunday. $.

The museum features authentic collections of ancient artifacts from the island's original inhabitants, and the center features a nature trail, exhibits, a pavilion, and a picnic area.

Where to Stay

Frisco Woods Campground, Highway 12; (800) 948–3942. Located on Pamlico Bay, this campground is very comfortable, with hot and cold water, a pool, playground, and more. It offers tent and RV sites. $

Buxton

Now get ready to climb. Buxton, farther north on Highway 12, is the home of the tallest lighthouse in the United States.

Cape Hatteras Lighthouse (ages 4 and up)
Highway 12; (252) 473–2111; www.nps.gov/caha/index.htm. Open 9:00 a.m. to 5:30 p.m. daily in summer and until 4:30 p.m. the rest of the year. $–$$ to climb.

At 208 feet, the Cape Hatteras Lighthouse is an international symbol for the North Carolina Coast and has gained more national attention over the past decade. Erosion from the treacherous sea began to threaten the lighthouse, and plans were undertaken to save it. As a result, in 2000, the lighthouse was moved about 1 mile inland. You can still climb the 268 steps to the top of the lighthouse and get a spectacular view of the surrounding area from the outside. Children must be old enough to make the climb on their own and be at least 42 inches tall. On the grounds of the lighthouse is the Cape Hatteras Visitors Center and Museum.

Where to Eat

Angelo's Pizzeria, Highway 12; (252) 995–6364. Specializing in Italian cuisine, featuring pizza, and calzones, Angelo's also has a game room. $

Buxton Munch Company, Highway 12, Osprey Shopping Center; (252) 995–5502. Salads, melts, burgers, quesadillas, subs, wraps, fried chicken, and vegetarian selections are on the menu here. $

The Captain's Table, Highway 12; (252) 995–3117. Across from the lighthouse entrance, the captain serves baby back ribs, local seafood, soup, pasta, salads, homemade desserts, and milkshakes. It has a kid's menu. $$

Diamond Shoals Restaurant, Highway 12; (252) 995–5217. Diamond Shoals serves local seafood and it's open for breakfast. $

Finnegan's Dining Haul, Highway 12; (252) 995–3060. Hot submarine sandwiches, hamburgers, hot dogs, pizza, seafood, and chicken are offered here. $

The Fish House Restaurant, Highway 12 Soundfront; (252) 995–5151. Fresh local seafood, pork, steaks, and pasta are all on the menu. $$

Orange Blossom Bakery & Café, Highway 12; (252) 995–4109. Breakfast including fresh baked goods and gourmet coffee are specialties here. It's also open for lunch and dinner. $

Pigman's BBQ, Highway 12; (252) 995–6900. BBQ pork, beef, and turkey are offered in addition to daily homemade specials. $

Wahini's Surf Grill, Highway 12; (252) 995–4900. Burgers, sandwiches, seafood, steaks, pasta, and a children's menu are offered here. $

Where to Stay

Buxton Beach Motel, Old Lighthouse Road (Oceanside); (252) 995–5972. Rooms, efficiencies, apartments, and cottages are offered here. $$$

Cape Hatteras Motel, Highway 12; (800) 995–0711. You'll find rooms, efficiencies, and apartments at this waterfront motel. $$$$

Cape Pines Motel, Highway 12; (252) 995–5666. This is a small motel, but it does have a pool and barbecue area. $$$

Falcon Motel, Highway 12; (800) 635–6911. The Falcon is a nice hotel for the price, offering rooms and apartments. $$–$$$

Lighthouse View Motel, Highway 12; (252) 995–5680. This is one of the larger and nicer accommodations in Buxton. $$

Tower Circle, 46423 Old Lighthouse Road; (252) 995–5353. Rooms and efficiencies are offered here. It also has a small playground. $$$

Rodanthe

Leaving Buxton and pointing your car north takes you through the small fishing village of Avon, gaining popularity among kiteboarders. A few restaurants and motels operate here but not much else. From there you drive about 15 more miles to the communities of Salvo, Waves, and Rodanthe, which seemingly blend into one. The entire northern end of Hatteras Island was once known as Chicamacomico (pronounced chik a ma COM i co), but in 1874 the postal service changed the name to Rodanthe.

Chicamacomico U.S. Lifesaving Service Station (all ages)

Highway 12; (252) 987–1552. Visitor center exhibits open during various hours; rescue drill held Thursday at 2:00 p.m. in the summer. Free.

The Chicamacomico U.S. Lifesaving Service Station, established in 1874, is one of North Carolina's oldest lifesaving stations. It includes two stations and five outbuildings. The villagers who have volunteered here have been credited with saving the lives of hundreds of sailors who found themselves caught in fierce winter and tropical storms. Reenactments of such rescues are performed weekly at the station during summer months.

Pea Island National Wildlife Refuge (all ages)

708 North Highway 64; (252) 987–2394; www.fws.gov/peaisland/. Open 9:00 a.m. to 4:00 p.m. daily April through November and weekends the rest of the year. Free.

Just north of Rodanthe begins the 5,915-acre Pea Island National Wildlife Refuge and part of the Charles Kuralt Trail, a series of refuges in coastal Virginia and North Carolina. You can use the observation platforms located throughout the area to view hundreds of species of local birds and any number of birds migrating to and from the refuge. The refuge also has a visitor center and nature trail, and bird walks and children's programs are held during the summer and fall.

Waterfall Action Park (all ages)

On Highway 12 north of Rodanthe on Hatteras Island; (252) 987–2213. Open 10:30 a.m. to 9:30 p.m. daily, May through September. Prices vary by attraction.

If the kids are ready for a little bit of modern adventure, try Waterfall Action Park. It's one of the area's largest fun parks and includes water slides, race cars, kiddy cars, miniature golf, bumper boats, bungie jumping, and more. This is the largest such park on the Outer Banks.

Laura Barnes **Shipwreck**

From Highway 12 you can see the *Laura Barnes* shipwreck of 1921. It is one of the few shipwrecks that is usually visible, depending on the shifting sands. The 120-foot ship, one of the last sailing schooners built in America, ran aground during a storm. A swimming area and a picnic area are available nearby.

Where to Eat

Boardwok South Restaurant, 24267 Highway 12; (252) 987–1080. Asian, American, and seafood are offered for lunch and dinner. $$

Lisa's Pizzeria, Highway 12; (252) 987–2525. Pizzas, subs and calzones are here. $

Uncle Pauly's Restaurant, Milepost 40, Highway 12; (252) 987–1623. Uncle Pauly has as much variety as any place in the area. $$

Where to Stay

Salvo Inn Motel, Highway 12, ocean-side, Salvo; (252) 987–2240. Efficiencies and cottages are available here. $$$

Sea Sound Motel, 24224 Sea Sound Road, Rodanthe; (252) 987–2224. This is a very small hotel, but it has a pool, basketball courts, and a picnic area. $$–$$$$

Coquina Beach

After you cross the bridge across the Oregon Inlet, still on Highway 12, you move out of the largely unpopulated areas and into a more traditional tourist area.

Bodie Island Lighthouse (all ages) 🏛

Highway 12, 8 miles south of juncture of US 158/64; (252) 441–5711. Free.

Bodie Island begins in the south at Coquina Beach, home of the Bodie Island Lighthouse. A visitor center, exhibits, and nature trail are open during daylight hours from May through September, but the lighthouse, built in 1872, is not open to climb.

Manteo

At Whalebone, Highway 12 encounters US 64, which crosses Roanoke Sound west onto Roanoke Island.

You may want to take this twenty-minute side trip into the late sixteenth century before continuing north to the popular Nags Head resort area, or plan on it as a day trip during your vacation. In Manteo there is plenty to fill a day and evening, or even several days and evenings. Roanoke Island is the site of the earliest English settlements sent by Sir Walter Raleigh beginning in 1584. Many sites and attractions here depict the lives of those settlers and others who helped shape the New World.

Elizabeth II State Historic Site and Roanoke Island Festival Park
(all ages) 🏛

Highway 64, across from the Manteo waterfront; (252) 475–1506; www.roanokeisland
.com. Open 10:00 a.m. to 6:00 p.m. daily (7:00 p.m. in summer), April through October,
with the last guided tour at 5:00 p.m. $$; free for children five and under.

Coming from Highway 64, your first stop might be the *Elizabeth II* State Historic Site
and Roanoke Island Festival Park. The *Elizabeth II* is a replica of the sixteenth-century
sailing ship that brought some of the first settlers to America. Your kids will love strik-
ing up conversations with the interpretive guides dressed as sailors who work for
Queen Elizabeth. They stay in character for the year 1585, so comments about televi-
sion or cars won't be understood. The kids might even get an opportunity to help
hoist the sails. After you tour the small vessel, you'll want to see the living-history
camp a short walk away. It's 1585 here, too, folks. You might find the queen's sailors
whipping up a meal, crafting tools, or preparing food for winter storage. More recent
additions include a fun, interactive museum, an art gallery, shops, and an amphithe-
ater for special performances. Picnic facilities and snacks are available on site.

Waterfront Shops 🔒
207 Queen Elizabeth Avenue.

After your visit to the *Elizabeth II*, journey through the quaint waterfront village on
Roanoke Sound. At the Waterfront Shops you can take your time and explore the
many unusual shops and restaurants, where you can find lunch or dinner. At the **Can-**
dle Factory (252–473–3813) you can watch craftworkers produce candles in the
shape of seashells, lighthouses, and more. Many more shops in the village will take
you back in time. **Manteo Blacksmith Shop,** 408 Queen Elizabeth Avenue, (252–473-
1709) is a working blacksmith shop offering live demonstrations of this age-old craft.
My Secret Garden, 101 Sir Walter Raleigh Street, (252–473–6880) is a fun gift shop
full of eclectic treasures. You'll also find a comfortable book store, jewelry, and more in
the Waterfront Shops.

Pirate's Cove Yacht Club (all ages) ⚠
Manteo/Nags Head Causeway; (252) 473–3906. Cruises run mid-May through mid-
October at 11:00 a.m. and 3:00 and 7:00 p.m. The evening tour departs at 6:00 p.m.
after Labor Day. $$–$$$.

At the nearby Pirate's Cove Yacht Club you can catch a sight-seeing cruise aboard the
Virginia Dare. The air-conditioned yacht leads you on a narrated trip through these
historic waters. You'll learn a lot about the rich history of the area, including pirates
who roamed the waters, early settlers, and the initial efforts at flight, while also learn-
ing about the natural features of the sound.

Amazing
North Carolina Facts

At an incredible 5.2 miles, the Virginia Dare Bridge, named for the first English child born in North America, is the longest bridge in the state. Opened in 2002, it takes motorists over the Croatan Sound, connecting Mann's Harbor and Manteo.

North Carolina Aquarium (ages 3 and up) 🐘

State Road 1116, also known as Airport Road; (252) 473–3493; www.ncaquariums .com. Open 9:00 a.m. to 5:00 p.m. daily; closed on Thanksgiving, Christmas, and New Year's Day. $–$$; **free** for children ages five and under.

Next take a jaunt on Airport Road, 3 miles north of US 64, to the North Carolina Aquarium. It's one of three such aquariums on the coast. In addition to the displays of fresh and saltwater habitats and a touch tank, the aquarium offers special programs and educational films throughout the year. At this aquarium you'll see sharks in a 285,000-gallon tank, alligators, and coastal environmental displays, including one on Outer Banks hurricanes.

Barrier Island Aviation (all ages)

Dare County Airport; (252) 473–4247; www.barrierislandaviation.com. $$$$.

This company offers thirty-minute scenic air tours of the Outer Banks with seating for up to three passengers. Tours fly over Wright Brothers National Memorial, Jockey's Ridge State Park, and lighthouses.

Kitty Hawk Aero Tours (all ages)

Dare County Airport; (252) 441–8687; www.flyobx.com. $$$$.

Shipwrecks are a cool addition to these tours that also fly over all of the sights. This operator also flies over Bodie Island Lighthouse.

Fort Raleigh National Historic Site (all ages)

US 64; (252) 473–5772; www.nps.gov/fora/. Open year-round during daylight hours. **Free.**

Back on US 64, it's on to Fort Raleigh National Historic Site. The site includes a visitor center with exhibits of artifacts from the original site constructed in 1585. The center features the Elizabethan Room, adorned with the paneling and fireplace from a sixteenth-century home. At the center you can also see a film on the attempts to establish the colonies and displays on colonial life. In addition, the National Park Service reconstructed the small earthen fort here in 1950 at the same location where it was originally built in 1585. Many of the artifacts, including a wrought-iron sickle and a Native American pipe excavated from the site, are on display at the center. Park interpreters present programs and special events at various locations of the site throughout the year.

Elizabethan Gardens (all ages)

1411 US 64/264; (252) 473–3234; www.elizabethangardens.org. Open from 9:00 a.m. to dusk daily. $–$$; children through age eleven are admitted free.

Plan to spend an hour or so wandering through the Elizabethan Gardens, located at the Fort Raleigh National Historic Site. Visitors entering the gardens through a replica of a Tudor gatehouse are led past myriad herbs, flowers, shrubs, water fountains, and trees.

The Lost Colony (all ages—look for an appropriate presentation) (♬)

1409 US 64/264; (866) 468–7630; www.thelostcolony.org. The two-hour production is presented from early June to late August at 8:30 nightly, except Saturday. $$–$$$.

Your trip to Manteo won't be complete without seeing *The Lost Colony* outdoor drama, which plays on the waterfront on the grounds of Fort Raleigh. Children and adults alike will be enthralled as the 150-member cast re-creates through drama, song, and dance the events leading to the mysterious disappearance of the men, women, and children who came here from England in 1587. Written by Pulitzer Prize–winner Paul Greene, *The Lost Colony* opened in 1940 and has been playing ever since. The play also commemorates the birth of Virginia Dare, the first European child born in the New World, who disappeared along with the other colonists. Exactly what happened to them remains a mystery. Weather changes rapidly on the waterfront, so bring along a jacket as well as bug repellent to keep the mosquitoes away.

The Lost Colony Children's Theater also presents other special productions for children who might not be able to make it through the evening show. These are performed at various locations on the Outer Banks throughout the season. Call the Lost Colony Box Office for times, locations, and ticket prices.

Where to Eat

Big Al's Soda Fountain and Grill, 716 US 64/264; (252) 473–5570. You can probably guess what kind of food you'll get here, so we'll skip it and say we just like the name. Try the homemade ice cream, though. $

Darrell's Seafood Restaurant, US 64/264; (252) 473–5366. If the old real estate adage "location, location, location" is true, Darrell's will be in business for a long time. Darrell's specialty is grilled marinated tuna, but the menu also includes a healthy portion of local catches, a good children's menu, and baskets for light eaters. $$

1587 Restaurant, 405 Queen Elizabeth Street; (252) 473–1587. This is a sort of casual, five-star restaurant on the waterfront. Great gourmet food is served in an elegant, yet comfortable, setting. $$$

Where to Stay

Dare Haven Motel, 819 North Main Highway; (252) 473–2322. This hotel has twenty-four rooms and is nice, but there's no pool. $$–$$$

Duke of Dare Motor Lodge, 100 South Virginia Dare Road; (252) 473–2175. This

is a AAA-approved facility with fifty-seven rooms. $$

Elizabethan Inn, 814 US 64; (800) 346–2466. This is a nice period-themed inn with mainly standard rooms. $$–$$$$.

Pirate's Cove Realty, US 64/264, Manteo/Nags Head Causeway; (800) 537–7245. This agency specializes in very upscale, elegant rentals on the waterfront and near the wildlife preserve.

Strawser Vacation Rentals, (252) 473–1170; www.cheapobxvacations .com

Nags Head

A little farther north from Whalebone, where you sidetracked to Manteo, on Highway 12 is Nags Head.

Here you'll find more of what you expect from a standard tourist center. Hotels, vacation cottages, and condominiums line the strip between the beach and Highway 12. You will find plenty of attractions, amusements, and eateries to choose from here. Until you get to Nags Head, the islands often aren't wide enough to accommodate much more than the highway, but this broader area has an array of services, including major retail chain and outlet stores. Here you also get a fair share of water parks, water slides, miniature golf courses, and gift shops. Nags Head is a good central location if you are planning to stay a week or more in the area. Not only can you enjoy the sand, sun, and surf, but there's also simply a lot to do, rain or shine.

Kitty Hawk Kites (ages 5 and up)
Several locations throughout the Outer Banks; (877) 359–8447; www.kittyhawk.com. Prices vary by activity.

For the ultimate family adventure, you might want to check in with Kitty Hawk Kites, just off Highway 12 on U.S. Highway 158, across the street from Jockey's Ridge State Park (it also has outlets at Avon, Duck, and Corolla). Kitty Hawk Kites offers lessons in kayaking, sailboarding, and hang gliding and sells kites and kite supplies. Even young children can be accommodated in kayaking tours, but you must weigh at least eighty pounds to take hang-gliding lessons.

Jockey's Ridge State Park (all ages)
West Carolista Drive; (252) 441–7132; www.jockeysridgestatepark.com. Open during daylight hours. **Free.**

If hang gliding is a little too adventurous for your family, it's almost as much fun to sit back and watch it being done at Jockey's Ridge State Park. This is the site of the largest sand dune on the East Coast, located on US 158. Most people come here to climb the 140-foot dune, while others come to fly kites in the wide-open, 414-acre park. Walking across the vast white sand almost makes you feel like you're walking across the desert. Unlike desert wilderness areas, it has picnic facilities available.

Nags Head Pier
Milepost 11, Beach Road; (252) 441–5141.

Anytime is a good time to try your fishing luck on the Nags Head Pier, one of the oldest and longest on the Outer Banks. Tackle is available for rent, as is a cleaning station. The pier is open twenty-four hours a day in spring, summer, and fall. The Pier House Restaurant located here will even clean and cook your catch.

A Fishy Tale

Even though the following story might not be completely true (don't be upset, Mom!), it's not a lie. It's a fishing story.

I took the kids to Nags Head Pier to get in a little fishing early one morning. I had given up on doing any serious fishing since I started taking the kids, but I was having just as much fun helping bait the hooks, untangling lines, and occasionally untangling my kids. We had spent about three hours catching small sea trout and other species with even the seasoned anglers on the pier around us doing the same. Then, suddenly, the big one hit. My daughter's pole bent to nearly breaking, the eight year old pulled back with all her might, and I sprung into action, saying, "Reel it in, Jessie, reel it in." After hours (well, OK, minutes) of fighting the blue at the end of the line, a crowd (well, OK, five people) gathered around us. "It's a blue," a shirtless boy said, examining the razor-sharp teeth in the fish's mouth. "What'd ya catch 'em with?" "Uh, Dad?" my daughter asked. "Calamari," I whispered. "Calamari," Jessie said, turning to the boy with an air of confidence. She immediately turned back to me and asked, "Dad, what's calamari?"

Where to Eat

The Dunes Restaurant, Milepost 16.5, Highway 12; (252) 441–1600. This family restaurant will offer more children's selections than most. $$

How Sweet It Is, 3941 South Croatan Highway; (252) 441–4485. Right across the street from Jockey's Ridge State Park, this shop also has sandwiches and features an old-fashioned soda fountain. $

Jockey's Ribs, Milepost 13, Beach Road; (252) 441–1141. Cute name for a cute barbecue restaurant. $

New York Pizza Pub, Milepost 10, 158 Bypass; (252) 441–2660. This place is unique in that the kids can get pizza and Mom and Dad can get steak. $–$$

The Pier House Restaurant, Milepost 11, Beach Road; (252) 441–4200. Treat the family to tasty local seafood in a casual dining atmosphere with an oceanfront view here on the Nags Head Pier. $$–$$$

Yellow Submarine, 5000 South Croatan Highway; (252) 441–3511. The owners probably aren't the first out of the '60s to think of the name, but you can probably guess what they serve. $

Where to Stay

We won't even attempt to list all the places you can find to stay in the Nags Head area, but here are just a few:

Beacon Motor Lodge, 2617 South Virginia Dare Trail; (800) 441–4804. This AAA- and Mobil Guide–approved facility has rooms, suites, and efficiencies. The kids will love the game room as much as the pool. $$$$

Blue Heron Motel, 6811 Virginia Dare Trail; (252) 441–7447. The Blue Heron offers rooms and efficiencies on the ocean. $$$$

The Dolphin Motel, 8017 Old Oregon Inlet Road; (252) 441–7488. You might find this motel a little more affordable. $$$

Nags Head Inn, 4701 South Virginia Dare Trail; (800) 327–8881. This inn is one of the larger ones in the area, with one hundred rooms. $$$$

Among the largest realty companies are the following:

Cove Realty, 105 East Dunn Street; (800) 635–7007.

Nags Head Realty, 2300 South Croatan Highway; (800) 222–1531.

Prudential Resort Realty, 2229 South Croatan Highway; (800) 458–3830.

Stan White Realty, 2506 South Croatan Highway; (800) 338–3233.

Village Realty, 5301 South Croatan Highway; (800) 548–9688.

Kill Devil Hills

Kill Devil Hills is just minutes from Nags Head. In fact, Nags Head, Kill Devil Hills, and Kitty Hawk all seem to blend into one vacation resort.

Wright Brothers National Memorial (all ages)

Milepost 8, US 158; (252) 441–7430. Open 9:00 a.m. to 5:00 p.m. daily and until 6:00 p.m. in summer; closed Christmas Day. $.

This is where human beings learned to fly. On December 17, 1903, two bicycle shop owners from Dayton, Ohio, named Orville and Wilbur Wright, took the first powered flying machine on a sustained flight. After several attempts that day they kept the machine aloft for fifty-nine seconds and traveled 852 feet. Today the Wright Brothers National Memorial, on US 158 north of Kill Devil Hills, stands on the same spot as a tribute to their accomplishment. It includes a museum on the history of flight and a demonstration of the principles they used, which are still instrumental to modern flight. Reproductions of the brothers' glider and the 1903 airplane are on display, and you will want to check out the reproduction of their camp workshop and hangar.

Kitty Hawk Aero Tours (all ages)

First Flight Airport, 171 Bay Drive; (252) 441–8687. $$$–$$$$.

Kitty Hawk Aero Tours offers a chance to take a flight from the same place the Wright brothers made so many attempts in their quest to fly. The tour flies over Oregon Inlet to observe the ocean life that includes sharks, porpoises, and sea turtles. You'll also be flown over the Bodie Island Lighthouse and Jockey's Ridge. Open cockpit planes are available, too. Call for reservations.

Nags Head Wood Ecological Preserve (all ages)

701 West Ocean Acres Drive, off US 158; (252) 441–2525. Admission to the preserve is free, but some programs may require a fee.

Now it's off to learn a little bit about one of nature's more unusual offerings at Nags Head Wood Ecological Preserve, where freshwater pools have bubbled up to create this 1,100-acre protected wetland. Walking trails and displays provide an interesting look at one of the last and most diverse forests on the islands. The woodlands include dunes adjacent to a majestic hardwood forest. The staff presents guided tours and educational programs throughout the year that explain the diversity of the area.

Amusements (all ages)

The Kitty Hawk/Kill Devil Hills area offers plenty of history, but don't forget about traditional family fun. You won't have any trouble finding these, but here is a short list of locations on the north end of the Croatan Highway: **Colington Speedway**

(252–480–9144) has three tracks available to please kids of most every age; **Professor Hacker's Lost Treasure Golf** (252–480–0142) has thirty-six holes complemented with waterfalls, dinosaur footprints, lost treasure, and a mining train that takes you to the first hole; **Wet 'n Wild Bumper Boats** (I don't think we need to say anything more).

Where to Eat

Bob's Grill, 1203 South Croatan Highway; (252) 441–0707. Bob's serves breakfast, lunch, and dinner and is open all night on weekends. $

The Coastal Cactus Southwestern Restaurant, 3105 North Croatan Highway; (252) 441–6600. Mom and Dad will enjoy the fajitas or the tequila-lime shrimp here, but the kids' menu is great, too. $$

Colington Cafe, 1029 Colington Road; (252) 480–1123. You'll have to make reservations well in advance to eat here. This is one of the nicest restaurants in the area, serving mainly French cuisine. $$$

Jolly Roger, Milepost 6.75, Beach Road; (252) 441–6530. Homemade Italian cuisine, seafood, steaks, and prime rib offers something for everyone. $$$

Kelly's Outer Banks Restaurant & Tavern, Milepost 10.5, US 158 Bypass; (252) 441–4116. Southeastern seafood, beef, and pasta is offered in a fine dining atmosphere in which children are welcome. $$$$

Miller's Restaurant, Milepost 9.5, Beach Road; (252) 441–7674. Seafood is the specialty here. $$

Where to Stay

Cavalier Motel, Milepost 8.5; (252) 441–5584. Rooms, efficiencies, and cottages make this a great place no matter what you're looking for. As a bonus, the Cavalier has a large swimming pool for adults, a small one for the kiddies, and a large playing area equipped with swings, shuffleboard, horseshoes, and volleyball courts. $$$

Ocean House Motel, Milepost 9.5, Oceanfront Road; (800) 699–1963; www.oceanhousemotel.com. Standard rooms are offered at Ocean House. $$$

Outer Banks Motor Lodge, 1509 Virginia Dare Trail; (877) 625–6343; www.obxmotorlodge.com. Rooms and efficiencies are offered here. $$–$$$$

Kitty Hawk

Kitty Hawk is just to the north of Kill Devil Hills.

The Promenade (all ages)
Barlow Road near the Wright Brothers Memorial Bridge. For information on golf attractions, call (252) 261–4900. For information on water sports, call (252) 261–4900. Fees vary by activity.

With dozens of activities for the entire family, The Promenade is a thirty-acre entertainment park that offers everything from golf to water sports. Yet it isn't a traditional entertainment center because the fun takes place in more peaceful surroundings. The eatery includes a coffee and draft house as well as ice cream and other snacks. You'll find a driving range, grass putting greens, a playground, and opportunity for kayaking or other water sports.

Kitty Hawk Kayaks—Kayak and Surf School (ages 5 and up)
6150 North Croatan Highway; (866) 702–5061; www.khkss.com.

Kitty Hawk Kayaks offers over a dozen guided tours, rental kayaks, and self-guided tours. Coastal studies field trips and overnight trips also available. They also offer a one-day surf school and a three-day surf camp. $$$$

Where to Eat

Jimmy's Seafood Buffet, 4117 North Croatan Highway; (252) 261–4973. It's noisy at Jimmy's, but that might work well with children. The food is good, but a little expensive for buffet-only. $$$$

John's Drive-In, 3716 North Virginia Dare Trail; (252) 261–6227. The milk shakes are why people go to John's, but you can get sandwiches here, too. $

Where to Stay

Atlantic Realty, 4729 North Croatan Highway; (800) 334–8401; www.atlantic realty-nc.com

Beach Haven, 4104 Virginia Dare Trail; (252) 261–4785. This is one of the prettier hotels among the northern beaches. It's AAA approved, has a putting green and bikes, and other beach items are available for a fee. $$$$

Kitty Dunes Realty & Rentals, (888) 860–3863; www.kittydunes.com.

Southern Shores Realty Services, (800) 334–1000; www.southernshores .com.

For More Information

Dare County Tourist Bureau, (800) 629–4386; www.outerbanks.org.

Corolla

It's a little out of the way, but a drive up Highway 12 to this northernmost point on the North Carolina coast may prove very relaxing. You will travel through the communities of Southern Shores and Duck before leaving Dare County.

Currituck Beach Lighthouse (all ages) 🏛

Highway 12 at Corolla Village Road; (252) 453–8152. Open Easter through Thanksgiving, 10:00 a.m. to 6:00 p.m. daily. $.

The Corolla area is one of the narrowest points on the barrier islands. Bordered on the west by Currituck Sound and the Atlantic Ocean on the east, sand frequently blows onto the highway from the dunes that line it here and at other narrow points on the island. Highway 12 ends at the Currituck Beach Lighthouse, a redbrick tower built in 1875. It is open for climbing.

Back Country Outfitters & Guides (all ages)

107-C Corolla Light Town Center; (252) 453–0877; www.outerbankstours.com. By appointment only. $$$$.

Backcountry Outfitters offers wild horse safaris in addition to other eco-tours. The wild horse safari is a two-hour journey to see the wild mustangs left behind by early explorers almost five hundred years ago. They take guests over 30 miles of back country and beach dunes.

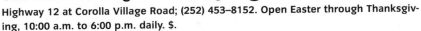

Amazing
North Carolina Facts

From one of the northernmost points in North Carolina, where Highway 12 ends at Corolla, to the Virginia border roam descendents of Spanish mustangs that apparently survived early sixteenth-century shipwrecks. Other theories suggest the horses survived as the Spanish settlers fell ill. You can still see them roaming the beaches in some protected areas, but development is forcing them into tourist and residential areas. In 1926 a National Geographic Society article estimated that there were as many as 6,000 horses roaming the land. Today, because some have been systematically removed and others killed, there may be as few as one hundred roaming the nearly 15,000 acres.

Corolla Wild Horse Museum (all ages)
1126 School House Lane; (252) 453–8002; www.corollawildhorses.com. Open 11:00 a.m. to 4:00 p.m. Monday through Thursday. Free.

This museum, dedicated to the preservation of the local wild horse population, is located in the Old Corolla Schoolhouse, in the heart of historic Corolla Village. Visitors see interactive displays and learn about local history and the story of the horses that inhabit this area. Kid's programs are held on Tuesday from 11:00 a.m. to 1:00 p.m.

The Whalehead Club at Currituck Heritage Park (ages 5 and up)
1100 Club Road; (252) 453–9040; www.whaleheadclub.com. Hours are 9:00 a.m. to 5:00 p.m. daily. Some tours require advance registration. $–$$.

Built in the mid-1920s to satisfy Industrialist Edward Collings Knight, Jr.'s passion for hunting waterfowl, the Whalehead Club is a spectacular landmark on the Currituck Outer Banks. Knight and his wife used the Corolla home as their winter residence from 1925 to 1934. It still boasts Tiffany lamps, cork-tiled floors, and brass duck head and water lily hardware. A Children's Tour and Treasure Hunt is offered for children ages six to twelve ($). This tour teaches participants about the history and art of the home and gives them a greater appreciation for the environment and geography of the area as well as giving them some navigational skills. A ghost tour ($) is recommended for guests age six and older.

Where to Eat

Barefoot Bernie's Tropical Grill & Bar, Milepost 4.5; (252) 261–1008. Seafood, steaks, pastas, salads, and sandwiches are offered in addition to live entertainment. $$$

Spanky's Grille & Pizza, Milepost 3.5; (252) 261–1917. Spanky's is a great place for breakfast or midday meal. $

Creswell

Now that we've explored the length of the Outer Banks, let's head back inland. US 64 is the quickest and easiest route out of the centrally located Manteo area. We will first head through the Alligator River National Wildlife Refuge.

Alligator River National Wildlife Refuge (all ages)
Located about 4 miles west of the US 64/264 split traveling west from Manteo; (252) 473–1131; www.fws.gov/alligatorriver.

The Alligator River National Wildlife Refuge is one of the most spectacular unspoiled areas in the state. It has great paddling trails, a wildlife drive, hiking trails, and a variety

of wildlife and habitats. Bogs, fresh and brackish water marshes, hardwood swamps, and Atlantic white cedar swamps comprise the area. Plant species include pitcher plants and sundews, cranberries, bays, white cedar, pond pine, gums, red maple, and a wide variety of herbaceous and shrub species. The refuge is one of the last remaining native homes of black bear on the Eastern Seaboard and it includes concentrations of ducks, geese, and swans. Other wildlife you might see there includes wading birds, shorebirds, American woodcock, raptors, white-tailed deer, raccoons, rabbits, quail, river otters, and, of course, American alligators. The area is also part of a red wolf repopulation project.

Pettigrew State Park

2252 Lake Shore Road; (252) 797–4475. Open during daylight hours. Free.

About 60 miles west of Manteo you come to Pettigrew State Park on Phelps Lake. The park includes 17,000 acres and plenty of room for camping, hiking, fishing, and picnicking on your way off the coast.

Somerset Place Historic Site

**Pettigrew State Park, 2572 Lake Shore Road; (252) 797–4560; www.albemarle-nc
.com/somerset. Open 9:00 a.m. to 5:00 p.m. Monday through Saturday and 1:00 to
5:00 p.m. Sunday, April through October, and 10:00 a.m. to 4:00 p.m. Tuesday through
Saturday and 1:00 to 4:00 p.m. Sunday, November through March. Free.**

You will want to see Somerset Place Historic Site while you are at Pettigrew State Park. Somerset is a fourteen-room manor built in the 1830s for Josiah Collins III, who was from Somerset, England. The rice plantation and Greek Revival mansion became a popular gathering place for the upper class of the time and served as an example of the South's slave-supported economy. Somerset, which houses an extensive collection of slave records, is the site of a homecoming for descendants of slaves and slaveholders. In recent years a number of Native American artifacts have been pulled from the lake. Two dugout canoes, possibly 4,000 years old, are on display year-round, but more of the artifacts and history are presented during **Indian Heritage Week,** held at Pettigrew the third week in September. Weekdays schoolchildren from the area visit to learn about the history of the Algonquin Indians, who were wiped out by European-imported disease.

Williamston

Staying on US 64 brings you west to this agriculturally based town.

Fort Branch (ages 3 and up)

Located on State Road 1416, 12 miles north of Williamston on Highway 125; (800) 776–8566; www.fortbranchcivilwarsite.com. Open 1:30 to 5:30 p.m. Saturday and Sunday, April through the first weekend in November. Free.

Most people who come here come to visit Fort Branch, an earthen Civil War fort. On display are eight of the fort's original twelve cannons, which Confederate soldiers pushed into the Roanoke River after General Lee surrendered at Appomattox in 1865. The Fort Branch Civil War Reenactment is held the first weekend in November, and the Fort Branch Spring Living History Program is another intriguing event this site offers.

Where to Stay

Green Acres Family Camping Resort, 1679 Green Acres Road; (252) 792–3939. A stay at this campground comes with a lot of extras, including a pool, a playground, a volleyball court, horseshoes, a miniature golf course, and scheduled activities. $

Robersonville

Back on US 64, heading west from Williamston, you can really pick up the pace if stock car racing is your thing.

East Carolina Motor Speedway (ages 3 and up)

4918 US 64; (252) 795–3968. Races begin at 7:30 p.m. Saturday, April through October. $–$$$.

This is a hard-surface racetrack, featuring late-model stock cars and sportsman-class racing.

Tarboro

Tarboro, west from Robersonville on US 64 at the junction with US 258, is another town with its roots grounded deeply in the history of the eighteenth century.

Historic District Recreation Trail (ages 5 and up)

Tour headquarters is located at 130 Bridgers Street; (252) 823–4159. Open 10:00 a.m. to 4:00 p.m. Monday through Friday and 2:00 to 4:00 p.m. Saturday, April through November. Free.

This is a prime location to study the architecture of the period, both in the charming downtown area and on the historic walking tour. The sixteen-acre Town Common includes an 1860 cotton press, herb garden, and nature trail. **Blount-Bridgers House** ($; **free** for children ages eleven and under) features the work of artist Hobson Pittman (1899–1972), whose works have been in collections at the Metropolitan Museum of Art in New York as well as the Corcoran Gallery in Washington, D.C.

Rocky Mount

The city of Rocky Mount is a great stopping point on the way to or from the beach. You can get here from Tarboro via US 64, heading west. From the north or south, Interstate 95 crosses the city's western edge. Numerous other roads also converge here.

Sunset Park (all ages)

4497 Sunset Avenue; (252) 952–1235. Open generally during daylight hours. Free, with fees for some activities.

Stop at Sunset Park, where you can take a break from driving and have a picnic. You'll also find a miniature train here as well as a merry-go-round, a skate park, and a spray park.

Children's Museum and Science Center

Imperial Center for Arts and Sciences, 270 Gay Street; (252) 972–1167; www.ci.rocky-mount.nc.us/museum/. Open 10:00 a.m. to 5:00 p.m. Tuesday, Wednesday, and Saturday, 10:00 a.m. to 9:00 p.m. Thursday and Friday, and 1:00 to 5:00 p.m. Sunday. $; free for children under three.

The Children's Museum and Science Center located at the Imperial Center for the Arts and Sciences includes interactive science exhibits, a digital planetarium, and other programming. Exhibits include Extreme Deep which brings the sea floor to the surface in dramatic fashion, giving guests the chance to walk on the ocean floor. Other exhibits introduce visitors to a variety of scientific concepts.

Where to Eat

Gardner's Barbecue, North Wesleyan Boulevard, (252) 442–0531; 841 Fairview Road, (252) 442–5522; and Westridge Shopping Center, (252) 443–3996. This is eastern barbecue country and Gardner's has built a reputation. $

For More Information

Nash County Travel & Tourism, (800) 849–6825; www.rockymounttravel.com.

Wilson

Head south on U.S. Highway 301 to the town of Wilson, one of the state's premier barbecue locales.

Imagination Station (all ages)

224 East Nash Street; (252) 291–5113; www.imaginescience.org. Open 9:00 a.m. to 5:00 p.m. Monday through Saturday and 1:00 to 5:00 p.m. Sunday. $; free for children under age four.

After grabbing a bite at one of the several restaurants recognized by *Southern Living* for quality barbecue beef, pork, and chicken, head to this unusual science center, which has exhibits that will make your hair stand on end. Included are daily science demonstrations on everything from chemistry to electricity, a state-of-the-art computer lab, and dozens of hands-on exhibits.

Where to Eat

Parker's Barbecue, US 301 and I-95; (252) 237–0972. Parker's has been in business since 1946. That has to mean something. $

Where to Stay

Village Motor Lodge, 2089 US 301 South; (252) 243–3331. This small lodge has both a pool and playground and offers basic rooms for short stays. $$

Windsor

If you choose to head north instead of west from Williamston, you can take US 17 to reach Windsor.

Livermon Recreation Park and Mini-Zoo (all ages)

103 North York Street; (252) 794–5553. Open 8:00 a.m. to 8:00 p.m. Monday through Friday, 9:00 a.m. to 8:00 p.m. Saturday and Sunday during the summer, and 8:00 a.m. to 5:00 p.m. daily during the rest of the year. Free.

Livermon Recreation Park and Mini-Zoo is a great place to stop if you're on the road. Take along the makings for a picnic (grills are available if you want to cook hot dogs or hamburgers) and let the kids run off some steam on the playground equipment. They can also tour the little zoo and see the thirty different varieties of animals, including birds, goats, and a llama. The zoo offers an opportunity to see the animals up close and even pet some of them.

Historic Hope Plantation (ages 5 and up)
132 Hope House Road; (252) 794–3140; www.hopeplantation.org. Open 10:00 a.m. to 4:00 p.m. Monday through Saturday and 2:00 to 5:00 p.m. Sunday, March 1 through December 23. $–$$.

Go west on Highway 308 about 4 miles, and you'll find the Historic Hope Plantation. This home of David Stone, one of North Carolina's governors, features an extensive library and a fabulous collection of eighteenth- and nineteenth-century furniture.

Murfreesboro

Historic Murfreesboro is located farther north at the intersection of US 258 and 158.

Renaissance in North Carolina (ages 5 and up)
Tours of the district are available starting at 116 East Main Street from 9:00 a.m. to 5:00 p.m. Monday, Tuesday, Thursday, and Friday. For more information call (252) 398–5922 or visit www.murfreesboronc.com.

This town has been painstakingly restored to its eighteenth- and nineteenth-century condition. Renaissance in North Carolina is one of the country's most ambitious renovation projects. More than twenty buildings have been restored in this riverport town, and several are open to the public. Ask about the annual Watermelon Festival held in the summer and about Colonial Christmas.

Sans Soucie **Ferry**

If you've taken a ferry on your trip to the Outer Banks or you're getting ready to, drop by and see the Sans Soucie Ferry on the Cashie River. The ferry isn't marked on state maps, but you can find it by taking Highway 308 east. Go about 10 miles and take a right onto State Road 1500. The ferry is one of three surviving two-car inland river ferries in North Carolina. It's open daily, and crossing is **free.**

Gatesville

Merchant Millpond State Park

State Road 1403; (252) 357–1191; www.ils.unc.edu/parkproject/visit/memi/home. Open during daylight hours. **Free,** but a fee is charged for camping and canoes.

If you and your family love nature, you'll want to stop at the Merchant Millpond State Park near Gatesville. The park is accessible via US 158 and Highways 32 and 37, but you rarely find big crowds here. With more than 2,900 acres, there is more than enough elbow room. The main feature is a millpond created when the gristmill and dam were constructed in 1811. You'll love canoeing through some of North Carolina's oldest cyprus trees, some of which may be more than 1,000 years old. Canoes are available for rent by the hour, day, or overnight—if you are ready to rough it in the park's canoe-in campground. You can also fish and hike, or you can enjoy one of the interpretive nature programs offered by the park.

Edenton

To continue your trip, take Highway 37 to Highway 32 south to Edenton.

Historic Edenton (ages 5 and up)

Two-hour guided tours of Historic Edenton are offered daily, beginning at the visitor center at 108 North Broad Street; (252) 482–2637. $.

Located at the head of Albemarle Sound, this place has been called one of the prettiest towns in the South, and as soon as you drive in, you'll see why. History abounds here, as it does in many of the coastal communities. Today Edenton is largely a retirement community, and many of the inns won't accommodate younger children. The scenery and history, however, make it worth the stop. On the tour you will see the 1782 home of Penelope Barker, who organized the Edenton Tea Party, in which fifty-one local women showed their support for banning consumption of British tea. It was considered one of the first occasions when women took part in a political act. In addition, the tour will show you the Chowan County Courthouse (circa 1767), a very distinguished building from the time; the James Iredell House (circa 1773), the residence of one member of the first U.S. Supreme Court; and the Cupola House (circa 1758), the state's oldest remaining wooden structure.

For More Information

Chowan County Tourism Development Authority, (800) 775–0111; www.visitedenton.com.

Hertford

US 17 takes you to State Road 1336 and to Hertford.

Newbold-White House (ages 5 and up)
151 Newbold White Road; (252) 426–7567; Open March 1 to Thanksgiving from 10:00 a.m. to 4:00 p.m. Tuesday through Saturday. $.

Newbold-White House, the oldest brick house in North Carolina, was built on this site, settled in 1685. Did you get that? 1685! That's old! The home has been restored to mint condition and is decorated with seventeenth-century furnishings.

Elizabeth City

On US 17 you can head east to Elizabeth City. The chamber of commerce (252–335–4365) can provide you with a map for a historic walking tour as well as information on the Albemarle Sound area.

Museum of the Albemarle (all ages)
501 South Water Street; (252) 335–1453. Open 9:00 a.m. to 5:00 p.m. Tuesday through Saturday and 2:00 to 5:00 p.m. Sunday. Free.

If you do nothing else in Elizabeth City, see this museum. This branch of the North Carolina Museum of History provides a fine overview, from prehistoric times to the present, of the all-important waterway and the ten counties that surround it. Here you will see Native American relics and other artifacts from the region. Crafted from Silver features an array of tea services, flatware, and other items. From a 1690 table-spoon to 1947 jewelry, the exhibit includes pieces made or owned by North Carolinians. Among those objects are spoons and sugar tongs produced by Edenton silversmiths during the eighteenth and nineteenth centuries. In addition, the museum offers a wide array of programs and special events throughout the year.

S-Shaped **Bridge**

As you travel farther east on US 17, you come to a rather obscure attraction. The S-Shaped Bridge is the only bridge of its kind in the country. Built in 1929, it was constructed to replace a floating bridge that historians have dated to 1798.

Other Things to See and Do
on the Northern Coast

- **Swing Zone,** New Bern, (252) 634–4263

- **Galaxy Golf, Nags Head,** (252) 441–5875

- **Nags Head Raceway,** Corolla, (252) 480–4639

- **Outer Banks Bear Factory,** Nags Head, (252) 441–1212

- **Blackbeard's Miniature Golf Park,** Nags Head, (252) 441–4541

- **Kitty Hawk Sports,** Kitty Hawk, (252) 441_6800

- **Portsmouth Island ATV Excursions,** Ocracoke, (252) 928–4484

- **Greenville Fun Park,** Greenville, (252) 757–1800

- **ExploraTown,** Greenville, (252) 321–0018

Appendix:
Events and
Celebrations

With glorious weather most of the year, the Tar Heel state has no shortage of fun festivals year-round. From mountain Christmases to fun-filled Fourths at the beach, you'll find plenty to suit your family. To get more information call (800) VISITNC or check out www.visitnc.com.

We've already covered some of the events North Carolina has offered for years, but here are some additional events that are the state's biggest and most unusual month by month:

JANUARY

Winterfest, Blowing Rock, (800) 295–7851

Kwanzaafest, Durham, (919) 683–1709

American Kennel Club Dog Agility Trial, Fletcher, (828) 687–1414

FEBRUARY

Southern Spring Show, Charlotte, (800) 849–0248

Anniversary at Moores Creek Battlefield, Currie, (910) 283–5591

Civil War Living History, Elizabeth City, (252) 335–1453

Annual Model Train Show, Kinston, (252) 527–2517

Kinston Bluegrass Festival, Kinston, (252) 522–5923

Sugar Bear's Birthday Celebration, Sugar Mountain, (800) 784–2768

Fort Anderson Living History Civil War Reencampment, Wilmington, (910) 371–6613

MARCH

Carolina Jazz Festival, Chapel Hill, (919) 962–1449

St. Patrick's Festival, Emerald Isle, (919) 354–6350

Anniversary of the Battle at Guilford Courthouse, Greensboro, (336) 288–1776

Maggie Valley Chili Challenge, Maggie Valley, (828) 926–1686

Pig Pickin' Contest, Newport, (919) 223–7447

NC Renaissance Faire, Raleigh, (866) 468–7630

APRIL

Festival of Flowers, Asheville, (877) 245–8667

Blowing Rock Trout Derby, Blowing Rock, (828) 295–7851

Food Lion AutoFair, Concord, (800) 455–3267

The Dogwood Festival, Fayetteville, (910) 323–1776

National Whistling Championship, Louisburg, (919) 496–4771

NC Gold Festival, Marion, (800) 959–9033

North Carolina Pickle Festival, Mount Olive, (919) 658–3113

Topsail Island Spring Fling, Surf City, (910) 328–4722

Blockhouse Steeplechase, Tryon, (800) 438–3681

Queens Cup Steeplechase, Waxhaw, (704) 843–7070

Merlefest, Wilkesboro, (800) 343–7857

North Carolina Azalea Festival, Wilmington, (910) 794–4650

MAY

Day Out with Thomas the Tank Engine, Blowing Rock, (800) 526–5740

White Squirrel Festival, Brevard, (828) 884–3278

Buggy Festival, Carthage, (910) 947–2331

Food Lion Speed Street, Charlotte, (704) 455–6814

Engelhard Seafood Festival, Engelhard, (919) 925–9461

Flat Rock Music Festival, Flat Rock, (828) 692–2005

Hang Gliding Spectacular, Nags Head, (877) 359–8447

Chicken Festival, Siler City, (919) 742–3333

Ham and Yam Festival, Smithfield, (919) 934–0887

Ramp Festival, Waynesville, (800) 334–9036

JUNE

North Carolina Rhododendron Festival, Bakersville, (800) 227–3912

Gates County Swampfest, Gatesville, (252) 357–0075

Hillsborough Hog Day, Hillsborough, (919) 732–8156

Wright Kite Festival, Kill Devil Hills, (877) 359–8447

JULY

Bele Chere, Asheville, (828) 259–5800

Brevard Music Festival, Brevard, (828) 862–2105

Day Out With Thomas the Tank Engine, Dillsboro, (800) 872–4681

Eastern Music Festival, Greensboro, (336) 333–7450

Coon Dog Day, Saluda, (704) 749–2581

AUGUST

Pirate Invasion, Beaufort, (252) 728–2503

Annual Sourwood Festival, Black Mountain, (828) 669–2300

Smokey Bear's Birthday Party, Brevard, (704) 877–3130

Lazy Daze Arts and Crafts Festival, Cary, (919) 469–4000

Virginia Dare's Birthday Celebration, Manteo, (252) 473–3414

Mountain Heritage Day, Mount Mitchell, (828) 675–4611

Sneeds Ferry Shrimp Festival, Sneeds Ferry, (910) 327–0432

NC Mineral and Gem Festival, Spruce Pine, (800) 227–3912

Waldensian Festival, Valedese, (888) 825–3373

SEPTEMBER

Ayden Collard Festival, Ayden, (252) 746–7080

Benson Mule Days, Benson, (919) 894–3825

Carousel Festival, Burlington, (336) 222–5030

Festival in the Park, Charlotte, (704) 338–1060

Charlotte Shout, Charlotte, (704) 332–2227

North Carolina Shakespeare Festival, High Point, (336) 887–3001

Thomas the Tank Engine, Spencer, (704) 636–2889

OCTOBER

Albemarle Craftsman's Fair, Elizabeth City, (252) 335–7276

Wooly Worm Festival, Banner Elk, (828) 898–5605

Cherokee Indian Fair, Cherokee, (800) 438–1601

North Carolina Chili Festival, Havelock, (252) 447–1101

NOVEMBER

Carolinas Carousel Parade, Charlotte, (704) 372–9411

Southern Christmas Show, Charlotte, (800) 849–0248

Toy and Hobby Show, Greensboro, (336) 373–7400

Turkey Bowl, Hillsborough, (919) 644–0339

Holly Festival, Holly Ridge, (910) 329–7081

Fall Living History Encampment, Kinston, (252) 522–4676

Hog Happenin', Shelby, (704) 739–7760

DECEMBER

A Dickens Christmas in the Village, Asheville, (888) 561–5437

Holiday Lights at the Garden, Belmont, (704) 825–4490

Tanglewood Festival of Lights, Clemmons, (336) 778–6300

Santa Express, Dillsboro, (800) 872–4681

First Flight Anniversary Celebration, Kill Devil Hills, (252) 441–7430

Crystal Coast Christmas Flotilla, Morehead City, (800) 786–6962

Santa Train, Spencer, (704) 636–2889

General Index

G

H

Activities Index

Historic Sites and Homes

Theme Parks

Zoos and Animals

About the Author

James L. Hoffman is a lifelong resident of North Carolina. He is a freelance writer and marketing director for Daniel Stowe Botanical Garden in Belmont. Hoffman has also been a newspaper reporter and editor and worked in marketing and public relations at Charlotte's Discovery Place science center. Hoffman coauthored *Day Trips from Raleigh-Durham*, also published by The Globe Pequot Press. He lives in Gastonia with his wife, Bonnie. They have five children.